IT AIN'T
NECESSARILY SO

IT AIN'T NECESSARILY SO

Investigating the Truth of the Biblical Past

MATTHEW STURGIS

Introduction by John McCarthy

HEADLINE

Copyright © 2001 John McCarthy (introduction), CTVC (TV series)
and Matthew Sturgis (text)

The right of Matthew Sturgis to be identified as the Author of
the Work has been asserted by him in accordance with the
Copyright, Designs and Patents Act 1988.

First published in 2001
by HEADLINE BOOK PUBLISHING

10 9 8 7 6 5 4 3 2 1

This book accompanies the television series produced by CTVC
for the ITV Network and first broadcast in 2001.
Executive Producer: Barrie Allcott
Series Producer: Ray Bruce
Writer and Director: Alan Ereira
Presenter: John McCarthy
Researchers: Siam Bhayro and Anna Thomson
Production Manager: Jill Dales

Endpapers: Detail of a relief on a Roman
sarcophagus depicting the Exodus (theartarchive)

British Library Cataloguing in Publication Data

Sturgis, Matthew, 1960–
It ain't necessarily so: investigating the truth of the biblical past
1. Bible – History of biblical events
I. Title
220.9

ISBN 0 7472 4506 1

Maps by ML Design

Typeset by Palimpsest Book Production Limited,
Polmont, Stirlingshire
Printed and bound in Great Britain by
Clays Ltd, St Ives plc

HEADLINE BOOK PUBLISHING
A division of Hodder Headline
338 Euston Road
London NW1 3BH

www.headline.co.uk
www.hodderheadline.com

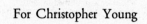

For Christopher Young

CONTENTS

ACKNOWLEDGEMENTS

In writing this book I owe several large and important debts: to Alan Ereira and Ray Bruce for their great generosity in sharing their deep and extensive knowledge of the subject, for their diligence in reading an early draft of the manuscript and their acuteness in suggesting improvements. They have saved me from numerous solecisms, and have refined many aspects of my narrative. John McCarthy has been unfailingly helpful in answering my queries, sharing his memories and bringing his own unique perspective to bear on the subject. Bill Dever, the doyen of American archaeologists, generously found time in his more than crowded schedule to read the manuscript and make many helpful comments. The staff of CTVC have been a model of support and efficiency, supplying me with research materials, videotapes and transcripts. And at every stage my editor, Lorraine Jerram, has provided encouragement, advice and deadlines in just the right proportions.

TIMELINE

This chart is constructed from the various different available chronologies. Its apparent exactness and detail are almost certainly deceptive, but it provides a broad framework for events.

CANAAN	EGYPT	MESOPOTAMIA & CO
LATE BRONZE AGE		
Under Egyptian control	New Kingdom dynasties 18–19	
	Thutmose III (1479–25)	Rise of Hittite empire: challenge of Egyptian control in Syria
	Amenhotep III	
	Akhenaten (1352–36)	
	Seti I (1294–79)	
	Ramases II (1279–13)	
	Merneptah (1213–1203)	Hittite empire collapses
Collapse of city states	Sea Peoples begin to invade	'Trojan War'
IRON AGE		
Israel emerges	Ramases III (1184–53)	Rise of Assyria under Tiglath-pileser I (1114–1076)

Philistines settle on
south-west coast

Period of book of Judges

United Monarchy in Israel
Saul (1025–1005)
David (1005–965)
Solomon (965–26)

Divided Monarchy:

JUDAH	ISRAEL		
Rehoboam	Jeroboam	Sheshon invades	Rise of Neo-Assyrian
(926–10)	(926–907)	Canaan (925)	empire
Abijam	Nadab		
(910–908)	(907–906)		
Asa	Baasha		
(908–868)	(906–883)		
	Elah		
	(883–82)		
	Zimri		
	(882)		
	Tibni		
	(882)		
	Omri		
	(882–71)		
Jehoshaphat	Ahab		
(868–47)	(871–52)		
	Ahaziah		Shalmaneser III
	(852–51)		(858–24)

		Battle of Qarqar (853)
Jehoram (847–45)	Jehoram (851–45)	
Ahaziah (845)	Jehu (845–18)	
Athaliah (845–40)		
Jehoash (840–801)	Jehoahaz (818–802)	Shamshi-adad (823–11)
	Jehoash (802–787)	Adad-nirari III (810–783)
Amaziah (801–773)		Shalmaneser IV (782–73)
Uzziah (773–36)	Jeroboam II (787–47)	Ashurdan (772–56)
	Zechariah (747–46)	Ashurnirari V (755–45)
	Shallum (746)	
	Menahem (746–37)	Tiglath-pileser III (744–27)
	Pekahiah (737–36)	Assyrian conquest of the Levant
Jotham (736)	Pekah (736–31)	
Ahaz (736–21)	Hoshea (731–22)	Shalmaneser V (726–22)
	Fall of Samaria (722)	Campaign against Israel, Samaria taken (722)

Hezekiah (721–694)		Sargon II (721–705) Sennacherib (705–681) Campaign against Judah, siege of Jerusalem (701)
Manasseh (694–40)	Egypt conquered by Assyria (671)	Esarhaddon (681–69)
Amon (640–39)	Psammetichus I (664–10)	Ashurbanipal (668–30)
Josiah (639–609)		Rise of Babylon under Nabopolassar (626–604) Fall of the Assyrian capital, Nineveh (612)
	Neco II (610–595)	
Jehoahaz (609)		
Jehoiakim (608–598)		Nebuchadrezzar (604–561)
Jehoiachin (597)		
Zedekiah (597–86)		
Fall of Jerusalem (586)		Evil-merodach (561–59) Neriglissar (559–55)
Babylonian Exile		Labashi-marduk (555) Nabondinus (555–39)

First exiles return (538)

Rise of Persian empire
under Cyrus (559–29)
Fall of Babylon (538)
Cambyses (530–22)
Persian conquest of Egypt
(525)
Darius I (522–485)

Building of the Second
Temple (520–15)

Xerxes (485–64)
Greeks repel Persian
invasions

Nehemiah governor of
Judah (c444–30)
Ezra arrives in Jerusalem
(398)

Artaxerxes I (465–24)
Peloponnesian war in
Greece (431–404)

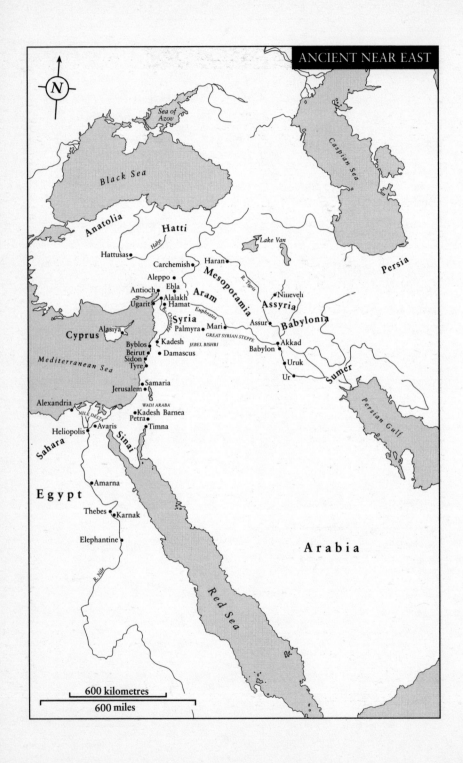

ANCIENT NEAR EAST

N

Sea of Azov

Black Sea

Caspian Sea

Anatolia

Hatti

Halys

Hattusas

Carchemish

Haran

Lake Van

Persia

Aleppo

Ebla

Mesopotamia

R. Tigris

Antioch

Alalakh

Aram

Nineveh

Ugarit

Hamat

Euphrates

Assyria

Alasiya

Syria

Mari

Assur

Babylonia

Cyprus

Palmyra

GREAT SYRIAN STEPPE

Byblos

Kadesh

JEBEL BISHRI

Akkad

Mediterranean Sea

Beirut

Damascus

Babylon

Sidon

Tyre

Uruk

Sumer

Samaria

Ur

Jerusalem

Alexandria

WADI ARABA

Persian Gulf

NILE DELTA

Kadesh Barnea

Heliopolis

Avaris

Petra

Timna

Sahara

Sinai

Amarna

Egypt

Thebes

Karnak

Arabia

Elephantine

R. Nile

Red Sea

600 kilometres

600 miles

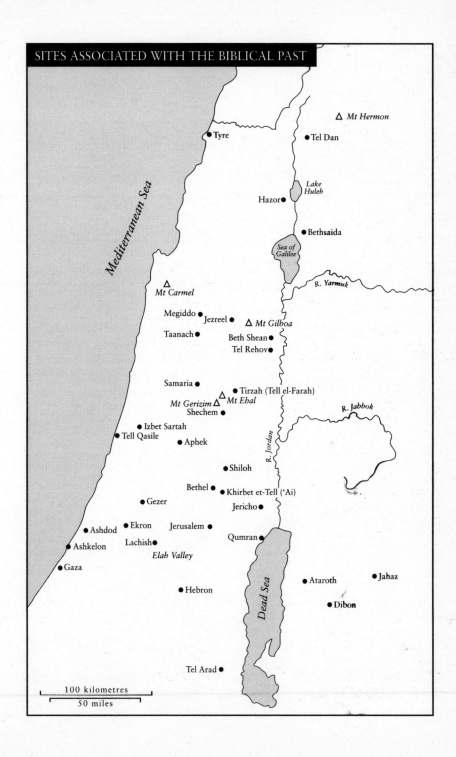

SITES ASSOCIATED WITH THE BIBLICAL PAST

△ Mt Hermon

● Tyre

● Tel Dan

Mediterranean Sea

Lake Huleh

Hazor ●

● Bethsaida

Sea of Galilee

R. Yarmuk

△ *Mt Carmel*

Megiddo ●
Jezreel ●   △ *Mt Gilboa*

Taanach ●
Beth Shean ●
Tel Rehov ●

Samaria ●
● Tirzah (Tell el-Farah)
Mt Gerizim △ △ *Mt Ebal*
Shechem ●

R. Jabbok

● Izbet Sartah
● Tell Qasile
● Aphek

R. Jordan

● Shiloh

Bethel ●
● Khirbet et-Tell ('Ai)
● Gezer
Jericho ●

● Ashdod
● Ekron
Jerusalem ●
Lachish ●
● Qumran
● Ashkelon

Elah Valley

● Gaza

Dead Sea

● Ataroth   ● Jahaz

● Hebron

● Dibon

Tel Arad ●

100 kilometres

50 miles

INTRODUCTION

W e were entering the outskirts of Nablus, a West Bank town under the control of the Palestinian National Authority. The soldier at the checkpoint nodded indifferently and glanced at our passports as our driver, also a Palestinian, explained we were a film crew making a series for British television. They chatted for a minute or two, our driver shaking his head a couple of times, then parted with a joke and a friendly handshake.

'No problems?' I asked.

'No problems – he was just saying if any of you were Jews you cannot go this way if you wanted to see Joseph's Tomb.'

According to the Bible, Joseph, of the amazing dreams and coat, was buried at Nablus, or Shechem as it is called in the Bible. The story goes that his father Jacob had bought the plot for one hundred pieces of silver. Jacob, son of Isaac, grandson of Abraham, changed his name to Israel under divine guidance. Joseph actually died in Egypt but, we are told in the Old Testament books of Exodus and Joshua, the people now known as the Children of Israel carried his remains here when Moses and then Joshua led them out of slavery to conquer Canaan, the Promised Land.

So Joseph's Tomb is a holy place, somewhere for pilgrims to visit perhaps, but not, one would have thought, a place of political significance. After all, we were visiting in the summer of 2000 and this story, if true, dates back more than 3500 years. But because of the story of Jacob's land purchase in Genesis xxxiii, 19, it is seen by some as legally belonging to the Jewish people and, since the Six Day War of 1967 when Israel seized the area, Palestinians have viewed the tomb as a symbol of Israeli occupation. Although now in an area of Palestinian control, Israeli soldiers were guarding the site and allowing only Jews to visit it.

Such things have been happening in the 'Holy Land' for thousands of years. Ever since the Bible deemed this small part of the Middle East (smaller than Belize) a *holy* place, people have fought over it, claiming an exclusive relationship with, or understanding of, the One True God and along with this claim the right – indeed the moral duty – to control the land and all the people who live in it.

In a small way I was caught up in the struggle for the Holy Land when I was held hostage in Lebanon for five years in the late 1980s. There I'd read the Bible closely, and while finding much solace, indeed entertainment in the book, I was shocked, physically sometimes, as I realised that the rockets, bombs and bullets unleashed in and around Beirut where I was held were just the latest chapter in a history of violence which began with the early history of the Israelites as recounted in the Old Testament. The Bible, with its accounts of God's covenant with the Children of Israel and their struggle to conquer Canaan, is the root of modern Israel's claim to the land. Since the Bible's record of events is so often quoted to support the claims of one side to live on and control this particular piece of the planet, it seems crucially important to evaluate how accurate that record is.

There is so much detail in the Bible stories that, while few people might accept that story of Jacob's purchase of a funeral plot as fact, it is not unreasonable to assume that the book's basic history has fairly solid foundations. But how can we be sure? The stories may have been 'spun' or even made up for the purposes of a particular group. Is the Bible's account of events backed up in other written records? The answer, I soon discovered, is an emphatic 'No'. So far, only two external sources have been found that even mention Israel up to the mid-ninth century BC. An Egyptian monument from about 1209BC commemorates a pharaoh crushing a revolt by various states and a people called Israel. There's nothing else until around 840BC when Mesha, king of Moab, celebrated his successful revolt against the Israelites. So for 350 years, during which the Bible details the triumphs and defeats of the tribes of Israel, culminating in the golden age when all twelve tribes were united under Kings David and Solomon, there is a black hole in the Israelites' history from external sources.

Maybe no one else wrote about it because they were themselves too weak to be writing history at the time. The Bible's history might be unique, but that doesn't make it wrong. I realised that without any written evidence the best way, indeed the only way, of finding out what truth lies behind the Bible's stories of the ancient Israelites is to go looking in the ground, at the archaeological record.

I hesitated before going back to the region but thought that as I wasn't actually going to Lebanon I should be all right emotionally. And anyway when I'd arrived in Beirut in 1986 I was the only Westerner on the flight but now I struggled out of Tel Aviv airport jostled by planeloads of tourists from all over the world. Nevertheless you immediately feel tension in the air; there are guns and checkpoints everywhere. It's odd that such a volatile place, often a war zone, is a major tourist destination, but that shows just how powerful the Bible is.

Heading away from the modern cities, the Jordan valley opened out before me, a wide, flat, dusty plain with parched hills shimmering at its edges. Driving through small villages where people sat out in the shade, often with sheep, goats — even a camel — standing nearby, I felt as though I had been transported back to ancient times and a landscape that looked like a picture from my childhood Bible. I was en route to start my archaeological search at Jericho where, so the story goes, the walls came tumbling down in the opening sequence of a long tale of ethnic cleansing, murder and mayhem that continued for a couple of hundred years.

When the great mound at Jericho was excavated in the 1930s and walls found that had indeed toppled, it was widely accepted that this proved the veracity of the Bible's account of the conquest led by Joshua. There is something about the Holy Land that must affect even the most cynical traveller: wherever you turn, you are looking at a sign to somewhere that you have heard about since your Sunday School days. With so many modern place names matching those in the Bible stories it is quite natural to be tempted to accept the Bible's history as the truth. This mix of myth and reality needs only a small leap of faith to have you jumping to conclusions. Looking down into a vast excavation trench at Jericho I could almost imagine the hordes of Israelites circling the city and blowing their horns.

Bill Dever, Professor of Near Eastern Studies at the University of Arizona, brought me back to reality. Listening to Bill — every inch the senior man in his field with his metal-rimmed spectacles, immaculately trimmed white beard, lightweight safari suit and pristine Panama hat — I began to realise that unearthing the truth behind the Bible stories was going to be a confusing and no doubt frustrating task.

Looking unreasonably cool and collected in the burning heat on the top of Jericho, Bill gave me a brief history of Bible archaeology itself. Starting late in the nineteenth century, Christians, looking for evidence of the Jesus story and the background to it, and then after 1948, Zionists, trying to connect the new Jewish state with ancient Israel, had gone looking at sites with Bible in one hand and spade in the other. They would 'read' their findings in the ground by comparing them with what was stated in the book.

The desire of many devout Jews and Christians around the world to have the Bible proved true put huge pressure on archaeology for many years. However, as the science of archaeology became more sophisticated and archaeologists less influenced by faith or believing sponsors, questions about the connections made between earlier finds and Bible history were raised. When the site at Jericho was reworked in the 1950s for example, it was discovered that the walls had fallen down long before Joshua and his people were supposed to have arrived – and that at that time Jericho was almost certainly unoccupied.

It struck me as ironic that not only do thousands still flock here, convinced that they are viewing the scene of an Old Testament miracle, but that this history, now dismissed by the archaeological establishment, is still promoted here by tour guides and not countered by the Palestinian Department of Antiquities who run the site. They have much political capital to gain by displaying the powerful evidence that the Bible's version of the place's history turned out to be wrong. But then the Department is a section of the Palestinian National Authority's Ministry of Tourism and looking at the busloads of tourists and pilgrims flocking through the site, lapping up their guides' unfounded story of Joshua's destruction of the city, I could appreciate the temptation for a poorly funded organisation to capitalise on the value of that story, however mythical.

As Bill spoke, the conquest of the Promised Land by the Children of Israel began to evaporate into the thin, hazy air in the hot belly of the Jordan valley. The fact that the archaeological evidence at Jericho – and at other sites mentioned in the Bible – refutes the conquest story, came as a shock. For pilgrims and sightseers having a story comfortably confirmed is one thing but when it has crucial physical, social and political importance for the people who live there, it seems incredible that the truth about the site is not better understood.

However, that monument in Egypt had talked about 'Israel' so even if Joshua's conquest was now unlikely, there was a people in the area who had the right name in that period. So who were they and where had they come from?

I went looking for them with Dr Adam Zertal of the University of Haifa and his friends as they surveyed the hills of what had been northern Samaria. While the book of Joshua talked of the conquest of the cities on the plains of Canaan, the book of Judges says that the Israelite invaders were up in these hills. Dr Zertal is convinced, through his surveys and study of pottery finds, that there was a gradual move westward from the Jordan by the ancient Israelites that confirms the Bible's account of their arrival, albeit as a slow takeover rather than a conquest.

I walked the beautiful, peaceful hillsides with Adam and his friends before we rested for breakfast, looking down on the timeless scene of an Arab village of mud-brick houses with a minaret rising elegantly above them. Adam had stopped off earlier to talk to the villagers who he has come to know over the years. The romantic view in the valley was blighted by a menacing sight on the top of the hill. High barbed wire fences and watchtowers indicated that this was a Jewish settlement. This part of the ancient Israel described in the Bible was not part of the modern state created in 1948. Israel took over the land, part of the West Bank, in the Six Day War. Adam told me how he once went to the settlement gates for some water and was warned off by a youngster with a gun. He has little time for the exclusivity and aggression of such settlers and we reflected on the sad irony that these modern 'Israelites' were once again up on the hills forcibly taking over 'Canaanite' land.

Adam's theory that the ancient Israelites at least echoed the Bible history and moved in from the east is not nowadays generally accepted. Archaeologist after archaelogist told me that while they agree that the Israelites developed in the hill-country, they maintain that these were disaffected people from the plains, or migrant herders. In the measured tones of university lecturers, they told me that not only was there no conquest of Canaan by Joshua and the Children of Israel (that was all a later invention) but that the Israelites were in fact Canaanites.

Such views seem to strike at the very essence of Israel's claim to the land. It is only in the past ten years or so that scholars have felt able to develop and express such 'radical' ideas even within the archaeological profession. Yet even today, when most archaeologists accept that the historical accuracy of some of the Bible's core episodes has been seriously questioned by recent finds, there is continuous and, judging by some published articles, vitriolic debate on the interpretation of that evidence. However, while the debate has raged in the archaeological world, at conferences and in learned journals, it rarely spills over into the public arena. In October 1999, however, Professor Ze'ev Herzog of the University of Tel Aviv's Institute of Archaeology published an article in the Israeli newspaper *Ha'aretz*, entitled 'Deconstructing the Walls of Jericho'. In it he put forward his views, also fairly widespread among his colleagues, that there had been no Exodus from Egypt, no invasion by Joshua and that the Israelites had developed slowly and were originally Canaanites. The article caused a furore. Strangely it was among secular Israelis that the response to Herzog's deconstruction of the Bible's historical veracity was the most virulent.

One of the more unexpected moments of my trip to the 'Holy Land' was sitting in the heart of the Knesset, the parliament of modern Israel, hearing politician Tomy Lapid, leader of the Shinui party, explain that he wanted to defend the Bible because, although not religious, he accepted it as his mythology. People like Herzog who want to diminish the stature of the Bible based on what he called 'archaeological nitty gritty' were, whether deliberately or not, destroying the justification for the Zionist existence of the Jews in Israel, according to Lapid.

Zionism, the movement for a Jewish national state in Palestine, came into being in eastern and central Europe during the latter part of the nineteenth century. Zionists argued that the only way to prevent the loss of Jewish identity to Western culture and to counter anti-Semitism was for Jews to have a homeland. Confusingly, Zionism, while being a secular movement, was built on a religious tradition, which it used to endorse the claims on Palestine.

Given the rumpus he had caused with his dramatic article and its powerful arguments I was expecting Professor Herzog to be larger than life, something of a firebrand. In fact when we met in a classroom at Tel Aviv University, he was a quietly spoken, diffident character. To his mind the views of modern archaeologists in Israel serve not to threaten the state but to help with its development by freeing it from messianic religious beliefs. Israel has existed for fifty years; why then does it need to keep going back to the Bible to justify its existence?

Although Ze'ev Herzog's article has caused an outcry, his life has not been threatened. Not so for another archaeologist whose name can't be mentioned for his own security. We met at a location overlooking the serene beauty of central Jerusalem on a bright, hot summer's afternoon where my informant played me the tape of a phone message that made my blood run cold. The caller, an ultra-Orthodox Jew, had denounced him as a 'Disgusting, disgraceful archaeologist. Your family should rot, your kids should get cancer and drop dead because you're doing disgraceful things to our forefathers.'

I had been surprised to hear from a number of archaeologists that no human bones had been found at ancient Israelite sites. Now I was hearing a different story; there were plenty of bones but my informant and other colleagues had been frightened off studying them by this kind of religious extremist.

Although it might be too dangerous to touch the *bones* of Israelites and Canaanites, the rules of DNA state that the *blood* of ancient people should run in their present-day successors. In the cool, clean environment of Jerusalem's Hadassah hospital, Professor Ariella Oppenheim gave me a brief introduction to genetics and explained how DNA tests are being used to see whether today's Jews and Palestinians might be descended from one group of people. The results have been amazing. They found that the two populations fit very closely together and that a majority of Arabs and Jews in Israel and the occupied territories of the West Bank and Gaza, have common ancestors who lived in the region as much as 8000 years ago.

This discovery that modern Jews share a genetic heritage with Palestinian Arabs seemed to back up the theory that Israelites and Canaanites were the same people. It was a relief to spend some time away from the heated atmosphere of archaeological interpretation and hear something that was based on pure science. And what's more, these DNA tests, suggesting that most inhabitants share a claim to having deep roots in the area, could be a valuable starting point for a peace process.

But of course the Bible insists that control of the land was covenanted exclusively to the Children of Israel. Its stories, which have encouraged modern Israel to treat the Palestinians as casually as the Canaanites were treated in the Old Testament, say that this divine sanction exists because the Israelites, alone of all the people at that time, adhered to a monotheistic religion; they worshipped the one true god, Yahweh.

Tel Rehov is a massive mound rising some seventy feet above the floor of the Jordan valley about twenty miles south of the sea of Galilee. Standing on the tell just after dawn is like being in a scene from *Raiders of the Lost Ark*, with groups of people working in the shadow of the black awnings that are dotted across the hillside. These awnings, staked out like massive bedouin tents, protect the exposed areas of this season's dig and the diggers from the heat of the sun. As the archaeological team sifts through the layers of time, the dust of ages swirls, dispersing itself across the landscape.

An American archaeologist, Diana Edelman, took me to a remote area of the site and showed me an altar, pointing out the small standing stones, each representing a god, and a hole where a wooden pole, symbol of the goddess Asherah, would have stood. I assumed that this must be a Canaanite cultic site but I was wrong. It was Israelite. The Bible refers to the gods of other groups in the region – Baal, Ashur, Chemosh, for example – and often gives them a certain credence and local legitimacy. In many stories the Children of Israel wander from the straight and narrow, shifting allegiance to other gods and subsequently paying a heavy price before seeing the error of their ways and returning to the exclusive worship of Yahweh.

In captivity, where I went through a painful process of self-examination, reviewing my weaknesses and strengths and hoping to lead a better life, the stories of the Israelites' backsliding and redemption were reassuring – people had been messing themselves up for thousands of years. Although I valued these stories for their human rather than theological message, I was stunned to find out from Diana Edelman and others that it now seems highly unlikely that the Israelites were fundamentally a monotheistic faith from way back.

For a start the word Israel means 'fighter for El' and El was a Canaanite god. What is more, the commonest religious objects found in excavations throughout Israel are small female figures. Two stones, dating from the eighth century BC, have been found with Hebrew inscriptions referring to Yahweh and his Asherah. Asherah was a female consort. So it seems the Israelites were worshipping God, Yahweh and Mrs God, Asherah.

The altar at Tel Rehov dates from the ninth century BC, after the time when, according to the Bible, David and Solomon had ruled all the tribes of Israel in the United Monarchy. After Solomon's death the country had split in two: Israel in the north and Judah in the south. Of course the Bible tells us that after the split, the northern kingdom lost its spiritual way and deviated from the worship of Yahweh, so perhaps this altar at Tel Rehov doesn't show us a true view of correct Israelite religious practices. Judah, however, is supposed to have remained faithful to the proper tradition.

The problem, as is so often the case with this subject, is to find evidence on, or rather in the ground to back up the Bible. The obvious place to look would be in Jerusalem where Solomon was supposed to have built his great temple. But that temple, and then a later one, was destroyed and built over again. So where can one see a temple that would reveal how Yahweh was worshipped?

Tel Arad lies on a desert plain. The low hill, although topped with a romantic fortress, seems to blend with the desert landscape, perfectly camouflaged. A temple from the eighth century BC was discovered inside the fortress. Surprisingly two or three standing stones were found in the temple's holy of holies, suggesting that *gods*, not *a* god, were being worshipped. Since the Bible tells us that Judah was remaining faithful to the true religion, maybe the true religion at that time wasn't the one we know from the Bible. I found my head beginning to spin again and it wasn't the desert heat.

Many archaeologists and biblical scholars believe that the Bible underwent some serious editing, probably in the late eighth and early seventh centuries BC. At the beginning of that period the whole region was being overrun by the awesome power of the Assyrian empire. In 722BC the Assyrian army destroyed Judah's northern neighbour, Israel, completely. The Bible tells us that ten of the original twelve tribes of Israel were lost forever.

The Bible recounts that around this time King Hezekiah of Judah was undertaking drastic reforms of the popular religion and the excavations at Arad show that the temple there was deliberately buried during this period. It could well be that Hezekiah thought Judah could placate their god and avoid the disaster that had befallen Israel by refining its religious practices. Also, by focusing all worship at his capital, Jerusalem, he strengthened his political power base. Unfortunately Hezekiah rebelled against the Assyrians in 701BC and his tiny kingdom's limited political and religious independence was drastically reduced.

However, sixty years later the Assyrian empire was on the wane so when Josiah acceded to the throne he saw the opportunity to restore his nation's fortunes and began a period of political and religious reforms. What better, or more likely a time for all the national stories to be brought together and edited into a new, rounded whole? Picking up where Hezekiah had left off, Josiah banned all foreign cults and had their altars destroyed. As the temple in Jerusalem was restored, an ancient scroll, supposedly Moses' book of Deuteronomy, was discovered which endorsed his reforms. So the Bible began to appear — a distillation of a whole range of folk tales, myths and oral traditions imbued with the social and theological beliefs of Josiah and his clique.

The puzzling thing about this theory is that Josiah is not exactly the most famous biblical character. How is it that he is now being proposed as the one who really defined the practices of Judaism and edited the history of the Children of Israel to create the Bible? What about David and Solomon? It's beginning to look as though those two kings owe their glorious reputation to Josiah and others who wanted Jerusalem and the house of David to be seen as having a special covenant with Yahweh in order to increase the prestige of the little state of Judah and its capital Jerusalem. This makes sense of another surprise that the hard evidence in the ground has thrown up. Three hundred years before Josiah, when, according to the Bible, under the United Monarchy Israel was a glorious whole, there seems to have been nothing at its supposed centre, Jerusalem. There is no archaeological evidence whatsoever that Jerusalem was a great city of palaces and temples at the time of Kings David and Solomon. Archaeologists have found much material from earlier periods, and much from later, but from the tenth century BC there is nothing.

During my time in the Holy Land I often heard the phrase 'absence of evidence is not evidence of absence'. Many people, from secular politicians to Christian pilgrims and Orthodox rabbis, told me that the archaeologists might yet find material in the ground that proves the Bible's history true and that it is very hard to prove that something did not exist.

Leaving Israel with my understanding of the Bible's historical worth completely revised, I felt liberated. The tales of conquest and genocide inspired or ordered by God that had disturbed me when I was a victim of the Middle East conflict, are now just stories – an understandable product of a time when a people had their backs against the wall, when self-preservation demanded a great national statement and historical justification.

It may well be due to the Bible that the Jews have managed to survive and maintain their culture of separateness through the centuries of exile and the book's social and theological themes have universal values. The Bible's great power is that we can read of our own daily struggles against each other and with ourselves, striving to understand the world, our place in it and the possibility of, or the need for an omniscient power for good. But the Bible has also formed the blueprint for many tragedies and from them we seem never to escape. It is a tragedy that blind adherence to what is now, clearly, uncertain history jeopardises hopes for peace now that the exile of the 'Children of Israel' is over.

Nowhere else would an ancient text have been given such historical credence in the first place. Any other book of tales would have been used only as a cross-reference at most, certainly not as an entirely reliable factual source. The creation of the Bible history is one of the finest examples of spin ever spun and it makes absolute sense to me in human terms. Basing a political argument on it and claiming an ordained right to territory in the twenty-first century, on the other hand, is sad and frankly mad. I share Professor Herzog's view that accepting that the Bible's history is flawed will benefit both Israel and her neighbours. The world continues to agonise over the rights and wrongs and the ebbs and flows of the battles between Palestinians and

Israelis for a homeland so why, if everyone in archaeology knows that this historical claim (which is so much cited in the dispute) is flawed, has it not been removed from the debate?

A few months after I visited Nablus, Palestinians in the town occupied and then wrecked Joseph's Tomb as another round of the 3000-year-old prizefight engulfed the country.

Apart from driving out an occupying force, this action reflects the influence of the Bible's story on the Israelites' relationship with the land. Destroying a site which is deemed holy is part of an effort to prove that something did not exist; that Israel, ancient and modern, has no greater claim on the land than any other inhabitant ancient and modern.

Even those who reject the Bible's version of history feel they have to argue with it. It is a tragedy that today's battle lines are still those drawn by the cultural draughtsmen of 3000 years ago.

John McCarthy

CHAPTER 1

The Book and the Spade

The Bible is the Number One best-seller of all time. Even in a world wary of publishing hyperbole the fact cannot be disputed. For almost two millennia the Bible has been read, copied, and quoted. Since the first days of printing in Europe it has been rolling from the presses. No book has been translated into so many languages. No book has been issued in so many editions, or in so many formats. Its influence is impossible to estimate, but difficult to exaggerate. It stands at the heart of two world religions: Judaism and Christianity. It has had a profound influence upon the origins of a third: Islam. It has been hailed as a great work of religion, of philosophy, of literature, of history. Its characters, stories and phrases permeate the very texture of Western thought and culture. From Milton's *Paradise Lost* to Tim Rice and Andrew Lloyd Webber's *Joseph and his Amazing Technicolor Dreamcoat* it has inspired art both sublime and banal. It is a book that has healed rifts and caused wars. Some see it as a book to live by, others as a book to die for. For many it is simply 'The Good Book'. Good it may be. But is it true?

This, of course, is a very big question. Much, much too big for a book like this to answer. Perhaps too big for any book to answer. At the core of the Bible stands its claim to reveal a universal and eternal religious truth. This truth may be disputed. Indeed it has been discussed, argued over, asserted, denied and elucidated for as long as the Bible has been read. But it is a question that can never be resolved – at least in this world. Ultimately it is a matter of faith.

But there are other truths. There is historical truth. And that is the truth addressed by this book. How accurate is the Bible as an historical record? The books of the Bible, from Genesis to Revelation, contain much that is apparently historical. The narrative is set in a recognisable historical and geographical world. Some of the people mentioned in the Bible – Nebuchadrezza, Sennacherib, Caesar Augustus – are well known from other contemporary sources. Many of the places in which the action unfolds can still be visited today. And yet, appearances can be deceptive.

Real historical characters, after all, appear in the plays of Shakespeare, in the novels of Walter Scott and even in the comic strips of Asterix and Obelix, but we would hesitate to call them accurate historical records. And even with more conventional historical accounts elements of bias and distortion always have to be taken into account. Often the demands of propaganda or the accidents of unconscious prejudice have a dramatic effect on the telling of a story. So the questions remain: did the events recounted in the Bible actually happen in the way described? Did they happen at all?

These are still very big questions. To narrow them down a bit further, this book will concentrate not on the whole Bible, but on just six books of the Old Testament (or Hebrew Bible as it is called by most Jews and biblical scholars): the books of Joshua, Judges, I and II Samuel, and I and II Kings. These books certainly look like history. They give a seemingly continuous narrative of heroes, battles, kings and coups. They tell of how the Israelites arrived in the promised land of Canaan, how they settled in it, established a great kingdom, and were then expelled from it and carried off to exile in Babylon.

For many centuries, although there were learned debates about how to read and interpret the religious truth of the Bible, the historical accuracy of the book was left unchallenged. Indeed any inquiry on that score was likely to produce an extreme response. The thumbscrew and the stake awaited those who questioned the veracity of the Bible's facts. Nevertheless over the years the spirit of inquiry has gradually taken hold. And it has advanced. The investigation into the historical truth of the Bible has moved forward along two main lines: biblical criticism and archaeology.

Biblical criticism starts from the text itself. It has a long history going back to the early studies of the Rabbis themselves when its first concerns were with interpreting meaning. Nevertheless it gradually began to impinge upon the literary and linguistic aspects of the Bible, and this led on to questions about the Bible's historical context and factual accuracy. As early as the eleventh century, scholars poring over the stories recounted in the Bible were surprised to discover inconsistencies, and even contradictions. For example, Isaac Ibn Yashush, a Jewish scholar in Muslim Spain, pointed out that the dynasty of Edomite kings listed in Genesis xxxvi named monarchs who lived long after Moses. How, then, could Moses be the author of the book of Genesis? They noted that sometimes a single incident would be described in two different biblical books with details that were often different if, not infrequently, flatly opposed. Initially much ingenuity was expended upon trying to explain and resolve these apparent discrepancies. But, over the centuries, the uncomfortable fact had to be faced: where two opposed accounts existed some doubt as to veracity must attach to at least one of the versions.

This was a major realisation. And it took until the mid-nineteenth century to become even remotely accepted and acceptable. Nevertheless it opened up the Bible to rigorous inquiry. The notion that the factual veracity of the Bible could be questioned and tested was now on the agenda.

Biblical critics have carried on this inquiry in all sorts of interesting directions. They have scrutinised the language and the form of biblical texts in an attempt to work out a chronology of their composition. Through their close study of the Bible's stories they have uncovered unexpected patterns and themes, and they have sought explanations for them in the concerns either of the biblical characters or the biblical authors. Their approach has both informed and complemented the work of the archaeologists.

Archaeology makes its discoveries on the ground. There was, even from the earliest times, a tradition of travellers coming to the Holy Land in search of the sites mentioned in the Bible. From at least the third century AD pilgrims have traversed the rugged terrain, seeking to breathe the air that Abraham breathed, or to look out upon the views that Moses saw. Most of these early religious tourists contented themselves with looking. But Helena, mother of Constantine, the first Christian emperor of Rome, went further. She launched a search for – and, indeed, discovered – the 'true cross' upon which Christ had been crucified. Or so she believed. Perhaps she has a claim to be considered the first biblical archaeologist. If so, she had to wait a long time for a proper successor. It was only during the nineteenth century that the endeavour really got under way.

The discipline had its origins not in the Holy Land itself but in the other regions of the ancient Near East: Egypt and Mesopotamia. The great discoveries, made by Henry Layard (1817–94) at Nineveh, the ancient capital of the Assyrians, or by Flinders Petrie (1853–1942) in Egypt's Valley of the Kings, revealed extraordinary treasures lying beneath the ground. These long-lost civilisations began to yield up their secrets. It was soon realised that not only were there valuable artefacts to be found, there was also a whole literary record waiting to be uncovered and deciphered. The hieroglyphs of the Egyptians and the cuneiform inscriptions of Mesopotamia preserved vivid contemporary accounts of life in the ancient Near East. These were fascinating in themselves, but they also threw an unexpected light upon another civilisation of the period: the civilisation depicted in the Old Testament.

What should we call this civilisation? Or the land in which it flourished? The nomenclature of the whole area is a minefield and a mess. Debates about the names ascribed to places and peoples can often turn out to be heated. What modern journalists call the Middle East, scholars – with perhaps rather more geographical accuracy – refer to as the Near East. The area, which is now largely taken up by the state of Israel, was called Canaan in ancient times. During the biblical period it included the twin kingdoms of Israel and Judah. The Romans regarded it as the province of Philistina or Palestina. For most of the Middle Ages it was simply the Holy Land. More recently it has been labelled Palestine. Although some modern Israelis consider the name Palestine too emotive, the majority of archaeologists – for historical reasons – still use it to define the region. Some prefer the broader – if scarcely less emotive – designation Syria-Palestine. And if the names that we choose to call this land are contentious, so are the terms by which we might try to fix the period under discussion. The old-fashioned designations 'BC' (Before Christ) and 'AD' (Anno Domini) are now thought to be too chauvinistically Christian for either a multi-faith or a no-faith world. They have been replaced with the more neutral BCE, which stands either for 'Before Christian Era' or 'Before Common Era', and CE (Common Era).

Geographically the Holy Land – Canaan, Palestine or what-you-will – runs as a narrow strip, bounded on the west by the Mediterranean, between Mesopotamia and Egypt. Throughout the second and first millennia BCE it was both a bridge and buffer between these two large and more powerful areas. This position brought opportunity and danger in equal measure, and it certainly ensured the area a colourful and crowded history.

During the biblical period the various regions of the ancient Near East were constantly connected with each other, by trade, migration and conquest. The stories of the Old Testament range across both the Euphrates and the Nile. According to the book of Genesis, Abraham's grandfather was born in the Mesopotamian city of Ur and his descendants became slaves in Egypt before launching their daring escape. To a Bible-reading public, such as existed in the mid-nineteenth century (and indeed continued into the early twentieth century), there was a real fascination in these connections – and a desire to find physical proof of them. It was recognised that the physical remains that might be discovered in the Holy Land were unlikely to be as spectacular in scale and value as those uncovered in Egypt and Mesopotamia, but they promised a different sort of excitement. The prospect of reaching back in time and making an actual physical connection with the world of the Bible was more than enough to encourage both the archaeologists and their backers.

One early and exciting discovery was made among the thousands of clay tablets recovered from what had been the Assyrian royal library at Nineveh. In 1872 George Smith, a young scholar who was restoring and cataloguing the tablets at the British Museum, came across the account of a great flood that seemed to echo the story in the Bible, even down to the detail about the white dove. It was a discovery that, if it did not actually confirm the facts of Noah's Flood, did suggest that stories about a massive and retributive deluge were part of a common ancient heritage.

It was not, however, until 1890 that the archaeologists turned their attention in earnest to the Holy Land itself. In that year Flinders Petrie began his excavations at Tell el-Hesi in the south-west of what he called Palestine. Over the previous decades the ground had been prepared, principally by the pioneering work of two erudite enthusiasts – Edward Robinson and Eli Smith. Together they made two important surveys, in 1838 and 1852. Riding over the country, they tried to match places mentioned in the Bible with actual sites on the ground. Smith, who worked as a missionary in Beirut, had an excellent knowledge of Arabic. He was able to quiz the local bedouin about current placenames and then relate those to the designations given in the Bible. It was ground-breaking work. They established the location of over a hundred biblical sites, most of which are still regarded as correct today. Most of these sites were no longer inhabited. They existed only as vast, scrub-covered mounds, known at tells, the long-abandoned remains of layer after layer of human habitation.

Robinson and Smith's pioneering work was followed up by others. Several countries established national archaeological societies to investigate the area. The Palestine Exploration Fund was founded in London in 1865. The American Palestine Society came into being five years later, and was followed by the German Palestine Society (1878) and the École Biblique (1890). A few tentative, exploratory surveys and digs had even been attempted at various sites before 1890, but it was Petrie who first placed operations on a formal footing.

Ironically Tell el-Hesi was not among Robinson and Smith's topographical successes. Petrie, when he chose the site, was under the impression that he would be excavating the ruins of Lachish, a great Judean fortress city mentioned several times in the book of Kings. He was disappointed. Nevertheless if his dig did not turn up any artefacts that could be linked directly to the biblical narrative it did open up a whole new era of endeavour and discovery. Archaeologists from all over the world – though principally from Britain, America, Germany and France – men of every shade of Christian belief, came to Palestine to dig.

The years between 1890 and the First World War saw the rapid growth of archaeology in Palestine. Many major sites were identified and excavated for the first time during this period. Many important discoveries were made. Advances in technique were continuous. It was Petrie who first recognised that tells were made up of different layers or strata, each one corresponding to a period of occupation. Although his formulation of this concept was over-simple (he imagined that each layer of the 'cake' was uniform and clearly distinct), he provided a model which others could refine. He also grasped that the key to establishing and dating the different strata lay in the tiny pottery pieces – or sherds – that were the most commonly found objects. Once a typological record of the region's pottery was established then a chronology could be attempted. Despite the increasingly scientific approach adopted in the technical details of archaeology, there was another element to the equation.

Behind the whole enterprise, guiding it and driving it forward, was the desire to recover the historical truth of the Bible. This, some commentators have suggested, was a particularly American concern. They point out that the British-based Palestine Exploration Fund had a broad scientific remit and was as interested in charting the natural history, geology and topography of the region as it was in uncovering specific archaeological sites. While the American Palestine Society declared in its founding charter that one of its aims was to prove the validity of the Bible. Under the influence of such aims the discipline developed swiftly from being archaeology per se into being something new and rather different called 'biblical archaeology'. It would not be putting it too strongly to say that for some of those digging in the Holy Land the goal was not to prove the historical truth of the Bible but to confirm it. After all, for many of these people it was beyond question that the stories in the Bible were true. Many of the early archaeologists were clergymen or missionaries. Almost all of them were firm believers. They worked, in the memorable phrase, 'with a spade in one hand and the Bible in the other'.

At their most extreme they used the biblical text both to direct their inquiries and to test their findings. If, say, the Bible mentioned that King Ahab built an ivory palace at Samaria they might locate the ancient site of Samaria, dig until they uncovered some fragments of ivory and then come swiftly to the conclusion that they had discovered Ahab's palace. If the Bible mentioned that Noah's Ark had come to rest on mount Ararat, they would head off to Turkey, and search on mount Ararat for the remains of a large boat.

Much of the funding for these early excavations came from religious groups. While museum-funded digs placed a burden on the excavators to uncover finds that would add lustre to the collections of the museum concerned, digs financed by religious groups placed a different sort of onus on the diggers. There was a hope, perhaps even an expectation, that the excavators' finds would confirm the biblical account.

The religious impulse, although strong, was not the only force driving archaeological exploration in Palestine forward. There was also a political motive – or, at least, a political context. Palestine was part of the Ottoman empire. And this empire, which had controlled the whole south-eastern corner of the Mediterranean for 400 years, seemed on the verge of collapse. The various European powers, most notably England, Russia, France and Germany, were jockeying for position, anxious to carve up the spoils when the once-great power finally imploded. As the world moved closer towards war, and it was feared that the Ottoman empire would align itself with Germany, against France, Britain and Russia, the situation became more urgent.

The surveys carried out by the Palestine Exploration Fund provided a useful cover for estimating the strength of Ottoman positions in the region. In 1913 the young T. E. Lawrence was part of a PEF expedition to the Wilderness of Zin, south of the Negev Desert. Zin is mentioned several times in the Bible: Moses and the children of Israel rested there during their wanderings. Although this biblical connection provided one ostensible reason for the expedition, the survey also gave Lawrence an opportunity to scout out the Ottoman military presence in an area that was close to the Suez Canal. It was information that he would put to good use three years later as one of the leaders of the Arab Revolt. The detailed and accurate maps of the Palestine Exploration

Fund would also provide General Allenby, the leader of the British forces in Palestine, with a decisive advantage in his campaigns against the Turks.

Having achieved victory, the British and French proceeded to divide the spoils between them. The newly formed League of Nations gave a mandate to Britain to control Palestine and the territory east of the Jordan (which subsequently became the kingdom of Jordan). The British mandate ushered in a new age of intense archaeological endeavour in the region. Biblical archaeology had definitely moved forward from being, to a large extent, the enthusiasm of antiquarian clergymen, to being an academically rigorous discipline. Under the direction of a newly established, and British controlled, Department of Antiquities Authority excavations became more coordinated and controlled. The indefatigable American archaeologist, W. F. Albright, through his work at Tell Beit Mirsim during the late 1920s and the 1930s, and his detailed analysis of the pottery found there, established a widely accepted chronological framework for the region.

The period after World War I, if it saw an advance in Palestine's archaeology, also opened up a new chapter in the region's troubled political history – a chapter that would have a profound impact on the development and direction taken by biblical archaeology over the coming decades.

The World Zionist Organisation had been campaigning since its foundation in 1897 for a homeland in Palestine for the Jewish peoples scattered throughout the countries of the world. Haim Weizmann, the organisation's leader, was a British citizen. He enjoyed widespread political support for his cause, and won the enthusiastic backing of the Foreign Secretary, Arthur Balfour. In 1917 Balfour issued the famous 'Balfour Declaration', stating that 'His Majesty's Government view with favour the establishment in Palestine of a national home for the Jewish people.' But he added the proviso that it should be 'clearly understood that nothing shall be done which may prejudice the civil and religious rights of the existing non-Jewish communities in Palestine', though he offered no proposals as to how this might be achieved.

There had long been a small Jewish community in Palestine, and during the recurrent pogroms which swept Eastern Europe (and especially Russia) during the late nineteenth and early twentieth centuries it had been swelled by new arrivals. The Jewish presence became more noticeable. Tel Aviv had been founded in 1909 as the first exclusively Jewish city in the region. The self-sufficient kibbutz movement was also established. Nevertheless in 1917 the Jews still remained a tiny minority in a country with an Arab majority which was itself striving towards independence. Following the collapse of the Ottoman empire, however, and the establishment of the British mandate, the drive towards the creation of a Jewish homeland gathered momentum. The Balfour Declaration was reiterated and fresh waves of Jewish settlers arrived.

Arab opposition to this new force was real but unfocused. Over the next two decades tensions continued to mount between the two communities. Riots, insurrections and killings were frequent. There was a full-scale Arab revolt in 1936. Britain's response, having put down the insurrection, was to announce a plan to end the mandate and partition the country between the Jews and the Arabs. The scheme, which was rejected by the Arabs, was overtaken by the outbreak of World War II. After the war, however, a revised version of this plan was sanctioned by the United Nations, despite continued Arab opposition. The Jews, who now represented about thirty per cent of the population, were to receive over fifty per cent of the land.

On 15 May 1948 the British mandate ended. The Jews declared the state of Israel the day before the British forces withdrew. The conflict that had long been simmering erupted in full force at once. The progress of this conflict, the exact reasons for it, and the exact results of it, were – and remain – highly contentious. Almost any attempt to describe the events, even in outline, is liable to fall foul of either – or both – camps. Nevertheless in the baldest possible terms: Arab forces both from

Palestine and the surrounding countries advanced, but, despite superior numbers, were repeatedly pushed back. By the time an Armistice was agreed in January 1949, eighty per cent of what had been Palestine was under Israeli control. Some 750,000 Palestinians had fled from their homes in fear for their lives. Arab rule was maintained on the West Bank and in East Jerusalem but it was exercised by the kingdom of Jordan. The coastal strip around Gaza, although it was placed under the nominal charge of an 'All Palestine Government', was controlled by Egypt.

Israel had achieved an extraordinary military victory. The new state had emerged with a miraculous swiftness that seemed – at least to some – to echo the story of the Israelites' conquest of the Promised Land as recounted in the Bible. It is perhaps not surprising that the rulers of the new state of Israel should wish to point up this inspiring parallel. One of the first things that the Israelis did after the war ended was to begin an intensive archaeological investigation of their new territory. The dividing line between military conquest and archaeological exploration sometimes became strangely blurred. At least one leading Israeli general, the great Yigael Yadin, became a leading Israeli archaeologist. Although American and European scholars continued to carry on excavations in the country, ever-increasing numbers of Israelis trained as archaeologists, eager to uncover the history of the land they now controlled. Under the direction of these enthusiasts, it has been suggested, the search to prove the truth of the Bible sometimes took on a further political dimension.

It was, nevertheless, a political dimension that continued to look to the Bible for its frame of reference. Shlomo Bunimovitz, an Israeli archaeologist of a younger generation, explains this attitude. 'They were not religious people,' he suggests, 'they were secular people. But for them archaeology – whatever came from the spade – was a proof of the connection between modern Israel and ancient Israel.' And the narrative of ancient Israel was to be found, they believed, in the Hebrew Bible. 'They looked at everything through the prism of the Bible. The books of the Bible that interested them most – and with which they sought to make a connection – were those of Joshua and Judges, the books that show how the Israelites came to be in their own land.' According to Bunimovitz's account, the prime minister of the new state, David Ben Gurion, had special meetings at his home with 'all these former generals who were now archaeologists', to learn of their discoveries, and to examine their newest finds. It was as if they were seeking a further confirmation for their claim to the land in recovering the distant past of the Hebrew Bible. They went to work with a spade in one hand, a Bible in the other and a machine-gun slung over the shoulder.

To many outside observers it seemed as if the distortions inherent in the overly scriptural approach of the nineteenth-century biblical archaeologists had been replaced by a new – and perhaps more dangerous – set of distortions. Hamdan Taha, who runs the recently founded Palestinian Department of Antiquities, considers that the whole history of archaeology in the area has been bedevilled by the over-excited and partisan expectations of successive archaeologists. 'Through archaeology,' he says, 'we cannot prove any religious, ethnic, or political claims; it is not the task of archaeology. This is ideology.' The distinction is now widely accepted among archaeologists, but – according to both Bunimovitz and Taha – in the 1950s and early 1960s it was less clear to many working in the field. At its most extreme, Israeli archaeology, Taha argues, 'inherited the basic attitude of biblical archaeology, but as a new phenomenon, which can be described really as Zionist archaeology. Archaeology was used directly to serve political claims on the land.'

Subsequent conflicts and territorial gains opened up new areas of the land to exploration and excavation. The Six Day War in 1967 gave Israel's archaeologists access to the Golan heights, the West Bank, the Gaza strip, East Jerusalem and Sinai. Not the least of Sinai's attractions to the Israelis seems to have been the fact that it was supposed to have been the scene of Moses' wanderings. Possession of the land would enable them to mount a search for some physical trace of this biblical drama. But because the United Nations did not recognise Israel's right to the territory, under international law they were not sanctioned to carry out any archaeological excavations there – unless there was a danger of a site being destroyed or damaged due to building work. The Israelis sprang through this legal loophole. All excavations in the area were designated as 'salvage digs'.

In recent years there has been a slow, fraught, and frequently stalled, search for some sort of peaceful political settlement in the region. In 1982 Israel handed back the Sinai to Egypt. In 1993, with the signing of the Oslo Accords, Israel agreed to withdraw from some parts of the long-occupied territories on the West Bank and Gaza strip, handing them over to a new Palestinian National Authority. But each small advance tends to be followed by a violent reaction. Progress is painful, and the way forward remains unclear. Nevertheless, moving in parallel with this slow-grinding peace process there has been the much more rapid and dramatic development in the area's archaeology. A new generation of archaeologists has emerged. Many – indeed most – of them are Israeli. But they are challenging the intellectual assumptions of their predecessors – and they are coming up with some very different, and very interesting, answers.

It would be too much to say that they have turned their back on the Bible completely, but they have certainly changed their attitude to it. In part this shift was prompted by a slackening confidence in the Bible as an historical guide. During the years since World War II it has become harder and harder to escape this sense of doubt. The expected discoveries of specific biblical artefacts and buildings were simply not being made, and certainly not at the rate that had once been hoped. Discrepancies between the biblical account and the ever-increasing archaeological record became more noticeable and harder to ignore.

Improved techniques of digging and dating have played an important part in this process of criticism and re-evaluation. The stratigraphical method of site analysis, mooted by Petrie at the beginning of the twentieth century and pioneered by the British archaeologist Kathleen Kenyon at Jericho in the 1950s, has become both universally adopted and steadily refined. Although it remains debatable whether archaeology itself is more properly classified as an art or a science, there is no doubt that it now makes great use of scientific expertise whenever it can.

Modern archaeology has become a multi-disciplinary enterprise. Satellite imaging is used to identify the location of new sites, geology adds an extra dimension to what is discovered in the ground, and paleo-botanical analysis has become a useful tool for evaluating and dating finds. Genetics, zoology, organic chemistry: all have a part to play in the full recording and analysis of an archaeological site. And, of course, all this information is now stored and ordered on computer.

And if the techniques of archaeology have advanced, so too have the planning and operation of excavations. Digs now tend to be carried out for shorter periods and with very specific aims in view. The art of archaeology is to ask the right questions of the right site. In that way more information is gleaned from less labour. But labour, of course, remains a major part of any archaeological enterprise. There is no short cut. The careful removal of layer after layer of earth from a series of 5×5 metre digging squares, using nothing more than a trowel and a brush, is – and must always be – painstaking, dirty and back-breaking work. Incredibly much of this toil is done by American and European students – who pay for the privilege. Israeli students seem to be less eager to sign up for a punishing regime of hard labour under the unforgiving sun.

While the excavation labourers often come from outside Israel, the archaeologists directing them tend to come from within. It is widely acknowledged that Israel is blessed with a whole generation of extremely gifted and charismatic archaeologists – men such as Amnon Ben-Tor, Israel Finkelstein, Ze'ev Herzog, Amihai Mazar, David Ussishkin,

Ephraim Stern and Adam Zertal. They are men who combine an exceptional command of the technical aspects of the job with a keen understanding of their work's wider intellectual context.

It is under the direction of men such as these that a new – and much broader – approach to the whole archaeological investigation of the period has been adopted. Rather than using the Old Testament as a field guide, the current crop of archaeologists is increasingly putting the Bible aside and working, not to prove – or disprove – individual stories, but to build up a fuller picture of the early life and culture of the whole region. The very term biblical archaeology has become tainted, and is now rejected by many academics. At their most austere the new archaeologists claim that their work is no more than a study of the material remains of the ancient Near East.

This, of course, is a bit disingenuous. The material remains of the ancient Near East are endlessly fascinating to the general public precisely because we think we know something of that world from the pages of the Bible. The possibility that there might be some connection between what is found on the ground and what is written in the Old Testament remains lurking in the background, however often some archaeologists try to deny it. It is no coincidence that very much more is known of the Early Iron Age of Canaan, than of the Early Iron Age of Outer Mongolia.

Nevertheless the order of precedence has gradually changed. The scrupulously objective approach of such pioneers as Kathleen Kenyon has become more widely recognised and adopted. Rather than taking the Bible as a starting point for an archaeological investigation, the new breed of archaeologists starts with the evidence of the excavations and then, only later, look to see whether an objective interpretation of the data relates in any way to the biblical picture. The old quest to confirm the historical truth of the events in the Bible has been replaced by a new agenda: to build up a full and detailed picture of life in the ancient Near East. If the Bible is consulted at all, it is approached with varying degrees of scepticism. The onus of proof has shifted: the text is now considered historically unreliable until proven otherwise. For the purposes of this book it might be useful to term this new generation of archaeologists as the 'Rejectionist' school. This is not to say that they reject the Bible outright, merely that they reject the conventional aims and old assumptions of biblical archaeology and the use of the Bible as a starting point for their investigations. Even within the school there are shades of opinion. The mainstream majority would probably classify themselves as no more than broadly critical of their predecessors' approach. Only a small minority of the newer generation – principally Herzog and Finkelstein – articulate their 'rejection' more sharply.

In this more extreme approach the newer generation of archae-ologists has encouraged – and to a lesser extent been encouraged by – a new school of biblical critics, centred – rather unexpectedly – upon the University of Copenhagen. The so-called Copenhagen – or 'Minimalist' – School, has consistently challenged the notion that the whole of the Hebrew Bible is an accurate historical chronicle. The 'Minimalists', as they have been dubbed by their critics, consider the corpus of texts that make up the Bible as literature rather than as a chronological history. They view the Bible as being much closer to a Shakespeare play or a Walter Scott novel than an historical account. It is literature, moreover, that was written long, long after the period during which the events which it describes may have taken place. Their proposed date for the composition of the text has slipped back through the sixth, fifth, fourth or even third centuries BCE, following the Jewish return from exile in Babylon. It now stands at the second century BCE. Its aim, they suggest, was to promote a particular contemporary ideology – the ideology of the post-exilic Jews.

This scepticism is bracing. The 'Minimalists' make some good points and challenge many received ideas. But theirs is only one approach. Very few scholars are prepared to relinquish the Bible so completely as a source for historical events. They dispute the very late dating suggested by the Copenhagen School, and argue that many of the materials used to make up the text are older, if not contemporary with the events they record. They suggest that the distinction between history and story, insisted on by the 'Minimalists' (who tend to see the text as all 'story' and no 'history'), would have been meaningless to the people who wrote the Bible.

Even among the newest generation of archaeologists there remains considerable suspicion of the 'Minimalists'. The archaeological fraternity seems to resent the fact that the 'Minimalists' do not themselves work in the field, that they are not trained archaeologists, but merely critics and theologians who make use of archaeological information, often in – what appears to the archaeologists to be – a cavalier and ill-informed way.

Disputes between the different factions are frequent. Debate rages. And it rages very fiercely, even by the heated standards of academe. There are constant salvos of argument and counter-argument. New theories are launched and then shot down in flames with a withering hail of scholarly invective. Fearsome insults are traded between the 'Minimalists' and their critics. And it is some surprise that – as yet – blows have not been.

In 1998 the editor of the *Biblical Archaeology Review* organised a face to face discussion between Thomas Thompson and Niels Peter Lemche – the two leading lights of the Copenhagen School – and William Dever and P. Kyle McCarter, two more cautiously sceptical scholars, the former an archaeologist, the latter a biblical scholar. It was a lively encounter not least because there was so much past animosity simmering away. Dever had allegedly condemned the 'Minimalists' for what he perceived as anti-Semitism; he was reported to have called the bustling, combative Thompson 'a nasty little man' (albeit in an unguarded moment). And the 'Minimalists' had countered by calling Dever a fundamentalist and much more besides. They found a few specific points of unexpected convergence and more areas of general disagreement. Sir Mortimer Wheeler once said, 'Archae-ology is not a science – it is a vendetta.' And the statement can sometimes seem more like a bald truth than an exaggeration.

Such scholarly spats are certainly entertaining. Sometimes they are even interesting. But they would be of limited significance if they were confined purely to academic circles. The Bible, however, cannot be confined to anything so narrow as an academic circle. It is too important to too many people. Questions about the historical veracity of the biblical narrative have a huge and powerful impact. They can disturb the convictions and provoke the passions of religious groups – both Jewish and Christian. And they have profound meaning for many of the people living in what once was Canaan. Some modern Israelis – particularly Zionists – see the new ideas put forward by 'Minimalist' scholars and 'Rejectionist' archaeologists as highly dangerous. For them the historical truth of the Bible has become inextricably bound up with Israel's view of its own legitimacy. To challenge the former is to undermine the latter. For this very reason other Israelis see any attempt to break the connection as a useful part of a process that might one day turn Israel into a modern secular state.

It is ramifications such as these that make the whole topic so important, so exciting, and so difficult. The search to uncover the truth of the Bible is arduous, but never dull.

CHAPTER 2

Jericho

The river Jordan is for the most part a surprisingly modest spectacle. For much of its course it is only a few yards wide. It is not deep. And although it flows briskly enough between its leaf-fringed banks to make one feel doubtful about the wisdom of wading across, there are traditional fording places along its route. Around, or above, the river there hangs an almost constant shimmer of haze. The narrow fold of the Rift valley along the bottom of which the Jordan traces its wandering path is hot. Very hot. This burning heat draws up the moisture of the river, giving an almost tropical density to the vegetation along the banks: the thick tufted tamarisk bushes and the tall stands of papyrus. But this placid scene is not the whole picture. The Jordan is prone to seasonal flooding. At such times it breaks its banks and, where it can, spreads out over the scrub-dotted flood plain along its margins, and then it becomes a mighty river indeed.

Today the river defines the boundary between the West Bank and the kingdom of Jordan. A few miles north of the point where it enters the Dead Sea, the river Jordan is traversed – and the border crossing is marked – by a narrow bridge, named, at least on the western side of the water, after General Allenby, the British Commander who drove the Ottoman Turks out of Palestine in World War I. In the time of Joshua, however, though the river, according at least to the biblical account, fixed a border between the lands of Canaan and the lands of

Moab and Ammon, there was no border guard on duty. Nevertheless it was no easy matter to get across, for there was no bridge either.

To make matters more difficult Joshua and the Israelites found the river in flood. They were obliged to rely on divine aid to get them safely across from their encampment at Shittim, over into the promised land of Canaan. Yahweh duly performed. According to the author of the book of Joshua, as soon as the priests carrying the Ark of the Covenant reached the 'brim of the water' and set their feet in the river, the flow was abruptly stopped and all the water piled up and stood 'upon an heap'. The river bed in front of them ran dry and they were able to lead the people across 'on dry ground' (Joshua iii, 15–17). It is a dramatic – if miraculous – opening to the story of Israel's return to the land of Canaan.

Nor is it the last apparently miraculous occurrence in the story. Nevertheless, despite frequent and spectacular evidence of divine intervention, much of the book of Joshua is decidedly brisk and practical in tone. The first twelve chapters appear to be nothing so much as a vivid historical record. They tell in graphic detail of how Joshua led the twelve tribes of Israel back into the promised land of Canaan after the long years of exile, spent first in slavery in Egypt and then in wandering through the wilderness of Sinai. The twelve chapters recount Joshua's successive – and bloody – victories over a whole constellation of established Canaanite cities, as he whirled across the country in a blitzkrieg campaign of conquest.

The picture is of a coordinated and planned operation sweeping across Canaan from east to west, from the banks of the Jordan up into the southern hill country and down to the coastal city of Gaza, before veering north towards Galilee, where Joshua wins his final victory over an alliance of northern cities led by Hazor. It is a tale of forced marches and surprise attacks. The distances covered are not enormous. It is important to keep in mind how relatively small the land of Canaan was – and is. It is little more than a corridor of land about 150 miles long, bounded by the Jordan in the east and the Mediterranean sea in the west: at its narrowest it is barely twenty miles wide. In area it is not much bigger than Wales or the state of Vermont. And yet within its narrow confines it boasts a wide variety of terrain and climate. Moving westwards from the arid depths of the Jordan valley, the land rises steeply into the central mountain range, rugged limestone hills cut by steep valleys. These central hills give way to the so-called Shephelah, a fertile band of rolling lowland, which in turn shelves down towards a narrow strip of coastal plain. These are the terrains, arranged as it were in four vertical stripes running down the length of the country, over which Joshua is supposed to have marched as he subdued the land.

In the biblical account the whole process of conquest takes just five years and twelve chapters. Having won the whole land Joshua is described as dividing it neatly among the tribes of Israel. Who were these tribes? According to the biblical tradition they were the descendants of the twelve sons of Jacob (or Israel, as he became known after he had met God and wrestled with him). The genealogy in the book of Genesis gives their names as Reuben, Simeon, Levi, Judah, Issachar, Zebulun (Jacob's sons by Leah); Joseph and Benjamin (his sons by Rachel); Dan and Naphtali (his sons by his concubine, Bilhah); and Gad and Asher (his sons by his concubine, Zilah). According to the account in Genesis and Exodus (and in *Joseph and his Amazing Technicolor Dreamcoat*), Joseph arranged for all his brothers — and their families — to join him in Egypt after he had achieved his position of influence at Pharaoh's court. And they all lived on there after Joseph's fall from power, multiplying away even during the harsh years of enslavement. All linked by their common descent from Jacob/Israel they became known as the children of Israel and it was as such that, according to the Exodus narrative, they escaped en masse from Egypt and set out for the promised land of Canaan.

Throughout the biblical account Joshua and the Israelite tribes are presented as a distinct and distinctive people, separate from and opposed to the indigenous Canaanite population. The recurrent emphasis of the biblical author is that the Israelites' distinction and distinctiveness derives from the fact that they are guided and supported in their triumphant course by their especial deity, Yahweh. It is common loyalty to Yahweh that binds the twelve tribes together and it is loyalty to Yahweh that makes them successful in battle.

Even with this theological element the story stands as a compelling tale of military conquest as exciting as any war memoir. It is enlivened by details of strategy and it appears to take place in a recognisable geography. The route that Joshua and his victorious armies are described as following can still be traced. The rivers they are said to have crossed, the valleys they are said to have passed through, the mountains they are said to have scaled, the towns they are said to have razed – almost all can still be found.

This is extraordinary enough, for the events described are generally thought to have taken place, if they did take place at all, at the end of the Late Bronze Age in the thirteenth century BCE.

This date, like almost every other date relating to biblical history, is not undisputed. The chronology of the Old Testament has traditionally been established by cross-reference with the chronology of the relatively well-documented ancient Egyptian dynasties. (Several named and anonymous pharaohs have walk-on parts in the biblical narrative.) The exact dating of the Egyptian chronology, however, remains contested. It has been substantially revised more than once. In recent years it has shifted by almost two centuries. And the biblical chronology has shifted with it. Most nineteenth- and early twentieth-century scholars – using the old model – placed the time of Israel's entry into Canaan much earlier, in the fifteenth century BCE. The new chronology, however, suggests a mid to late thirteenth-century BCE date.

Although it is generally accepted that the book of Joshua was not written down in its present form until some centuries after the events it describes, and it is also acknowledged that the intentions of the author – or authors – were more theological than historical in the modern sense of the word, the work cannot be dismissed out of hand as an historical record. To many it seems probable that the authors based their composition on earlier sources, either oral or written. Is there, however, any reason for supposing that these existing traditions were themselves either very early or very accurate? And how can they be untangled from the later, theologically inspired material? What is the kernel of historical truth, if any, at the heart of Joshua's story?

Biblical scholars have for many years been counselling caution. Their close reading of the biblical text has suggested many grounds for doubt. There are many elements of the account that don't quite ring true. Relatively small though the land of Canaan was, Joshua does not seem to have fought enough battles to have really conquered it. Victories at Jericho, 'Ai, Gibeon, Gaza, Hebron, Hazor and the other cities listed, when mapped out, simply don't add up to a fully achieved conquest. Also, rather curiously, there are two different versions of the division of the land given one after the other – in chapter xiii and then in chapters xiv–xviii. They don't agree with each other. Nor do they match the list of the territories captured. Discrepancies such as these have been enough to raise a question mark against the notion of Joshua's conquest, but they can only be taken so far.

Other evidence has to be looked for, either to corroborate the story or to explode it. Evidence for Joshua from literary sources outside the Bible is, unfortunately, non-existent. He is not mentioned in any contemporary Egyptian inscriptions or histories, nor in any of the other written records from the Near East which, amazingly, survive. So it is to archaeology – the physical remains left in the ground – that historians have had to turn in their quest for the truth of the biblical narrative. The search for evidence of Joshua and his campaigns has been a long one. Indeed it is still going on. But it must always begin at the same place: Jericho.

Generations of archaeologists have come to Jericho, to the site of

Joshua's first and most memorable victory, in the hope of uncovering the truth behind the story. The story of how Joshua, having sent spies to infiltrate the city and reconnoitre its defences, then besieged and took the place is one of the great set-pieces of the Bible, and one of few enduring memories in most people's rather sketchy general knowledge of the Old Testament.

For six days he marched his troops, his priests, and the Ark of the Covenant, around the walls of the city each morning. 'And it came to pass on the seventh day, that they rose early about the dawning of the day, and compassed the city after the same manner seven times: only on that day they compassed the city seven times. And it came to pass at the seventh time, when the priests blew with the trumpets, Joshua said unto the people, Shout; for the Lord hath given you the city. And the city shall be accursed, even it, and all that are there in to the Lord . . . So the people shouted when the priests blew with the trumpets: and it came to pass, when the people heard the sound of the trumpet, and the people shouted with a great shout, that the wall fell down flat' – or, in the more sprightly phrase of the popular song – the walls came tumblin' down.

After this second seemingly miraculous intervention on the part of Yahweh, the Israelites 'went up into the city, every man straight before him, and they took the city. And they utterly destroyed all that was in the city, both man and woman, young and old, and ox, and sheep, and ass, with the edge of the sword . . . only the silver, and the gold, and the vessels of brass and of iron, they put into the treasury of the house of the Lord.' (Joshua vi, 21, 24)

Although the mention of iron might sound surprising, given that the fall of Jericho took place before the arrival of the so-called Iron Age, such neat distinctions cannot, apparently, be made. And in other respects there is a certain broad plausibility about the tale in most of its external particulars. That Joshua should have wanted to take Jericho is not surprising. The city stands only a few miles from where he is supposed to have crossed over the Jordan. It is situated on what was one of the principal routes running from the east side of the Jordan valley up into the western mountains of Canaan. Set in the lee of the steep cliffs that fringe the western edge of the broad Jordan valley it enjoys a sheltered position and a favoured climate, with hot summers and mild winters. And most importantly it is the largest oasis in the Middle East. It boasts an abundant freshwater spring, the Ein es-Sultan, or Elisha's well. If this water source is harnessed to any sort of irrigation system the oasis soon prospers, presenting a tempting and fertile respite from the dry lands surrounding it. It can, as it does now, produce a whole range of temperate and tropical crops: avocados, green vegetables, wheat and dates. And although the fertility of the land is not a natural phenomenon but depends on the upkeep of the irrigation system it is clear that even in biblical times the city had a reputation for its dates: it is sometimes referred to as the 'city of palm trees' (Judges iii, 13).

The modern town of Jericho sprawls along the fertile valley, circling the remains of the ancient city, or cities, which are preserved in the compacted layers of Tell es-Sultan. Here, in this large mound, some sixty foot high and ten acres in area, over the millennia, peoples have built their mud-brick houses using the ruins left by the previous inhabitants as the foundations for their own buildings. Like a layered cake the site has grown and grown. It is a story repeated all over Israel and the Middle East. But perhaps nowhere is the cake so multi-layered as at Jericho.

Archaeologists have traced the site's origins back to the Mesolithic period (around 12,000BCE), many, many thousands of years before the supposed time of Joshua – if not well before the time of everyone else in the Bible, with the exception of Adam and Eve and their immediate family. Evidence has been found that Stone Age hunters, at this time, camped around the spring and built a low oblong structure out of clay, possibly for religious or agricultural purposes. By the ninth century BCE there are clear signs of mud-brick based houses on the site. Indeed Jericho has good claims to be considered as the oldest city in the world. Nor is this Jericho's only claim to distinction: at 840 feet below sea level it is certainly the world's most low-lying city.

Although these early Stone Age discoveries are interesting, it is the notion of Jericho's connection to the biblical story that has drawn people to the place. And it is rather nearer the top of the tell's archaeological mille-feuille that the search for Joshua's city has been made.

Jericho, because of its starring role in the Old Testament drama, was one of the first sites to be investigated when archaeologists began to take an interest in the possibilities of the Holy Land during the second half of the nineteenth century. Charles Warren, a young officer in the Royal Engineers (who subsequently became Chief Commissioner of the Metropolitan Police and received a knighthood) was the first man on the scene. Under the auspices of the recently established Palestine Exploration Fund he dug a number of trenches and sank several shafts into the mound. He narrowly missed discovering the imposing Neolithic stone tower that dominated one of the very early settlements (his shaft passed within a few feet of it), but he did uncover evidence of an Early Bronze Age (c2600–2300BCE?) town wall, and found a few small artefacts – pottery shards and stone mortars.

These finds were scarcely thrilling but they were enough to convince Warren that the tell at Jericho – along with others in the vicinity – was indeed a man-made structure rather than a geological phenomenon, a fact that had, up till then, been in some doubt. Displaying the natural prejudice of a military man he came to the conclusion that the site was probably a military one: 'The fact that in the Jordan Valley these mounds generally stand at the mouths of the great wadies is rather in favour of their having been sites of ancient guard-houses or watch towers.'

After Warren's visit the site was thoroughly surveyed by two other English engineers, Claude R. Conder and H. H. Kitchener in the 1880s, but the next archaeological expedition proper to the tell was not until early in the next century. Between 1907 and 1911 an Austro-German team, under the direction of Ernst Sellin and Carl Watzinger, carried out an important series of digs at the site. Their excavations revealed much of the Early Bronze Age town wall as well as the revetment (a masonry faced embankment) which ran around the base of the tell providing a first line of defence. They also uncovered evidence of houses dating from a later period within the line of the wall. Although the excavations were carried out with exemplary thoroughness, the interpretation and dating of the finds was hampered by the lack of any established chronology based on pottery typology. As a result much of their work was highly speculative. Nevertheless Watzinger, after reconsidering his initial opinions, did suggest that the city was probably unfortified and uninhabited in the Late Bronze Age (c1550–1200BCE), the period when Joshua was supposed to have taken the town.

It was partly to elucidate, if not to challenge, this point that John Garstang, a British archaeologist from the University of Liverpool, led his expedition to Jericho in the 1930s. From 1930 to 1936 he investigated the site. Archaeological methods and techniques had increased in sophistication over the previous twenty years and though his work might sometimes appear crude by today's standards it was a marked advance on the procedures of Sellin and Watzinger.

Garstang uncovered much interesting new material both on the tell and at the nearby necropolis, west of the site. Among other things he discovered the traces of the very early Mesolithic and Neolithic settlements. On the Joshua front his discoveries seemed no less exciting. He uncovered an inner and an outer city wall running around the summit of the tell, providing a double line of defence. He dated the find to the early part of the Late Bronze Age (c1500–1350BCE). He also carried out careful work on a section of what appeared to be a residential area on the south-eastern slope of the tell in the area between the two walls. He believed that the houses here dated from the same period as the city walls.

Both the walls and the houses showed evidence of violent destruc-tion. The walls had indeed collapsed and house remains revealed clear signs of having been burnt. Basing his estimate on the pottery types found in the debris from the layer of destruction he concluded that the city had fallen in about 1400BCE. And, given that this was then supposed to be the approximate date of the Israelites' settlement of Canaan, it was a very short step for him to claim that the destroyer must have been Joshua himself.

As Garstang put it in *The Story of Jericho*, his popular book on the subject, 'In a word, in all material details and in the date the fall of Jericho took place as described in the biblical narrative. Our demonstration is limited to material observations: the walls fell, shaken apparently by earthquake, the city was destroyed by fire, about 1400BCE. These are the basic facts resulting from our investigations. The link with Joshua and the Israelites is only circumstantial but it seems to be solid and without flaw.'

It was a conclusion that helped to established Garstang's reputation and seemed to furnish proof of the Bible's historical accuracy. The notion that the walls had fallen as a result of an earthquake gave a scientific basis to the event without obliterating its miraculous content. It was, after all, miraculous that Yahweh had sent the earthquake at just the right time to just the right place. In support of the idea it was pointed out that the Rift valley was prone to seismological activity. Indeed the notion that the walls of Jericho were brought down by an earthquake was connected by some to the apparently miraculous crossing of the Jordan. Perhaps that too, it was suggested, might have been the result of a geophysical upheaval. It was found that there were not infrequent records of mud slides along the Jordan valley arresting the flow of the river. The descriptions of these events were remarkably similar to that enshrined in the biblical account.

The book of Joshua (iii, 16) describes the halting of the waters of the Jordan with precise geographical detail: 'The waters coming down from above stood and rose up in a heap far off, at Adam, the city that is beside Zarethan, and those flowing down toward the sea of the Arabah, the Salt Sea, were wholly cut off; and the people passed over opposite Jericho.' It seemed an extraordinary coincidence that the town of Adam, or Damiya as it is now known, had been the site of a major mud slide in 1927, only three years before Garstang first came to Jericho. The mud had cut off the flow of the Jordan for almost two days – just the amount of time it might have taken to get the twelve tribes of Israel across in safety . . .

Jericho had been a place of interest to European travellers in Palestine since as early as the fourth century AD. Indeed there is an account of a visit to the city in AD333 written by the so-called Pilgrim of Bordeaux. But Garstang's claims instituted a new wave of excitement. Jericho developed almost into a place of pilgrimage. It assumed a position as a pre-eminent attraction in any tour of the Holy Land.

In the 1950s, however, this sense of certainty was dented. Another British archaeologist, the formidable Kathleen Kenyon, began an investigation of the site. Her dig, it must be admitted, was undertaken partly at the prompting of Garstang himself, who seems to have begun to doubt some of his former theories. Kenyon worked at the tell from 1952 to 1958, bringing to bear not only her own scrupulous attention to detail but also all the latest refinements of archaeological method. Although much of the site had already been excavated by the previous expeditions, Kenyon opened up three, large, new trenches on the north, west and south sides of the mound. She employed sophisticated new stratigraphic excavation techniques, involving the close analysis of soil and debris layers, in an attempt to elucidate as accurately as possible the chronology and development of the city's various fortification systems.

Her conclusions swung the pendulum back towards Sellin and

Watzinger. She suggested that the great double ringed city wall, which Garstang supposed had fallen to Joshua's trumpeters in about 1400BCE, in fact had its origins in the Early Bronze Age, over 1000 years earlier. She noted that not one, but two cataclysmic destructions of the walls had occurred – one in about 2300BCE, the other in about 1550BCE.

Even the later of Kenyon's two new dates removed the destruction of Jericho from the world of Joshua by several centuries, especially when it was coupled with the general revision of the Egyptian chronological framework, which seemed to suggest that the emergence of Israel in Canaan was not even a late fifteenth-century BCE phenomenon, as had been thought, but belonged to the thirteenth century BCE. Kenyon suggested that Jericho might have been destroyed by the Hyksos, the Canaanite settlers who ruled Egypt as pharaohs for almost a century, until they were overthrown and expelled by a new native Egyptian dynasty in about 1550BCE. They fled back into Canaan, and it is at least possible that either they, or the pursuing forces of the new pharaoh, destroyed the walled city.

More certain, at least in Kenyon's mind, was that, after each catastrophe, Jericho remained undefended and largely uninhabited for long periods. It was, according to her reckoning, almost a ghost town throughout the whole of the Late Bronze Age (1550–1200BCE). It was resettled in a minor way in the eleventh century BCE but did not achieve any renewed prominence until some 400 years later. Kenyon's reading of the archaeological evidence has been widely accepted. Many regard it as a valuable warning.

Bill Dever is a dapper man with a short, neatly trimmed beard, and owlish spectacles. Even among seasoned archaeologists he has a richer appreciation than most of the issues involved. The son of an American preacher from the Deep South, he spent his childhood touring the Bible Belt giving sermons alongside his father to congregations that believed every word of the Bible to be the literal truth. He later converted to

Judaism, but now considers himself an informed agnostic. Since the 1960s he has devoted himself to the archaeology of the ancient Near East. His views are sometimes controversial; his battles with the biblical 'Minimalists' have already been mentioned, but he is widely regarded as one of the leading figures working in the field. Jericho still makes him shake his head.

'Jericho,' he says, 'is nowadays regarded as one of the great scandals of biblical archaeology: where we really went wrong.' Standing on top of the tell, amidst the scarred remains of so much archaeological endeavour, he adopts a tone of half-amused exasperation, in trying to explain how it happened: 'We're looking here at one of the city walls of the third millennium BCE which was destroyed in about 2300. This is the wall that John Garstang, working for the British in the twenties and thirties, identified as Joshua's wall, and he thought the destruction was the destruction described in the book of Joshua, and he dated the wall to the fifteenth century BCE. And in those days the Exodus was dated to around 1440BCE. So he was obviously influenced by the biblical story.'

Such influence is, of course, very difficult to escape. It is a continuing force even in modern archaeology and scholars fight a constant battle to try and prevent it distorting their interpretations of the physical evidence that they turn up. And for Garstang, operating some eighty years ago, the pressures were even greater. Dever admits as much: 'He may have been influenced already by the biblical story. He may have been influenced by his backers. They were a group of evangelical conservative Christian businessmen, and they may have had a certain result they desired. And also pottery chronology wasn't very exact in those days. So what his personal motivation was I don't know.'

Dever, however, suggests that even the new dating of the site has its miraculous dimension. 'I always say to people if you want a miracle, here's your miracle: Joshua destroyed a city that wasn't even there.'

Although Kenyon's description of Jericho's history has now

achieved a position as the current orthodoxy, it is not undisputed. For some scholars the superficial echoes between the narrative of the book of Joshua and some of the physical remains at Jericho – the fallen walls, the burnt houses, the full grainstores (cited as evidence that any siege of the city was remarkably short) – are just too attractive to be given up. The objections that Kenyon raised to Garstang's picture of events were matters of chronology, and the dating of archaeological finds is a notoriously difficult matter. As a result there has been at least one attempt by an eager reactionary to challenge Kenyon's own conclusions, and to bring the date of the city's destruction forward once again by a few centuries.

In an article in 1990 the archaeologist – and staunch traditionalist – Bryan G. Wood questioned Kenyon's dating of the event. He suggested that she had based her arguments too heavily on the absence of imported Cypriot pottery in the destruction level of the site. Although the presence of such pottery would certainly have indicated Late Bronze Age habitation, its absence – Wood argued – does not constitute a proof that there was no such habitation. He made the further point that the houses uncovered in Kenyon's excavation seem to have been in the poorest quarter of the town where it is unlikely that fancy imported pottery would have been in use. He contended that the city's destruction should be dated to c1400BCE, citing in support of his argument not only his own reassessment of the pottery types found at the site but also the radiocarbon dating of a lump of charcoal taken from the destruction layer which was placed at c1410BCE.

A series of scarab amulets, carved with the names of successive pharaohs had been found in the nearby necropolis. One scarab was inscribed with the name of Pharaoh Amenhotep III who died in 1349BCE, suggesting that town might not even have been destroyed until the fourteenth century.

Although Wood's theory moves the date of the city's destruction back to the time originally suggested by Garstang, 1400 BCE is now, of course, considered by most scholars to be too early a date to connect with the arrival of Joshua. The general consensus places the Israelite appearance in Canaan some 150 years later.

In an effort to overcome this difficulty some popular publications on the topic have prescribed a resort to drastic measures. In his book *A Test of Time* David Rohl, for instance, has recently suggested that the currently accepted Egyptian chronology needs to be drastically re/revised by almost 350 years. Not the least significant effect of his proposal would be to place Joshua once more amid the ruins of Jericho – at least in theory.

Such hypotheses hold little sway with academics in the field. In 1993 when Israel agreed that some of the West Bank should be returned to the control of the Palestinians under the Palestinian National Authority, Jericho once again changed hands. It also changed names. The modern city is now also known by its Arabic designation, Ariha. At the tell, though, rather less has altered.

The current archaeological work at the site – a joint Italian–Palestinian dig carried out under the auspices of the recently constituted Palestinian Department of Antiquities – has confirmed and emphasised the dates and conclusions established in outline by Kathleen Kenyon.

Hamdan Taha – the codirector of the dig – thinks that Jericho's demise might even have been slightly earlier than suggested by Kenyon, and that it may have been final. Standing on top of a run of ancient brickwork at the tell he can feel history firm beneath his feet. 'The only wall that has been anchored here,' he says, 'dates back to the sixteenth century BCE. And there are earlier walls below it, of course. We are standing on a mud/brick structure dating back to about 1600BCE, and, as you see, this is the surface of the tell, so no occupation took place after the abandonment of the site in the sixteenth century [BCE].'

Hamdan Taha and his team have searched for traces of later habitation without success. 'There is no evidence,' he says, 'of a fourteenth- or thirteenth-century occupation that would fit with the biblical story.' Like Kenyon before him he has had to conclude that 'Joshua must have come to an abandoned city. There is nothing, at least from archaeological results, to indicate that the site was inhabited when Joshua came to the site, at least according to the biblical account.'

Some scholars, seeking to make a connection between the conflict-ing facts of the Bible story and the archaeological record have suggested that the account of Joshua's destruction of Jericho perhaps enshrined some much earlier tradition about the city's destruction. A local folk memory about the walls of Jericho falling down (perhaps as the result of an earthquake) became, in the hands of the biblical authors, part of the drama of the early Israelites. The story they created has gripped the imagination of millions for well over 2000 years. But almost everyone agrees that it is not true. This verdict seems final. It is certainly made with confidence by Hamdan Taha and his team. But you wouldn't guess that it had been made at all if you visited the site.

Whatever the political capital that might be made from such evidence, the commercial realities of the situation cannot be ignored. Jericho and its historic tell have, since the time of Garstang, prospered as a tourist site. Still they flock here from all over the world in their thousands, people anxious to stand upon the ruined walls of the fabled Jericho and imagine the circling armies of Israelites and the fatal, final trumpet blasts. By an ironic quirk of bureaucracy the Palestinian Department of Antiquities is actually part of the Palestinian Office of Tourism. And for the moment the demands of tourism seem to outweigh archaeology, an all too common phenomenon at historic sites the world over.

But away from the realities of mass cultural tourism, it seems that the picture of Israel's entry into the Promised Land continues to fragment in interesting and unexpected ways. The ground-breaking work carried out at Jericho by Kathleen Kenyon has had repercussions throughout the region. Other archaeologists and scholars have not been slow to follow her lead, and to subject the whole narrative of Joshua's conquest of Canaan to close scrutiny against the evidence of the ever-growing number of excavated sites.

Excavations at Et-Tel, a large site close to the town of Bittin on the West Bank, are believed by many scholars to have revealed much of 'Ai, the second city that Joshua is supposed to have conquered. The results have been thoroughly confounding. As at Jericho, despite repeated excavations, all the evidence suggests that in the late thirteenth century BCE, the period of the supposed conquest, the site was deserted. Indeed the site appears to have been abandoned in the late third millennium BCE and not resettled until the end of the thirteenth century BCE, after the supposed date of the conquest, and then only on a very modest scale. This was not a surprise to some commentators. Even in the very beginning of the twentieth century some biblical scholars had pointed out that the very name 'Ai means ruin, suggesting that the site was first known to the early Israelites not as a great city but as a ruin. On the basis of this evidence it was plausibly claimed that it could only have been at a much later date, after they had forgotten this derivation, that the Israelites sought to explain the ruined site as being the result of their supposed early military conquest. Was this another example of an old, local tradition being used by the Bible's authors to create a mythic Israelite conquest?

Of course to those scholars reluctant to surrender the colour and drama of the Joshua story even this evidence is not conclusive. Fighting a brave rearguard action to uphold the tradition of military conquest, they have questioned whether modern archaeologists have in fact located the correct site of the ancient 'Ai. Perhaps it is not at Bittin, but somewhere else.

Nevertheless the Jericho story has been repeated again and again, with variations. According to the latest count (carried out by Bill Dever and Lawrence Stager) of the thirty or so cities Joshua is said to have conquered, almost all of them were found to have been uninhabited in the thirteenth century BCE or destroyed by other agents or not destroyed at all.

In these latter cases, of course, a degree of caution should be exercised. As has been stated earlier it is a truism of archaeological research, indeed of all research, that 'absence of evidence is not necessarily evidence of absence'. Many successful conquests leave almost no archaeological trace. The Norman conquest of England might be an example, or the Persian conquest of Babylon. If it were not for the written records we would know little or nothing of them.

Such arguments have allowed – and, one suspects, will always allow – those scholars who wish to use the Bible as at least a partial source to challenge the assertions of their 'Minimalist' peers. It is all but impossible to prove that something did *not* happen, while it only takes one lucky find to prove that something *did* occur. Perhaps somewhere beneath the earth of Israel there lies a contemporary inscription describing the victories of a war leader called Joshua.

While some scholars do continue to cherish such hopes, the majority are sceptical. And getting more so. The almost total absence of direct archaeological evidence for Joshua's blitzkrieg is too suggestive to be passed over. And if direct evidence is lacking, so too is indirect corroboration.

Modern archaeologists of the broadly 'Rejectionist' school have in recent years done much to illuminate the whole context of life in the Middle East during the Late Bronze Age period. Working self-consciously without reference to the Bible narratives, they have tried to build up an independent picture of Late Bronze Age Canaan. It is an approach that has produced some interesting and challenging results, results found at places such as Aphek, an archaeological site only a few miles to the north-east of Tel Aviv.

Perched on its little hill, slightly off the main road, Aphek now seems a refuge from the metropolitan bustle and sprawl of Tel Aviv. The land is owned by the National Parks Authority, and the site – when not crowded with school parties – has a tranquil, well-tended air. But in former times this was a thriving place. Its position, close to the junction of a main coastal route and a road running inland, up to the central hills, gave Aphek strategic importance. Today the site presents the aspect of a mediaeval castle. The hilltop is dominated by the imposing walls of a sixteenth-century Ottoman fortress. But the military history of the place stretches back millennia. Excavations have revealed evidence of Byzantine and Roman settlements. Part of an impressive Bronze Age city wall has been uncovered. But – most interestingly – archaeologists have discovered that, between the fourteenth and mid-twelfth centuries BCE, Aphek was a major military and administrative centre for the Egyptians. It was, moreover, one of several.

Evidence of the Egyptian presence has been found throughout Canaan. Numerous small, Egyptian-built sites have been identified along the coast; some appear to have been military outposts, others were more palatial. Nor did the Egyptians restrict their interests to the Mediterranean littoral. They controlled Beth Shean, the settlement that dominates the eastern end of the Jezreel valley close to where it crosses the Jordan. At several cities – such as Megiddo and Tell Beit Mirsim – they erected imposing mansions, which seem to have served as residences for Egyptian (or Egyptian-appointed) officials. Some archaeologists consider the fact that so many Canaanite towns remained unfortified during this period to be the result of Egyptian control.

The exact reasons for Egypt's interest in Canaan during this period are argued over by historians. Some contend that the Egyptian presence was principally to maintain a buffer zone between Egypt and the neo-Hittite empire based in what is now central Turkey. Others have suggested that the Egyptians wished to control the important trade routes that ran through the land, north to Mesopotamia, south into Arabia, and west across the Mediterranean. Whatever brought them into Canaan, the Egyptians soon found themselves embroiled in the political dramas of the country. Some of the colour and detail of these dramas has been miraculously preserved in a cache of letters and other documents which was discovered in the late nineteenth century at a site in Egypt.

Tell el-Amarna, on the east bank of the Nile, some 200 miles south of Cairo, was once the site of the pharaoh Akhenaten's capital city. In 1889, peasants digging among the ruins, in search of decomposed mud bricks (which they used to fertilise their fields), began to turn up numerous clay tablets inscribed with a cuneiform script. Although some of these tablets doubtless did become fertiliser, archaeologists were able to recover almost 400 of them. They turned out to be part of the diplomatic correspondence of Akhenaten and his predecessor. Many of them related to Canaan. They touch on the constant bickerings and conflicts that flared up between the local vassal kings and city states, as well as on the not infrequent threats posed by encroaching Hittite campaigns. Egypt was frequently obliged to intervene, in order to restore stability. The references to interventions seem to confirm the Egyptians' administrative network of control. And each such intervention doubtless gave them an excuse for extending it. It is probably not too much to say that from the fourteenth to the twelfth century BCE Canaan was a province of Egypt.

This is a startling realisation to make when held up against the narrative of the Old Testament. The whole drama of the Exodus story depends upon the theme of the people of Israel escaping from Egypt and Egyptian rule, and making their way to the promised land of Canaan. And yet, it seems, that if the events described did happen, the children of Israel would never have escaped Egyptian rule at all. They would merely have passed from one Egyptian controlled land to another. The curious anomaly of this situation is suspicious at the very least.

The fact that the Egyptians are not mentioned at all in the book of Joshua is one of the best clues to the fact that the story does not describe actual historical events happening in the thirteenth century BCE. If there was a single prominent political element in Canaan in the thirteenth century BCE, at the time of the great Ramases II, that element was the Egyptian administration. The strange silence of the biblical sources upon this key political fact has led scholars to question not only the story of Joshua's conquests but also the whole narrative of the Captivity in Egypt and the Exodus. If the children of Israel did not sweep into Canaan and conquer it, did they ever escape out of Egypt and cross the wilderness? Indeed, were they ever in Egypt?

The Exodus story, they point out, is mentioned nowhere in the various contemporary Egyptian sources. That a whole tribe – or confederation of tribes – could escape from the most powerful and authoritarian state in the region without the fact being recorded is, they suggest, unlikely, if not impossible. Recently Egyptologists have done something to question these confident assertions. In an effort to redress the balance, they point out that only so much can be argued from the absence of evidence in the Egyptian records. Inscriptions tend only to record major triumphs. News of insurrection might well be preserved on papyrus documents. But very, very few papyri have survived, especially from the Nile Delta region where the Exodus story is supposed to begin. The climate there is simply too wet; any papyri that might have existed would have rotted away over the years.

Moreover some Egyptologists suggest that the picture of life in Egypt painted in the Bible is confirmed in a surprising number of points by contemporary records, even down to the details of brick manufacture and workers' wages. The discovery of an elaborate tomb at Sakkara in Egypt containing the remains of a senior government official called Aper-el has intrigued some scholars. Aper-el is a distinctively Semitic name. He provides a possible parallel with Joseph, the son of Israel who rose to high office at the Pharaoh's court. There is also an interesting reference in a letter written by an Egyptian border guard in the thirteenth century BCE. The man, stationed at a 'border crossing' between Egypt and Sinai, refers to two slaves who, having fled from the city of Ramases during the night, managed to cross the border and escape into the desert. The reference, however, cuts two ways.

If the escape of a pair of slaves has been recorded, it might be argued, surely the flight of a whole nation — many thousands, if not millions, strong — would have been preserved too. Especially if it occurred after a series of cataclysmic plagues. By the same token it could be supposed that such a throng of people wandering for forty years through the vast tracts of the Sinai desert might leave some trace. Nevertheless physical details of the whole Exodus story remain elusive. They have not been provided by archaeology, though not from want of effort. After gaining control of Sinai from Egypt in the Six Day War of 1967 Israeli archaeologists could barely wait to explore the area. But despite intensive searches no trace of the Israelites' presence has ever been found. There was an exciting moment when one archaeological survey came across dozens of beehive shaped limestone structures, known to the local bedouin as *nawamis*. According to bedouin tradition they had been built by the wandering Israelites as protection from mosquitoes. The word *nawamis* means mosquitoes in Arabic. Closer inspection, however, revealed that the structures were tombs.

The site of Tell el-Qudeirat, in northern Sinai, which was iden-tified as ancient Kadesh-Barnea, also proved disappointing. Kadesh is mentioned several times in the book of Numbers as a place where the Israelites camped. Miriam the sister of Moses is even said to have died there. Extensive excavations, however, showed no traces of use or habitation at the site before the tenth century BCE, three hundred years after the supposed sojourn in the wilderness.

Nevertheless the whole story of the enslavement and Exodus, the wanderings in the desert, the Covenant on mount Sinai (or mount Horeb), and the final arrival in the Promised Land is such a powerful one — and one that echoes throughout the rest of the biblical narrative — that some of the more Bible-minded scholars cannot bear to part with it completely. They argue that, although the experience of enslavement and escape may not have been common to the whole people of Israel, it might have been the story of a single family, or group of families.

This story was then expanded, over the years of retelling, to embrace a nation. One theory recently put forward is that the biblical tribe of Levi could be that family.

The picture of twelve neatly ordered, commonly related tribes, as delineated in the Bible, is – most scholars agree – a mythical construction. Certainly the order suggested in the Genesis genealogy is not even maintained elsewhere in the Bible. In the numerous tribal lists scattered throughout the various books of the Old Testament there are frequent inconsistencies as to the numbers and names of the tribes. In several listings, Joseph's sons Ephraim and Manasseh are listed as separate tribes. And on one occasion Micha the son of Manasseh is given a tribe in place of his father. Simeon and Levi are often omitted altogether. But, aside from this confusion about the names, it seems clear to most commentators that the whole notion of the early Israelite conquest being carried out by well-organised family based clans claiming a common ancestry and acting in concert is a literary fiction, the pious invention of a much later date.

Nevertheless the various tribes do seem to have emerged as entities at some later stage of the Israelites' development when they came to have the names ascribed to them in the Bible. Levi was one of those tribes, though always a small and idiosyncratic one. In the Bible the children of Levi are always marked out as different from the other tribes. In the account given in the book of Joshua they received the office and duty of the priesthood while all the other tribes were allotted land. Perhaps, some scholars have argued, they owed this distinctiveness to the fact that they had a special and separate history from the other tribes. And perhaps, it has been suggested, that history lay in Egypt. It has been pointed out that several distinctive Levite names, such as Hophni, Phineas and, indeed, Moses, are Egyptian rather than Hebrew in origin.

It is an attractive notion but one that leaves the majority of scholars unconvinced. For them – in the absence of archaeological evidence – the Exodus – like the story of Joshua's conquest – remains an exploded myth. The Israeli archaeologist Ze'ev Herzog has been one of the most forthright in expressing such views. 'The Israelites never were in Egypt,' he says with an air of firm but understated certainty. 'They never came from abroad. This whole chain is broken. It is not an historical one. It is a later legendary reconstruction – made in the seventh century [BCE] – of a history that never happened.'

When Herzog published an article in an Israeli national newspaper airing these theories and showing how they were based on the current state of archaeological knowledge, it created a major furore in the country. Although the claims made in the article were not particularly new – indeed they had been circulating in academic circles for some years – the wider public had proved remarkably good at ignoring them. Confronted by them in the national – and the international – press (Herzog's article was picked up by the *Sunday Times* and the *International Herald Tribune*), however, they were forced to take note. It was a painful experience.

Many people, it seems, just do not want to hear about the unreliability of the biblical narrative. They are not comfortable with it. And by and large this discomfort is echoed on the other side of the academic divide. There has been a general reluctance among scholars to impose their discoveries upon the wider world. They don't want to force their theories on anyone. They are sensitive to – and respectful of – the religious faith of others and have no wish to compel anyone to change his or her beliefs. Among the critics of Herzog's article were several prominent archaeologists who seemed to think he had in some way broken the code by publishing his ideas in a newspaper.

When confronted with ideas such as those Herzog put forward, many modern Israelis find it very difficult to come to terms with them. The Orthodox community, by and large, dismiss them outright. But even among secular Jews the impact is profound. The notion that there was no Exodus and no Joshua-led conquest seems – at least to some – to strike at the very heart of Israel's national identity. After Herzog's article appeared a national debate on the subject was hastily arranged. The discussion was chaired by a senior government figure who reflected the general air of hostility. 'In his presentation at the opening of the speech,' Herzog recalls, 'he said that once he read this article with my statement that there was no Exodus and that we did not come from Egypt – he could not sleep for three days. And he is a secular person. And he has a position in the Ministry of Education.'

The feelings stirred up by Herzog's claims reflect in part the divisions in modern Israel, divisions that achieve an almost symbolic shape in the very different cities of Tel Aviv and Jerusalem. Herzog and his colleagues belong to the world of the former; they teach in the Department of Archaeology and Ancient Near Eastern Studies at Tel Aviv University. Tel Aviv is a modern city unencumbered by the weight of historical and religious significance that rests upon Jerusalem. It is unequivocally secular, contemporary and cosmopolitan. It is a city of skyscrapers and beaches.

Jerusalem, by contrast, is the ancient city par excellence. For the last two millennia it has been a religious focal point for a large part of the world. To the Israelis it is the city of David and of Solomon and of the Wailing Wall. It is home to the holiest sites of Judaism. And for good measure it is also a key centre for two other world religions: Christianity and Islam. It is a city the very fabric of which is steeped in history and religion. Its topography is mapped in the pages of the Bible. And it is the biblical past that informs its present. For some modern Israelis this is the glory of the place, for others it is a fetter that holds the country back.

Herzog genuinely holds that his theories, besides being historically correct, could – and should – prove liberating for modern Israelis, rather than undermining their sense of self. 'I believe,' he says, when discussing the ramifications of his ideas, 'that this development will contribute very nicely to the progress of Israel into a modern state – a more enlightened community freed from messianic and strong religious beliefs – so that it can be part of the modern world as I would wish it to be.'

For many, however, the sense of a God-given right to a land first conquered by Joshua underpins their whole understanding of the state. Cast doubt upon that God-given right – upon the signs of Yahweh's direction of his chosen people across the Red Sea, through the wilderness, over Jordan and into Canaan – and you cast doubt upon the very legitimacy of modern Israel.

Intriguingly it has tended to be the secular conservatives – people like the man from the Ministry of Education – rather than the religious ones who have been exercised by Herzog's claims. Tomy Lapid, the sprightly leader of Israel's thoroughly secular and liberal Shinui party, is among the sternest critics of the current trend in biblical criticism. Sitting in his modern parliamentary office, he explains his thinking: 'I'm in a strange position,' he admits, 'of being the most extremely anti-religious member of this parliament, totally secular, and yet defending the Bible. But I'm defending the Bible exactly because I'm not religious.' For Lapid, the Bible stands at the heart of Jewish culture regardless of its religious content. 'It is the basic book of our existence, our justification in history. The Bible is the basis of modern Hebrew literature. We are the only people in the world who can read exactly something that was written three thousand years ago and understand every word. The Greeks can't do it, the Chinese can't do it; we can. The Bible is our language. The Bible is our geography. I can travel in Israel today by the Bible. And of course the Bible is our mythology even if you are not religious. And therefore people who want to diminish the stature of the Bible based on the archaeological nitty-gritty are really aiming to destroy the justification of the Zionist existence of the Jews in Israel nowadays.'

The faith of the devout is not so easily shaken. At one level they are supported by a belief in the higher truth of the Bible above and beyond whatever the book's mere historical accuracy, or inaccuracy, might be.

At another level there is a recognition that archaeology is an imperfect science. Evidence is open to different interpretations. Old theories are constantly having to be modified in the light of new discoveries. And there are still many new discoveries to be made.

As one Orthodox rabbi put it, 'I'm not an archaeologist, but my understanding is that even among the archaeologists there are differences of opinion. But, I think it doesn't really make any difference to me. Not because I'm a closed-minded person and I've got my views set, but rather because I have a document. What they haven't yet found in the ground they haven't yet found in the ground. It doesn't mean that tomorrow they won't find something else in the ground that will put them on the right track.'

This, of course, is an apparently irrefutable argument. And it is also, to some extent, a true one. Archaeologists *are* constantly finding new things in the ground – things that might indeed 'put them on the right track' or, at least, make them modify their existing theories. One site that, in recent years, has yielded much interesting new information is Hazor.

The ancient tell of Hazor stands in the far north of Israel, near the mouth of the Hula valley and some three miles from the not very lovely modern town of Hazor. From the sheer scale of the tell it is clear that the ancient city of the same name was a considerably more impressive foundation. And, according to the Bible, it attracted the attention of Joshua and his all-conquering Israelites. The book of Joshua relates how Jabin, king of Hazor, led a confederation of Canaanite cities in the battle against Joshua at 'the waters of Merom'. To avenge this opposition it is recounted that 'Joshua turned back at that time, and took Hazor, and smote its king with the sword; for Hazor formerly was the head of all those kingdoms ... and he burnt Hazor with fire ... But none of the cities that stood on mounds did Israel burn, except Hazor only: that Joshua burned' (Joshua xi, 10–11, 13). Although this account rather ignores that fact that Joshua was said to have burned both Jericho and 'Ai, it presents a vivid picture of the town's destruction as something spectacular and special.

At Hazor, as at Jericho, the tell reveals evidence of long and varied occupation, although on a much larger scale. The site is composed of two distinct parts: the tell itself, an area of some eighteen acres, which marks what was once the upper city. And then a huge lower city sprawling out over a rectangular plateau to the north of the tell, covering almost 200 acres.

From the archaeological record it appears that the upper city is the earliest part of the site. It was first settled in the Early Bronze Age. The town grew up as a point on the trade route running along the coastal strip, linking Egypt and Mesopotamia. It became one of the great cities of Canaanite civilisation, and a major commercial centre in the region. It is mentioned in many early Egyptian and Canaanite texts from the nineteenth to fourteenth centuries BCE. In the mid-eighteenth century BCE, the lower city was established. Hazor continued to grow and prosper. By the fourteenth century BCE it was the largest city in the whole of Canaan. And although this heyday had passed by the time of Joshua, even in the late thirteenth century BCE it would have been an imposing and important city.

In the late 1950s large-scale excavations at the site were conducted by the Israeli archaeologist (and former general) Yigael Yadin, under the auspices of the Hebrew University of Jerusalem, the Palestine Jewish Colonisation Association and the Anglo-Israel Exploration Society. He discovered evidence in the Late Bronze Age strata that the city had been violently destroyed. Across both the upper and lower cities he found a destruction level made up of fallen mud bricks, ash, burnt wood and other debris. In some places it lay more than three feet thick. There was evidence too of what seemed to be the deliberate desecration of religious artefacts and cult objects: statues of deities with their heads knocked off, inscriptions defaced. Yadin fixed the date of this destruction in the last quarter of the thirteenth century BCE and attributed it to the action of Joshua and the Israelites.

Over the last decade the Israeli archaeologist Amnon Ben-Tor, who worked under Yadin, has been carrying out further excavations in the upper city. Ben-Tor is one of the magisterial figures of modern Israeli archaeology. His mischievous sense of humour, drooping moustache and floppy sunhat cannot disguise the rigour of his approach, nor the total control he exerts over every aspect of his excavations: few sites are as beautifully dug and as clearly delineated as Hazor. His findings have expanded, if they have not always confirmed, the picture delineated by Yadin. Ben-Tor has uncovered more evidence to suggest that a truly enormous fire did indeed destroy most of the city at some point in the Late Bronze Age. The fire that consumed the city was so intense that the great basalt stairs of the palace shattered. The broad cedar floorboards, which covered the floor 'like something out of Versailles' as Ben-Tor puts it, were turned to charcoal, and the mud bricks became so hot they turned to glass. 'It must have been like a volcanic eruption,' says Ben-Tor. 'For mud bricks to become vitrified the intensity of the heat must have been more than thirteen hundred degrees.'

Ben-Tor has pieced together a plausible explanation as to why such an inferno engulfed the city. The enormous amount of heavy timber used in the construction of the palace buildings (not only the floors but also the ceilings were made of cedar boards) would certainly have provided a great deal of fuel for any fire. But Ben-Tor believes that it was the combustion of the large quantities of olive oil on the site (he has uncovered the remains of twenty or thirty large oil storage jars) that resulted in such intense heat levels. He also points out that the site of Hazor is – during the summer season – subject to a strong easterly wind each afternoon. Such a wind, blowing steadily throughout the latter part of the day, might well have fanned the flames, and brought the fire to its extraordinary pitch of intensity. The fire that destroyed Hazor was, as Ben-Tor succinctly puts it, 'the mother of all destructions'.

But was this great destruction really wrought by Joshua? Did he start the great fire of Hazor? Ben-Tor admits that we just do not know the answers to such questions. He agrees broadly with Yadin's dating of the destruction level of the site to the Late Bronze Age, but admits that this is a fairly broad band. He concedes that there are certainly other candidates beside Joshua and the Israelites.

It is known, for instance, from Egyptian inscriptions that Pharaoh Seti I destroyed Hazor around 1300BCE. And it has been suggested that this was the moment of the great conflagration that marked the end of the city. Some scholars have drawn out this line of argument to suggest that – as perhaps happened in the case of Jericho – the memory of this cataclysmic destruction lived on vividly in the area, and that – years later – the Israelites appropriated the incident and ascribed it to Joshua. Ben-Tor, however, remains sceptical. His reading of the site convinces him that the city revived after its destruction by Seti I, albeit on a slightly reduced scale, and it was in this state that it was finally obliterated by the great fire.

It has been argued by some that this second destruction was perhaps the work of another pharaoh – Ramases II – who marched past Hazor on his way home from the battle of Qadesh in c1274BCE. Others have put forward as the likely candidates the marauding 'Sea Peoples' who – according to contemporary sources – troubled much of the region during the late thirteenth century BCE. And still other scholars have contended that Hazor was probably destroyed by a rival Canaanite city state. Ben-Tor, however, remains unconvinced by the various candidates. No firm evidence supports their claims. And Ben-Tor has put forward arguments against each of them.

He is also mildly exasperated that so many modern scholars seem prepared to entertain almost any theory – but one. 'I would say every possibility has been advocated [with regard to the destruction of Hazor] except one, and that is the biblical one.' The idea that the Israelites may have destroyed the city is 'automatically excluded simply because that is what the Bible says happened'.

Ben-Tor is critical of what he regards as the extreme position of some of his more pronounced Rejectionist colleagues. He admits that the Old Testament has to be treated with great caution as an historical source but argues that this should not be a reason for excluding it entirely. Although he hesitates to suggest that the Israelites *did* destroy Hazor, he argues that it must at least remain as a possibility – if only until some more concrete evidence comes to light. It is, he contends, quite as plausible as the suggestions put forward by other scholars. 'Of course it is not necessarily so as in the book of Joshua,' he concedes, before adding with an almost mischievous twinkle, 'but also it is not necessarily *not* so.'

CHAPTER 3

Judges

M odern archaeology has not been kind to the book of Joshua. Although the verdict on Hazor may still be open, the stories of the river Jordan and the walls of Jericho, of lightning strike military campaigns and glorious victories against the odds are not – it seems – necessarily so. Indeed they are almost certainly fabrications. Although some scholars continue to dispute details of this picture, the general verdict is accepted among the majority of experts in the field. But, if it didn't happen as it says in the book of Joshua, if there was no military conquest, what was there? And how did it happen? And when? A new explanation is required. A new picture of this period when the Israelites are supposed to have arrived in Canaan needs to be drawn.

The approach of the current generation of scholars and archaeologists has been to try and draw this new picture without using the Bible as their field guide and their narrative frame. At its most extreme this approach was crystallised by one biblical website which recently issued a challenge to its users: to write a history of the ancient Near East without any reference to the Bible at all. The challenge, however, for all the novelty of its formulation, is not entirely a new one.

Over the past three or four decades, archaeologists have made considerable advances in this direction. Although, as always, the physical evidence that they have uncovered is mute. It requires arrangement and interpretation. And the arrangements and interpretations put forward by different scholars tend to vary, if not to conflict. Nevertheless certain clear elements have emerged from their findings.

A broad framework has been established. It is agreed that whatever occurred in Canaan during the Late Bronze and Early Iron Ages took place against the background of a general and cataclysmic collapse that reverberated throughout the whole eastern Mediterranean world during the thirteenth century BCE. The reasons for this collapse remain unknown. Its exact course is also obscure. Details of its impact are, however, apparent over a wide area. Cities were abandoned or destroyed. Whole populations migrated or disappeared. In some civilisations, accomplishments such as literacy evaporated abruptly.

In Canaan the immediate impact of the cataclysm seems to have been the abandonment of some cities and the fortification of others. Many rural areas appear to have become depopulated at this time. The subsequent political and demographic changes that occurred during the Early Iron Age which followed have been harder for the archaeologists to determine, and yet harder for them to explain. It has taken several decades to gather the evidence.

When the borders of modern Israel were first set in 1947 much of the old land of Canaan lay outside them. But after the war of 1967 the Israelis came to control most of this territory. One of the schemes initiated in the wake of the war was an extensive and well coordinated archaeological surface survey of the whole terrain. It has been an amazing undertaking, carried out by men of great dedication and resilience.

Not the least dedicated, and almost certainly the most resilient of the surveyors, is Adam Zertal, who has led the team surveying the central terrain of what is designated northern Samaria. The region now makes up part of the West Bank territory. Every Friday for more than twenty years Zertal has led a team of enthusi-asts over the rough ground of this territory, patiently searching for traces of early life or habitation. And he has done it on crutches.

'I was an officer in the Israeli army,' he recalls without rancour, 'and I was injured near the Suez Canal. I was more than a year in hospital. Then I received a wheelchair. And finally I got my crutches. But this, I believe, became a kind of challenge for me. It keeps me going. That, and the curiosity. I want really to know: is the Bible – which is so important all over the world – is it true historically, or untrue?' It is a curiosity that continues to drive him.

A day spent in the field with Zertal and his volunteers, trekking in a cordon across the dry scrub, is an exhilarating introduction to the art of surveying. The ancient past is, it seems, under our very feet. 'The art of surveying – I call it an "art",' Zertal explains, 'but really it is art and science together – is to concentrate on the ground and to look for little tiny pieces of pottery, but then – also – at the same time to keep in mind the bigger picture of the whole territory, the period it was in use, the other sites you have discovered. You must learn to put together the wide angle of the hills and mountains, and the very narrow angle of the pottery.' The pottery angle can be very narrow indeed. The ceramic fragments lying on the ground tend to be tiny and dust covered; to the untrained eye they can look exactly like just another stone. But to someone of Zertal's experience they are full of interest and information. A little sherd of pottery, barely an inch across, serves not only as an indication of previous human habitation but it can also allow archaeologists to date finds and to assign them to a particular cultural group – Canaanite or Egyptian or Roman or whatever.

Not all the objects marked by Zertal and his team are so tiny. The surveyors are constantly on the lookout for vestiges of old walls and buildings. And they are adept at spotting them. A few stones littering the hillside suddenly take on life and character as Zertal approaches them. 'There is an architecture appearing here,' he exclaims, pointing with his crutch to what appears to be no more than a low run of rough field stones on the barren hillside. Even as he takes in the details of the site, the various elements arrange themselves into a clear pattern. 'This is a kind of wall, an enclosure wall,' he ventures with gathering conviction, indicating the continuous contour of stones half hidden in the sparse mountain grass. 'And there is more and more pottery on the ground. I think,' he concludes confidently, 'we have just discovered a site here.' What looks very like a pile of large rocks reveals itself, under Zertal's expert prompting, as an Early Iron Age settlement.

It is the sort of discovery that Zertal and his colleagues have been making on a regular basis over the past decades. The dry climate, the preferred stone building materials and the relative remoteness of these parts, are all elements that have combined to ensure that remains dating back many millennia are still there, visible on the surface of the earth. The land survey has greatly extended scholarly understanding of the early development of Iron Age Canaan. Indeed it has revolutionised thinking upon the subject. The surveyors have brought to light over 300 previously unrecognised sites, which archaeologists have dated to the Early Iron Age, late thirteenth to early twelfth centuries BCE.

Most of these newly discovered sites are concentrated on the western slopes of the band of central hill country running down the middle of the country, from Galilee in the north to the Negev desert in the south. The surveyors have located areas of particularly dense settlement in the hills around Shechem and Shiloh, and – further south – in the hills surrounding Hebron. There is also a distinct grouping of new villages in the region immediately to the west of the Sea of Galilee. All these were areas that in the previous era – the Late Bronze Age – had been very sparsely populated, if not absolutely vacant. As a result archaeologists have found few signs of displacement or destruction.

The villages seem, almost exclusively, to have been built on new sites, not upon the ruins or remains of previous habitations. Although, as the Iron Age developed and the number of villages increased, there is evidence for the appropriation of existing sites by these new settlers on the outer margins of the hill country.

Almost all of the villages appear to have been modest in form. Perched, for the most part, on knolls and hilltops, the settlements were enclosed but not defended by low walls. Although there is evidence of growth and development during the course of the Iron Age period, with some of the villages increasing in size or changing slightly in form, they remained relatively small. Village populations seem to have ranged from a couple of hundred to a couple of dozen.

Who were these villagers? Where did they come from? Why did they settle? And how did they live? These are among the great questions of Near Eastern archaeology. They are questions that exercise many of the leading scholars in the field. Theories abound, and not many of them agree. There is a constant clamour as rival schools of thought strive to make their theories heard. Among the contending voices perhaps none carries further than that of the Professor of Archaeology at Tel Aviv University, Israel Finkelstein.

It is not that Finkelstein's theories – or his excavations – are necessarily better than those of his colleagues and rivals; it is just that he is very, very adept at putting them across. Finkelstein is the nearest thing that ancient Near Eastern archaeology has to a media star. He has that combination of good looks, a questioning intelligence, and a fondness for boldly formulated hypotheses which appeals to the journalistic mind. Like almost all archaeologists he has a beard, but it is short and well looked-after, its blackness only slightly flecked with professorial white. International TV crews are never far away from him or his excavations. Not that he plays unduly to the camera. And that, of course, is why he looks so good on film. Unlike some of the professional overenthusiasts who front popular archaeological programmes he has mastered an engaging line in self-deprecation coupled with a close control of the minutiae of his chosen subjects.

His enormous success at promoting his views inevitably provokes varying degrees of wonder, envy, anger and frustration among his colleagues. Some are exasperated by what they see as his habit of frequently changing his ground, others by his perceived attacks on their own particular theories. Some feel that the media focus on Finkelstein's work inevitably distorts the broader picture of current archaeological practice. None, though, can deny the impact that he has had. The archaeology of Early Iron Age settlement sites has been one of the abiding intellectual passions of his career. Indeed it was where his career began.

As a young archaeologist, some twenty years ago, Finkelstein participated in a dig at Izbet Sartah, a small site just north of Tel Aviv. Returning to it two decades on much has changed; the long grass has grown back, obscuring the exposed stones of the site. And nearby, where once there was nothing but countryside crackling with insect life, there is now the dull roar of a major road. Nevertheless he can still trace the distinctive features of the excavation. 'The first settlement of the site was some sort of an oval camp,' he explains. 'It was about a hundred metres across, no more than that. In the middle there was an open court with a few silos, but not much else.'

In the second stage of the site, just slightly later in the Iron Age, this arrangement was superseded. The archaeologists found traces of oblong houses. Oblong houses had, of course, existed in Canaan before the Iron Age, but these buildings were of a new and distinctive type. From their ground plans it seemed that they represented an innovation in domestic architecture. But it was not an innovation confined to this site. The same type of house has been found in almost all of these new Early Iron Age settlements.

Archaeologists have described it as the 'four-room' or 'pillared' house. Although slight variations were played upon the theme, the basic arrangement was of two to four ground floor rooms divided by a double row of pillars, with more rooms on an upper storey, and a flat roof on top. It is a format that could provide not only living space for a family upstairs, but also accommodation for the family's animals and a storage room of their produce downstairs. The cooking area was, archaeologists suppose, in the central, pillared ground floor space, and that – along with any animals that were housed in the lower rooms – would provide warmth for the living and sleeping quarters upstairs. It has in many respects become a classic farmhouse design.

Interestingly these Early Iron Age villages seem to have been made up almost exclusively of such 'farmhouses'. Archaeologists have found no traces of monumental buildings or temples at any of the sites. There are no material signs of organised civic life, or indeed of hierarchical structure. The picture that is conjured up by the sites – at least in the minds of most archaeologists – is one of simple family based agrarian communities operating a virtually self-sufficient economy.

In an effort to find out more about the people living in these communities the archaeologists have turned, inevitably enough, to the pottery. They were surprised to discover that the potsherds found at the various newly established sites were not very exciting. Indeed the pottery appeared to be very like – if not exactly the same as – the traditional Canaanite ware that had been common throughout the region since the previous era. There were no signs of major innovation or of foreign influences. This remarkable continuity of manufacture and design has convinced many scholars that the settlers who established these new villages came – not from outside the country – but from inside Canaan itself.

But just what sort of Canaanites were they? Why did they settle in the hill country? Did they develop a separate cultural identity? And, if so, when? Dozens of suggestions have been put forward in answer to these questions. None of them is entirely satisfactory. Finkelstein's theory is that the new arrivals in the hill-country were pastoralist nomads who – for economic and social reasons – were obliged to abandon their traditional pastures and traditional ways of life to become sedentary farmers. According to this argument the network of urban markets and secure trade routes upon which the herd driving nomads depended to sell their wares, and buy agricultural produce, broke down during the Late Bronze Age cataclysm. The nomads, as a result, needed to settle down to try and produce their own crops. And they chose to settle in the central hill district, precisely because the land was largely uninhabited.

Israel Finkelstein is convinced that the arrangement of some of the earliest sites shows clear signs of pastoralist influence. The oval enclosure at Izbet Sartah is, he believes, a significant and revealing detail. 'This kind of settlement,' he explains, 'where you have an open court like that is, I think, a clue that these people had many animals. They were pastoral people and then became agriculturalists. Now when we look at societies in the Middle East today which are going through this same process – which is a gradual one – you see something very interesting: they tend, in the first stage of the sedentary agricultural village life, to keep the traditions of the tent and tent encampment of their former pastoral way of life.' The stone-walled, oval village enclosure seems to be a very close echo of the unwalled pastoral encampment.

Nevertheless even among the scholars who claim that pastoralist nomads were involved in the period of early settlement, there is some division as to exactly where these pastoralist nomads came from. One theory has suggested that the nomads might have come from the area known – at least in biblical times – as Midian, which corresponds roughly with northern Arabia. This theory connects the incoming pastoralists with a nomadic people called the Shasu, who are mentioned in several Late Bronze Age and Early Iron Age Egyptian texts.

Modern scholarship has largely discounted any exact identification of the Shasu and the early Israelites, but a few contemporary archaeologists continue to hold on to elements of the theory. Adam Zertal, for instance, has suggested that the early settlers of the hill-country were nomads who migrated en masse from east of Jordan, very much as described in the book of Joshua, but that, rather than conquering the land, they settled its empty areas peacefully. This notion, which has been labelled by Bill Dever as 'secular fundamentalism', has not received widespread support.

To many archaeologists the apparent exact match between traditional Canaanite pottery and the pottery found in the new hill settlements suggests that whoever settled in these villages came from inside Canaan; so, if nomads were the settlers, they must have been nomadic peoples who had previously been wandering around in Canaan.

This new refinement of the nomad theory, as it is called, is certainly attractive. But it has its limitations. Although Finkelstein has been an able advocate for the idea, the theory has proved difficult to flesh out with archaeological evidence. Archaeologists have, for instance, struggled to build up a full picture of the material life of the pastoralist nomads in Late Bronze Age Canaan. And without such a picture it is hard to make claims about the continuity (or otherwise) of that culture in the new Iron Age settlements. The difficulty is, of course, not surprising: nomads, by the very nature of their mode of life, do not leave much trace in the archaeological record.

And beyond the negative evidence of archaeological silence there is also the more positive argument of anthropology. Archaeologists and historians have in recent years been adopting more and more what they term an interdisciplinary approach. They have tried to expand their picture of early Canaanite society by comparative studies from other cultures, which have gone through similar courses of development. From such studies scholars have made several telling criticisms. Some have argued that the new settlers appear to have developed agricultural skills too quickly for it to be likely that they were novices at arable farming. Others, like Dever, and Larry Stager of Harvard University, have concluded that the indigenous population of Canaanite nomads would simply not have been big enough to explain all the new settlements in the hill-country. Nomads may have been an element of the new settlement, but according to Stager and others they cannot account for the whole picture.

In the late 1960s and early 1970s a new theory was put forward to explain the emergence of the Israelites. It became highly, if briefly, fashionable. Two American scholars, George E. Mendenhall and Norman Gottwald, elaborated what has been termed the peasants' revolt hypothesis. They saw the birth of early Israel in terms of revolutionary class war. For them the early settlers were not nomads but oppressed Canaanite peasants and town dwellers rebelling against the exploitation they endured within the established economy of the lowland city states, and seeking a new freedom and autonomy up in the hills outside the control of the existing power networks.

Once again the development was placed within the context of the more general Late Bronze Age cataclysm and its aftermath. It was argued that, faced with widespread economic collapse across the region, the Egyptians centralised and tightened their control over the greatly reduced urban centres of Canaan. Power became more concentrated. Taxes were increased and levied more efficiently. In the face of these harsh new conditions, it was suggested, many Canaanites chose to flee. They made their way to the hills and established new communities beyond the pale of Egyptian control.

Rather as the German scholars equated their nomads with the Shasu, Mendenhall and Gottwald equated their revolting peasants with another distinct group: the so-called 'apiru. The 'apiru seem to have been a social – rather than a racial or political – phenomenon of the Near East throughout the Late Bronze Age period. They are frequently mentioned in early Near Eastern texts as a motley, if ill-defined, group living on the margins of society in Egypt, Mesopotamia, Canaan and elsewhere. They had, it seems, little social status and, according to the sources that mention them, survived either through menial work, mercenary service or banditry.

The peasants' revolt hypothesis, however, has waned in popularity of late. There is too little archaeological (or, indeed, literary) evidence of widespread revolution and revolt in Late Bronze Age Canaan. Where there are signs of decline in the Canaanite cities it is often gradual rather than cataclysmic. And where there is evidence of destruction, such upheaval is just as likely to have been the cause of popular unrest rather than the result of it. Moreover, beyond these specific doubts thrown up by archaeology, the peasants' revolt hypothesis has also suffered as a result of shifting intellectual fashion. It is seen now as too obviously a product of its time. It is too clumsy in its reduction of the question to the Marxist equation of class conflict. Nevertheless the notion that some of the Early Iron Age settlers many have come from the world of the Canaanite cities remains attractive to many.

While the various theories jostle for position modern scholars are forever seeking new approaches, and trying out new arrangements of the known facts. As is so often the case in such academic debates, there is a tendency to combine elements of all the existing explanations to produce something richer, more complex, and – it is hoped – nearer to the truth. It is now being argued in many quarters that the settlement was not simply a matter of nomads adopting a new sedentary way of life, nor of a disaffected underclass fleeing from the centres of urban control, nor – indeed – of military conquest from outside; it was, perhaps, a little bit of each. That, at least, is the theory adopted by scholars such as Bill Dever and Larry Stager, and it is achieving a position close to a new orthodoxy.

At the risk of repetition, the new synthesis suggests that the general Late Bronze Age upheaval led to a decline in the power of the established Canaanite city states, and an increase in the control exercised by the Egyptian provincial administration that stood behind them during this period. This political arrangement encouraged a centrifugal process of ruralisation. As central power became both weaker and more demanding many peasant farmers sought to evade it by heading for the hills – literally. On the free land that they discovered there, they established small, largely self-sufficient agricultural communities with networks of interdependence for defence.

At the same time groups of nomadic pastoralists were moving into the same area mostly from within Canaan, but perhaps also from across the Jordan. The decline in the established economy – which maintained the traditional routes and markets upon which they depended – encouraged these nomads towards a more settled and self-sufficient mode of life. Although, for the most part, this settlement was carried out peacefully on otherwise vacant land, as it continued there were inevitably points of friction and conflict both with old-established Canaanite communities on the edges of the new settlement areas and among the new settlers themselves.

The picture is certainly rich and complex. It is also, to anyone with a more than passing knowledge of the Old Testament, somewhat familiar. It echoes in its general outline – if not in its details – the story told in the book of Judges.

Although the book of Judges appears to carry the story of the Children of Israel forward from the period of Joshua's conquest, through to an era of growing political consolidation, in fact – as biblical scholars have long recognised – this sense of seamless continuity is deceptive. If you read the book of Joshua and then read the book of Judges, it can seem as if you are being treated to two very different histories of the same event. The book of Joshua describes a brief, united blitzkrieg campaign. The Israelites conquer everything and then distribute it. In the book of Judges the Israelites are also shown distributing the land. But now they are presented, not as a united body, but as divided among themselves. They seek to expand their territories. But they find themselves confined to the hill-country. Despite their best efforts, they cannot get down to the fertile plains near the coast because there are too many military obstacles in their way.

There is a strong tribal flavour to the book. As titles go, 'the book of Judges' is perhaps unfortunate. To English ears at least it conjures up the image of serious men in full-bottomed wigs and flowing robes, displaying a baffled ignorance of all manifestations of popular life and culture. To the ancient Israelites, however – or at least to the authors of the Bible – these judges were rather different. They were not senior figures of the legal establishment. They were tribal heroes who emerged at times of crisis to fight off the enemies of the Israelites or the individual tribe.

There was Gideon who led a daring night-time raid on the Midianites, equipping his small force with trumpets, and with lamps concealed in pitchers. His men stealthily surrounded the Midianite camp, and then, at a given signal, broke their pitchers, held up their lamps, and blew their trumpets. In the ensuing panic, the enemy was easily routed and despatched. And there was Jephthah who ingeniously tracked down the remnants of the fleeing Ephraimite army by setting up checkpoints at the fords over the river Jordan, and then making everyone who wished to pass over say the word 'shibboleth'. The Ephraimites – apparently unable to cope with the initial sibilant – pronounced the word 'sibboleth' and were thus exposed, and (following the unvarying pattern of most of these stories) summarily executed.

And of course there was Samson, the least judicial of all the 'judges', who tore a lion apart with his bare hands. He waged a series of personal battles against the Philistines, often armed with nothing more than an ass's jawbone, before succumbing to the fatal charms of Delilah. She betrayed the secret of his great strength to his foes. He was captured, blinded and led away in chains – only to wreak a final and devastating revenge when he brought down the pillars of the Philistines' temple upon himself and his enemies. The stories are rich in incident, colour, and blood. They are stories which, taken together, appear to tell of the emergence of the tribes of Israel as a powerful unified force in the land of Canaan. But are they true?

There is much about the book of Judges that is immediately unconvincing from an historical standpoint – and not just the notion that one man could kill 1000 adversaries with an ass's jawbone. For one thing the chronology seems impossible. If all the time periods mentioned in the book are added up the total comes to over 400 years. Even in the ever shifting and poorly signposted world of biblical chronology this is recognised to be far too long a span. According to most current estimates the stories in the book of Judges take up at least twice the time they should.

Given the disparate nature of the various tales, it would seem that the book is really a collection of stories taken from various sources which have then been strung together into a continuous – if spurious – narrative. This is clearly a flaw, but does it make the book useless as an historical source? How early and authentic are the various traditions that have been incorporated into the book? Is there any chance that they preserve memories of actual events?

On this score scholars have been much intrigued by the discovery of an Early Iron Age Philistine temple at Tell Qasile. Archaeologists working at the site uncovered the bases of two supporting columns. While not exactly massive (the bases are only 27 inches in diameter) the columns would have supported a considerable load. In earlier times the find might have prompted an overenthusiastic scholar to announce that here was the very site of Samson's final act of self-destructive vengeance, a living proof of the Bible's factual accuracy. Such claims are now frowned upon. Nevertheless even for archaeologists determinedly rejecting the undue influence of the biblical narrative, the connection between Samson and the columns has been hard to ignore completely. It is a connection that, when put into its proper context, opens up some interesting possibilities.

Archaeological evidence suggests that the Philistines, after settling on the coast of Canaan in the Early Iron Age, quickly adopted many of the habits of the Canaanites. Within a couple of generations they were, it seems, constructing temples that did not require or make use of supporting columns. Although there is much scholarly disagreement over when the Bible was written down, it is generally agreed that it was long after the period recorded in Judges – and long after the period when the Philistines ceased to use columns to support the roofs of their temples. And yet the memory of this long-vanished practice (a practice only recently rediscovered by archaeology) is recorded in the story of Samson's suicidal act of defiance. It is enough to suggest that this story at least has its origins in a very old, if not a contemporary, tradition.

While the echoes between some specific incidents and the archaeological record are certainly interesting, it is not the truth, or otherwise, of the individual stories that is suggestive. It is the more general picture that emerges from such readings. The opening chapters of the book of Judges seem to hint at a process, not of conquest, but of settlement – a process, moreover, that has been only partial and piecemeal. Much of chapter 1 is taken up with listing all the places that have *not* been settled. And the whole cumulative effect of the book, with its descriptions of frequent small-scale conflicts, limited territorial gains, and fluctuating alliances, suggests many disparate groups – or tribes – acting for the most part individually. It is a picture of a fragmentary tribal society only slowly coming together, first into a loose, occasional confederation and then into a more formal and centralised polity – a kingdom.

This is the picture that seems oddly familiar. Could it perhaps be the early Israelite tribes described in the book of Judges were one and the same as the Iron Age settlers identified by the archaeologists as colonising the central hill-country? It is a tempting notion. But is it a chimera? Is it – in the context of modern 'Rejectionist' scholarship – even a legitimate question? In other words, if we did not have the Bible would we ask it at all? Well, as it turns out, we might . . .

There is a large polished stone that would prompt us to pose the question: the Merneptah stela. The stela is a black granite pillar, standing over seven feet high, dedicated to the pharaoh Merneptah. It was discovered by Flinders Petrie in a temple at Thebes, in southern Egypt, in 1896. Merneptah's dates are now generally given as 1213–1203BCE. His stela – according to this chronology – was erected in 1209BCE to commemorate an impressive list of military victories. Towards the end of the long and vainglorious inscription that covers one face of the stela there is a hymn detailing the pharaoh's campaigns in Canaan. Various cities and places are mentioned. But one name stands out – at least to biblical scholars and archaeologists – Israel.

> The Princes are prostrate, saying 'Mercy'!
> Not one raises his head among the Nine Bows.
> Now that Tehenu has come to devastation,
> Hatti is pacified.
> The Canaan has been plundered with every sort of evil;
> Ashkelon has been overcome;
> Gezer has been captured;
> Yanoam is made non-existent;
> Israel is laid waste and his seed is not;
> Hurru is become a widow because of Egypt!
> All lands together, they are pacified.

There is, as has been pointed out, a certain irony in the fact that the very inscription that provides the first proof of Israel's existence should be announcing – rather prematurely – Israel's destruction. But the importance of the find remains: here is an early, extra-biblical and contemporary documentary reference to an ancient Israel.

Although the mention is brief, Egyptologists have been able to extract an impressive amount of information from it. The inscription not only seems to confirm the existence of Israel at this early period but it also suggests something of Israel's nature. Within the broad territory of Canaan, Israel was clearly seen as something a bit different. The three Canaanite city states, or kingdoms, of Ashkelon, Gezer and Yanoam, which Merneptah also boasts of vanquishing, are all treated grammatically in one fashion, while Israel is presented syntactically not as a city or kingdom, but as a people. At this stage – the late thirteenth century BCE – it would seem that Israel, though a definite entity and an adversary worth crowing over, was still only a rural and tribal grouping rather than anything more formal.

Further details are absent. Just who this group were, where they came from, where they settled, when they settled, and what distinguished them from their neighbours – all this is left unstated and unclear. Nevertheless the inscription does place a people called Israel in Canaan at the beginning of the Iron Age. And that, of course, is what the book of Judges does too. The connection cannot be made any more emphatically than that; the book of Judges, unfortunately, does not make any reference to Merneptah's campaign, and Merneptah's scribes make no specific reference to any of the heroes mentioned in the book of Judges. Nevertheless most scholars are prepared to accept that the Israel mentioned in the inscription at Thebes is directly linked with the Israelites who came to write down the book of Judges. The coincidence of the two names has been enough to put the early biblical Israelites onto the historical map. Just where to locate them on that map remains a challenge.

The very fact of the Merneptah stela's inscription, however, makes it legitimate to pose the question: are the early Israelites of the book of Judges and of Merneptah's campaign the same people as the Iron Age settlers of the central hill-country?

Even among many broadly 'Rejectionist' archaeologists and

scholars, the connection has proved just too tempting to pass up. The archaeologists have found evidence of a wave of new settlement in the hill-country; the book of Judges describes a wave of new settlement in the hill-country. There must be at least a strong possibility that the two things are related in some way. In an attempt to assess just how close – or tenuous – this relation might be, scholars have been obliged to look again at their Bibles.

The Old Testament has crept back into the scholarly frame. It has been argued, not without justice, that if any other comparable Near Eastern literary source existed it would not be completely passed over by archaeologists. It would be treated with caution, certainly. It would not be used to direct research and excavation. But it would be used after the excavations had taken place, in the general effort to explain and interpret the material uncovered. The Bible, though it does not deserve a privileged position, does not warrant an extremely unprivileged position either. It should be treated simply as another ancient Near Eastern text, and scrutinised for what it can offer in building up a picture of the past.

Close study of the book of Judges has revealed some interesting points of connection with the discoveries and ideas of recent archae-ology. Intriguingly the nomad theory – or theories – elucidated by Finkelstein, Zertal and others were prefigured by similar ideas evolved merely from textual analysis of the Bible. The great German biblical scholar Albrecht Alt, as early as the 1920s, long before the archaeological survey had even revealed the nature and extent of the Iron Age settlement in the central hill district, elucidated a broadly similar theory based on a close study of the territorial divisions listed in the book of Judges. This picture was attractive to Alt and his followers not least because it seemed to be reflected in the broader biblical narrative: the tales of Abraham and Isaac and their flocks. It also suggested a process of social evolution: a progress from a wandering life in tents to a settled life in houses. Although notions about social progress are no longer fashionable, and modern scholars are extremely sceptical about the historical authenticity of Abraham and Isaac, the basic theory – derived from the biblical subtext – that nomadic pastoralists played a part in the settlements of the early Israelites chimes with the ideas of many archaeologists.

Another possible point of connection between the extra-biblical and biblical worlds is suggested by the aforementioned 'apiru. Some scholars have maintained that the word Hebrew – which very early on became a near synonym for Israelite – is derived from the word 'apiru (or habiru as it appears in Sumerian texts). The derivation, if correct, would seem to confirm the central role of the 'apiru in the establishment of early Israelite society. But, needless to say, the derivation is not undisputed. Indeed nearly all etymologists now doubt the connection. The similarity in sound between the two words is, they claim, deceptive: they almost certainly derive from different roots. They contend that the word Hebrew comes, more probably, from the verb abar, meaning to cross over, suggesting that the Hebrews were defined as those who crossed over. Exactly what they crossed over remains unstated: the river Jordan has been suggested, and so has the Euphrates. Other scholars argue that the word has its origins in the genealogies of the book of Genesis where Eber – the grandson of Shem – is listed as one of the forefathers of Abraham.

The picture built up by archaeologists of the social structure that existed in the early Iron Age villages, for all its apparent novelty, finds a surprising number of echoes in the biblical text – both in its detail and its outline. Several scholars have been struck by the fact that the quite distinct familial arrangements that can be traced 'on the ground' in the settlement patterns and village plans of the hill-country, are very similar to those suggested, or alluded to, in the descriptions of early Israelite life in the book of Judges.

According to such readings, the four-room house represents the nuclear unit. The clusters of such houses, often built around a common courtyard, which have been noted in many villages, might be equivalent to the biblical *bêt 'āv*, or house of the father, the extended, multigenerational family, presided over by its patriarch. The next level of social organisation – suggested by the biblical narratives – was the *mishpaha*, or clan, which probably consisted of all the clusters in the village. Beyond that was the *shebet* or tribe. And then there was *benei-Israel*, perhaps equivalent to the emerging ethnic group, a confederacy of the various tribes.

Although, as has already been suggested, the biblical picture of the early Israelites comprising twelve (or thirteen) neatly designated fraternal tribes all claiming common ancestry from a great patriarch, was almost certainly mythical, it is also generally agreed that early Israelite society probably was tribal. And it is at least possible that the various tribes did – at least in time – come to bear the names ascribed to them in the Bible. Nevertheless it cannot be assumed that the tribes were well organised. Nor, apparently, did they conform to the popular notion of a tribe as some sort of nomadic or semi-nomadic group. In Early Iron Age Canaan, scholars have suggested, the term tribe was probably used to denote settled groups of people – rural or even urban – who claimed a common ancestry.

Using only the internal evidence of the book of Judges, scholars have suggested that the principal function of the tribe seems to have been not so much social or political, as military. The tribal unit is shown as providing a militia in times of danger. And, if the danger was exceptional, then various tribal militias might seek to ally themselves against a common enemy.

As far as the author – or authors – of the book of Judges are concerned this sense of the possibilities and responsibilities of tribal coalition was an important element in Israel's developing sense of itself. Certainly it is this sense that can be clearly seen running through the Song of Deborah, a passage that some biblical scholars consider to be among the earliest parts of the book of Judges. A few critics date it to as early as the late twelfth century BCE, very close to the probable time of the events it purports to describe. George Foot Moore has gone so far as to call it the 'only contemporaneous monument of Hebrew history' before the tenth or ninth centuries BCE. And even if few other critics are quite so bullish in their estimates of its antiquity, many biblical scholars do regard it as early, at least in origin.

The poem tells of how Deborah and her general, Barak, lead a confederation of Israelite tribal militias to victory over the superior Canaanite forces commanded by Sisera. After his troops are routed at Taanach 'by the waters of Megiddo' the Canaanite general flees, and is memorably finished off by Jael, who drives a tent peg through his temples while he is taking a nap. Israel, in the poem, is presented as a loose confederation of ten (not twelve) tribes bound by a common adherence to Yahweh. Four of the tribes (Reuben, Gilead, Dan and Asher) are – for various reasons – unable to answer Deborah's call to arms. It is left to the other six to provide the men to fight. The practicalities of the arrangement are given in such detail that some scholars are convinced they must relate to some actual event.

The picture of Iron Age settlement in Canaan painstakingly built up by the archaeologists does not, indeed cannot, deal with such matters. Although it can suggest a certain amount about the basic social organisation of village life, less tangible concerns such as tribal service and tribal responsibility tend to leave no trace in the archaeological record. Military conflicts, however, often do.

Archaeologists working at the site of Taanach 'by the waters of Megiddo', (Judges v, 19), in the Jezreel valley have uncovered a destruction layer that can be dated to around 1125BCE. Although they have not claimed – as once they might have done – that here is clear evidence of Deborah's famous victory, the find – taken together with destruction layers from the same period at other sites (some mentioned in the book of Judges, some not) – does at least contribute to a picture of conflict on the fertile fringes of the hill-country towards the end of the twelfth century BCE. And this is a picture that matches, in some respects, the one adumbrated in the book of Judges.

Nevertheless despite its elements of historical plausibility – if not historical accuracy – there are other aspects of the Song of Deborah that seem to demand caution. The author of the poem clearly saw the early Israelites as fundamentally different from and opposed to the Canaanites. This, to many scholars, is suspicious at the very least. The discoveries of modern archaeology suggest that in all probability the majority of early settlers of the central hill district were indigenous Canaanites. If, as is increasingly accepted, these settlers were or became the early Israelites, then the early Israelites must, in fact, have been Canaanites. In the early period of settlement any distinction – such as that suggested by the Song of Deborah and most of the other stories in the book of Judges – would probably have been very difficult, if not impossible, to make.

The notion that the early Israelites did not arrive as conquerors from outside the country, but emerged as settlers from within the indigenous Canaanite population, is arresting. It seems – at first acquaintance – rather shocking. And, as it sinks in, it seems more shocking. A God-given conquest of the Promised Land and a distinct racial identity as God's Chosen People: these are the two great planks of Jewish tradition. Take them away and it seems to realign radically the accepted story of the Old Testament. It undermines the entire dynamic of the biblical narrative. And it suggests that extreme caution must be exercised in attempting to use the book of Judges as an historical source.

This notion that the early Israelites were probably Canaanites, though not undisputed in academic circles, is now widely accepted. It recently received some unexpected pictorial support. It turns out that there is, very probably, a vivid illustration of the fact among the carved Egyptian reliefs at Karnak. One series of reliefs which was previously thought to show the campaigns of Ramases II, has recently been re-ascribed to the time of his successor, Merneptah. The carvings are now believed to depict his victories over the three Canaanite city states (Ashkelon is specifically captioned) and over the people of Israel – as described in his victory stela at Thebes. The Israelites, shown being trampled under the hooves of the rampant Egyptians, are – significantly – not distinguished by dress or hairstyle from the Canaanite inhabitants of Ashkelon and the other cities. From this evidence, at least, it would seem that the Egyptians regarded the people of Israel as Canaanite.

The idea that the Israelites and the Canaanites might share a common racial heritage has repercussions beyond the confines of Near Eastern archaeology and biblical scholarship. The notion – like so many others in this field – has struck a powerful chord in modern Israel. Any suggestion that the Palestinians (who see themselves as the descendants of the biblical Canaanites) and the Israelis (who see themselves as the descendants of the biblical Israelites) might all come from the same stock is intriguing or appalling, depending on your point of view.

It is a hypothesis that could perhaps be elucidated by modern DNA testing. But, for such tests to be carried out, the scientists would need the bones of some of the early Israelite settlers. Bizarrely, archaeologists and surveyors claim that no such bones have ever been found. Certainly Adam Zertal will not admit to having come across any during his digs or surveys. 'There are no human bones,' he laments with an air of puzzled resignation. 'In the early Israelite sites, no cemeteries, no human bones have ever been found. It is one of the big mysteries of biblical archaeology: why there are no human bones of the early Israelite time.' And other archaeologists are eager to echo such sentiments. Nevertheless there is evidence to suggest that this may not be the whole picture.

One Near Eastern expert, who wishes to remain anonymous, claimed that the mystery might have a darker side. 'The bones were there,' he claims. 'We have an awful lot of skeletal material from that period here in Israel. But if there is anyone here in Israel today who is carrying out this research I am positive they are not willing to speak about it publicly.' The reason for this reticence – indeed the reason for the expert's desire for anonymity – is fear. 'Over the years,' he explains, 'the archaeological community has suffered tremendously as a result of religious fanaticism.' Death threats and curses are commonplace. For some people in modern Israel the work that the archaeologists are doing stands as an insult to their religion. Many Orthodox Jews regard any interference with the remains of the dead as sacrilege. It is a subject that calls forth strong feelings and some extremists are moved to vent their anger against archaeologists in abuse and threat.

Nevertheless, even if the bones of the early Israelites are not readily available for research, some work on the question can still be carried out. The genes of the ancient Israelites and the ancient Canaanites are surely present in the population of modern Israel. Each man carries in his Y chromosome a full record of his male line: his father, his father's father, his father's father's father, and so on back through all the generations to the beginning of human history. By looking at the records of a section of a population it is possible to trace these lineages back to a point of common paternal ancestry. A research project being carried out at the Hadessah hospital in Jerusalem is trying to build up a picture of the origins of the local population.

'Our research is focused on the Arabs who live in this area,' explains Dr Ariella Oppenheim, one of the team carrying out the project. 'We have tried to see what their relationship is with the Jews.' The experiment has had some very intriguing results. The researchers have discovered that it is possible to trace all Palestinians and Jews back to a common paternal ancestor. This, in itself, is not, apparently, surprising. If we traced our lineages back far enough we would find that we all came from a very small handful of common ancestors. What surprised the researchers was that the fork in this family tree when the Jews and the Palestinians separated from each other, occurred *after* the fork when the other Arab peoples of the Near East separated from the Palestinians. In other words the Palestinians appear to be more closely related to the Jews than to the rest of the Arab world.

It is a discovery that chimes with the archaeologists' theories about the Canaanite origins of early Israel. Nevertheless it can only be taken so far. At the moment it is impossible for scientists to determine the date of these genetic events. Did the separation in the patrilinear lines of the Palestinians and the Jews happen in 1200BCE, 1800BCE or AD600? It is not known. But techniques are advancing and it is hoped that in time a fuller answer will be given. In the meantime scholars are cautious of pressing the point too forcefully.

For some modern Palestinians, of course, such discoveries have a political as well as an historical dimension. If the Israelites were originally Canaanites, they claim, the modern Israelis should be viewed, not as something separate, but as just a strand of the single ancient and continuous Canaanite cultural tradition. And as such they should have no special rights to large sections of the former land of Canaan.

Modern Palestinians can indeed point to the continuity of at least some aspects of ancient Canaanite culture. The vernacular pottery still made in many Palestinian communities today bears remarkable similarities to the earthenware produced in the same area during the biblical period. But it is a large distance to leap from pottery to land rights and, not very surprisingly, few contemporary Israelis are prepared to make such a jump.

Moreover, even if it is established – as seems likely – that the early Israelites were indigenous Canaanites, the question still remains: what made them different from their neighbours? What distinguished them from other Canaanites to such an extent that, even by the end of the thirteenth century BCE, Pharaoh Merneptah could refer to them as the people of Israel?

The Bible, of course, has no doubt what it was that made the Israelites different and special: adherence to the one true God, Yahweh. The special relationship between Yahweh and his people, the Israelites, is the great theme of the whole Old Testament or Hebrew Bible. It is certainly the dominant motif running through the book of Judges: the tribes of Israel desert Yahweh and worship foreign gods; Yahweh in turn deserts them, and as a result they are defeated and oppressed by their neighbours. Just as extinction threatens, they call upon Yahweh for assistance and He obligingly sends a leader – or judge – to deliver them. All the dramas and battles of the various heroes and heroines are fitted into this recurring pattern. Most scholars, however, are wary of this picture. They argue, from studying the text, that the pattern of religious distinctions and religious division was imposed on the narrative at a comparatively late date, certainly many years after the land settlements described in the book of Judges. Just because Yahwism became the religion of the Israelites and the dominant motif of their narratives, they argue, there is no reason to suppose that it always held this position. Indeed there is much evidence to suggest that it did not.

The very name Israel is a Canaanite word. Its exact meaning is argued over by scholars, but it is universally agreed that it is made up of two elements – *Isra* and *el*. El is both the Canaanite word for god, and the specific name of the leading deity in the Canaanite pantheon. The *Isra* element means something close to fighter with/for/of/etc. The book of Genesis explains the name Israel as meaning fighter with God or he contended with God, and claims that it was a title first conferred on Jacob after he wrestled with God – or God's angel – at Wadi Jabbok. But it is, apparently, just as possible to translate the word as fighters for El, with El being the presiding Canaanite god. In other words the early Israelites may have defined themselves by their close adherence to the Canaanite god El.

One of the most interesting Iron Age religious sites uncovered in the region, while it revealed no obvious trace of Yahweh, did yield a small bronze figurine of a bull. The little statue is almost certainly an image of Bull El, one of El's most popular manifestations.

Some commentators remain unimpressed by such arguments. They place Yahwism at the centre of their explanation of events. Norman Gottwald, for instance, suggested that it was the new cult of Yahwism that provided the ideological motor for the supposed peasants' revolt, and the moral framework for the egalitarian communities that the revolting peasants established. Most recent scholarship, however, has been more circumspect, reluctant to move beyond what archaeology can reveal. Thus far, archaeology has revealed nothing to connect Yahweh directly or specifically to the new settlement sites. For Dever, as for many others, Yahwism was almost certainly a later development, perhaps much later, 'not the cause of Israel's rise but the consequence'.

If archaeology has not revealed the presence of Yahweh among the early settlers, it has concentrated its energies upon trying to discover some trait – or traits – that might mark the Iron Age hill sites as distinctively different, and thus distinctively Israelite. Some of the more obvious aspects of this new material culture have been mentioned already: the four-room house, the simple village plans. Among the pottery, some archaeologists have detected a new form of large collar-rim storage jar, which they regard as characteristic of the early hilltop settlements. Other elements found in these villages – and thought to be distinctive and new – include rock hewn, plastered water cisterns, subterranean stone lined grain silos, some simple iron tools, and terracing for hillside farming. All these traits have been put forward as distinctive markers, potential indicators that here is what may be termed an Israelite settlement as opposed to a Canaanite one. Each has held a glimmer of hope, but then has been undermined by discoveries elsewhere. Similar jars, houses, grain silos and tools have been found at well-attested and long-established Canaanite sites, or across the Jordan in Ammon or Moab.

Perhaps the greatest – and most sustained – flurry of excitement has been stirred up by a recent discovery. 'In the highlands we saw something quite surprising,' explains Israel Finkelstein. 'Pig bones disappear altogether from the archaeological record. We had them before. And we have them again later. But at this time – the Iron Age – the time of biblical Israel, if you wish, they disappear. At the same time in the lowlands we not only *have* pig bones, we have a lot of them.'

The evidence clearly suggested that the highland settlers had made a decision to take pork out of their diet at this time. And this, of course, makes a connection with established Jewish dietary taboos. No scholar, however, would argue merely from the absence of a few spareribs from the archaeological record that the early Israelite settlers had adopted a fully formulated kosher diet at this early stage; there may have been cultural, economic, agricultural or even gastronomic reasons for dropping pork from the menu. The evidence is mute upon such matters. Nevertheless it did seem as if an exciting breakthrough had been made. Here might be a means of distinguishing Israelite settlements from Canaanite ones.

The first flush of optimism occasioned by these findings has now passed. Finkelstein's argument has been challenged, even if it has not been decisively overturned. A recent study by a pair of American zooarchaeologists has painstakingly examined the bone records of Iron Age archaeological sites throughout the Near East. Its findings indicate that by the latter half of the second millennium BCE pig consumption may, in fact, have been almost non-existent throughout the entire region – from Babylonia through to Egypt. Remains are very scarce. There were a few exceptions. As Israel Finkelstein argued, there are indeed plentiful pig bones dating from this period in the lowlands of what was Canaan. Substantial numbers were found in the Philistine cities of Ashkelon, Ekron and Timnah.

Nevertheless even these finds may not be enough to confirm that pork eating and abstention from pork eating can be regarded as defining ethnic markers. Some other Philistine cities appear to show no traces of pig bones. And, interestingly, even at Ashkelon and the other pork eating settlements, pigs appear to have gone out of fashion within a hundred years or so. Their bones cease to crop up in the archaeological record after the tenth century BCE. Pigs, it seems, were perhaps just not very well suited to life in the ancient Near East. Maybe they required too much water and too much supervision.

The search to find valid and effective ways of separating the Canaanites from the Israelites remains one of the ongoing challenges for archaeologists working in the field. It is a difficult business. Sometimes it feels as if a mist has descended upon the whole subject, blurring everything and making clear definition impossible. It is at such moments that one turns with relief to Adam Zertal standing upon the bright sunlit crags of mount Ebal.

Mount Ebal is the one of the highest peaks in Israel. It rises above the surrounding central hill-country to a height of over 3000 feet (940 metres). From its summit it commands views over the Mediterranean to the west, and as far as the mountains of Gilead, across the river Jordan, to the east. The hills surrounding Jerusalem, over thirty miles away, can be seen to the south.

Mount Ebal plays a starring role in the biblical story. Or, rather, it is a co-starring role, shared with its southern neighbour, mount Gerizim. In the book of Deuteronomy (chapters xxvii and xxviii) Moses commands the Children of Israel, after they have safely entered the Promised Land, to gather in two groups, one upon mount Ebal, the other upon the facing slope of mount Gerizim. The former group was to issue curses upon the Children of Israel, should they fail to keep the Commandments, the latter group was to bless all those who kept God's law. This ceremony was to be preceded by a solemn sacrifice on a great altar which the Children of Israel were to set up on mount Ebal.

The book of Joshua (viii, 30–32) describes in some detail how Joshua carried out this commission.

> Then Joshua built an altar unto the Lord God of Israel in mount Ebal, as Moses the servant of the Lord commanded the Children of Israel, as it is written in the book of the law of Moses, an altar of whole stones, over which no man hath lifted up any iron: and they offered thereon burnt offerings unto the Lord, and sacrificed peace offerings. And he wrote there upon the stones a copy of the law of Moses, which he wrote in the presence of the children of Israel.

After this ritual, the party divided in two, one group stayed on mount Ebal, the other went and stood 'over against mount Gerizim', and they duly issued their respective blessings and curses. It is a vivid if curious story, and one that places mount Ebal at the heart of the biblical narrative.

Mount Ebal is not only tall, it is large: in area it covers some six and a half square miles (18sq km). As such it presented a major challenge to Zertal and his team of surveyors. It took them the best part of two months – starting in February 1980 – just to cover the ground.

It was towards the end of this period – on what Zertal recalls as 'a cool, spring afternoon in April' – that he and his fellow surveyors came upon a large heap of stones set in a little natural amphitheatre on the mountain's 'second step'. It was not the first that they had encountered. The landscape of ancient northern Samaria is littered with such heaps. Most of them were created by early farmers as a means of clearing at least some of the land for cultivation and use. They provoke little interest. Zertal learnt that the local population around mount Ebal refers to the heap of stones as *el-burnat*, which means the hat in Arabic. But to his eyes there was something different and special about it. For a start it was larger than the usual type. And among the stones were numerous fragments of broken pottery.

These potsherds were distinctive enough in design and manufacture to enable Zertal to date them confidently to the Early Iron Age (1220–1000BCE), exactly the period at which it is thought the Israelites emerged as a distinctive group in Canaan. This was exciting, if not entirely surprising. Zertal's survey of northern Samaria had revealed numerous sites dating from exactly this period, most of them small-scale domestic and agricultural buildings. And the area, at least according to biblical tradition, was one of the heartlands of early Israel. Nevertheless the new find displayed several novel and distinctive features.

It was uncharacteristically isolated. Although Zertal found a dozen other sites on the mountain they were all of a much later date. There was no evidence of other Iron Age settlements nearby. While the rest of northern Samaria appears to have been scattered thickly with sites from the Early Iron Age, on mount Ebal there was only this one. It was an anomaly that prompted Zertal to find out more.

'We began to uncover the pile of stones,' Zertal recalls. The mystery deepened: 'We did not know what was there but we could see some walls emerging from the pile of stones.' It was clear, however, that more serious resources were going to be called for. Zertal began raising funds in order to excavate the site.

Excavations did not in fact begin until late in 1980. They continued until 1989 and much was uncovered that seemed strange and unexpected. The principal features of the site were soon exposed, simply by removing the pile of stones. Underneath the 'hat' Zertal discovered an imposing rectangular structure some $24 \times 29\frac{1}{2}$ feet. The walls, built from large, unhewn field stones were five feet thick and stand even now almost nine feet high. The area enclosed by these stout walls had been completely filled in. Excavation revealed that this filling was composed not of mere debris or in-fill but of carefully built-up and distinct layers of 'field stones', earth and ashes, arranged in order.

Amongst the earth and ashes there were more pottery fragments, all dateable to the early Iron Age. At the bottom of all these layers of filling, Zertal was surprised to discover no obvious floor covering or foundation; the walls were built directly on to the bedrock. Even more curiously there was no doorway into the structure.

Adjoining the south-western side of this strange edifice were two paved courtyards, each containing several small, stone built structures. Some of these little installations had been paved with crushed chalk. They contained either pottery vessels or ashes.

Separating the two courtyards was what appeared to be a massive, if rather decayed, stone wall. On closer inspection Zertal recognised it as a shallow ramp, some three feet wide and twenty-three feet long, running up to the top of the main structure at an incline of twenty-two degrees. The highest point of the ramp is actually a foot higher than the wall it touches, suggesting that the main structure was once slightly higher than it now is. This complex of stone structures – and a large area around it – is enclosed by a low stone wall. And beyond the ellipse of this first wall there are traces of another, larger in scale and older in date.

What did it all mean? Zertal's finds were certainly puzzling. Initially he had supposed that the main structure was a farmhouse. But he could not relate its layout to other farmhouses from this period – or, indeed, from any other period. The absence of a doorway made it difficult to view the building as essentially domestic in function.

Perhaps it was a watchtower. Certainly the height and thickness of the walls would make it a good and defensible vantage point. But to Zertal's mind there were problems too with this interpretation. There was, after all, nothing to watch for. No major routes, let alone major roads, passed over mount Ebal, and no one lived nearby. The mystery, it seemed, remained.

A possible answer arrived unexpectedly. 'I remember it vividly,' recalls Zertal. 'It was a Thursday, the morning of 13 October 1983.

A friend of mine, a young archaeologist named David Etam, visited the site, and I gave him a tour. I was explaining the site to him, especially the difficulty we were having understanding the function of the strange central structure that had been filled. David interrupted me: "Why don't you think the opposite? Why don't you think that the filling is the important part, rather than the building?"'

It was, Zertal considers, a brilliant insight, and one that sent him back to his Bible. He turned to Exodus xxvii, 8, a passage which gives instructions on how to make a portable tabernacle altar. 'Hollow with boards shalt thou make it; as it was shewed thee in the mount, shall they make it.' *The Biblical Encyclopaedia* expands on this picture: 'The Tabernacle altar is described as having four walls'; it was filled with earth and stone to its full height. On this filling the fire was burned. This construction method is well known from Assyrian altars. That is why the altar is described – in the Exodus passage – as being 'hollow with boards'.

Zertal was convinced that here was a possible answer: the structure might be a massive altar. It was certainly a theory that would resolve many of the site's mysteries: the absence of a doorway, the large ramp (Exodus xx, 26 specifically condemns the use of steps in altar construction), the neatly ordered layers of filling, the signs of fire. The low elliptical wall encircling the site became explainable as a temenos wall, such as is frequently found enclosing sacred places in early cultures.

Zertal's vision of the altar was, moreover, found to chime extraordinarily closely to a second century AD description in the early rabbinic Mishnah of the great altar in the Second Temple in Jerusalem, before it was destroyed by the Romans in AD70.

Other evidence also seemed to support the theory. The bones, which had been found in such large quantities among the ashes in the main structure, were sent for scientific analysis at the Hebrew University in Jerusalem. It was discovered that they belonged to only four different types of animal: bullocks, rams, goats and fallow deer. All were male and all were young. Most of them appeared to have been burnt on open fires at low temperature. The book of Leviticus, which gives detailed instructions about the correct sacrificial procedures, lists bullocks, rams and goats as the animals to be used for burnt offerings. The absence of fallow deer from the list cannot be ignored, but it should be noted that they are – like the others – kosher animals. They can be eaten, and it is at least possible that during the early Israelite period, they could also be used as sacrificial victims.

A good deal of pottery has been found, both in the installations in the courtyard spaces next to the main structure which Zertal identified as an altar and in several other little stone structures uncovered away from the altar but inside the temenos wall. Almost two-thirds of the pots that have been discovered are large storage jars with distinctive, collared rims. These, Zertal believes, would once have contained offerings. There are also significant numbers of jugs and chalices, and small vessels, which were perhaps for votive use. Of domestic pottery, however, there is almost no trace.

Altars are mentioned frequently in the Bible. And although some of the references are to small incense burning altars, most are to altars used for burnt offerings. Although they were often associated with – and connected to – major temples, there are also references to independent, free-standing altars. Some scholars argue that these independent altars are related to the sacred high places – or *bama* – which are sometimes described as places of sacrificial offering. In I Kings iii, 4 there is an account of how Solomon 'sacrificed and burnt incense in high places. And the king went to Gibeon to sacrifice there; for that was the great high place [*bama*]: a thousand burnt offerings did Solomon offer upon that altar.' Perhaps, Zertal argues, the altar on mount Ebal and its surrounding site constituted just such a *bama*.

The very mode of the site's preservation seems, at least to some, to suggest that it must have been a spiritually important place. The large structure appears to have been deliberately and carefully buried under its pile of stones, almost as if its power needed to be covered and contained.

If it is accepted that this curious edifice on mount Ebal is an altar, then it becomes tempting to take the argument one step further and suggest that here might be the very site where Joshua made his famous sacrifice in fulfilment of Moses' command. Any such suggestion is, of course, well calculated to irritate the 'Rejectionist' school of archaeologists. Even if they were to admit that it was a cultic site, there is nothing material to connect it definitely with Joshua – or indeed the Israelites. No inscriptions have been found. Zertal himself hesitated to take the step. 'I must confess,' he sighs, 'it was not easy for me [to accept that this was Joshua's altar]. It took me, I would say, four years of excavating at the site. As a scientist, as a rationalist, as an archaeologist, I refused to accept the fact. It was very hard for me. But finally I had to surrender. And I think it somehow liberated me from that conception that the Bible, the early Bible, is all mythology – is all a collection of legends.' The location of the site, the narrow dating band it can be placed in, and the unique spirit of the place, have all combined to convince him that this is one of those rare cases 'where biblical tradition and concrete archaeological evidence coincide, [and] cannot be ignored'.

There are, it must be admitted, some problems with this particular coincidence of biblical tradition and archaeological evidence. Not the least difficulty is mount Gerizim. During the early years of biblical archaeology, when scholars were striving to discover the lost sites of the Old Testament, several efforts were made to locate Joshua's great altar on mount Ebal. None of them was successful. The early archaeologists, following the story set down in the book of Joshua, concentrated their searches on the southern slopes of the mountain, the slopes facing mount Gerizim. The biblical account suggests that the two groups were probably in sight of each other as they issued their blessings and maledictions.

The structure uncovered by Zertal is on the north flank of the mountain, out of sight of, and facing in the opposite direction from, mount Gerizim. It is a problem that Zertal has sought to defuse by suggesting that perhaps generations of scholars and millennia of tradition have mislocated mount Gerizim: it is not – as is generally supposed – the large mountain to the south of mount Ebal, but another, not quite so large, mountain to the north. This new mountain has the advantage – for Zertal's argument – of being in clear view of his 'altar'. Such ingenuity has not gone down well in many quarters. Not least it has offended the Samaritans, a Jewish sect that regards mount Gerizim as its holy mountain. They are not keen to see their most sacred site suddenly relocated.

Predicatably Zertal's assertions have also provoked hostile debate in academic circles. Fellow archaeologists and historians have rushed forward with rival theories and arguments. Nadav Na'aman has suggested that the site, rather than being Joshua's altar, might be the tower of Shechem, the cultic centre of the people of Shechem, also mentioned in the book of Judges. He interprets the central structure as the house of El-berith in which the people took refuge from their king, Abimelech (Judges ix, 46).

Other scholars, such as Israel Finkelstein, while admitting the cultic – and even the Israelite – nature of the site, do not follow Zertal in seeing it as an altar. Michael David Coogan, a leading American archaeologist, has misgivings about ascribing the site to the Israelites, feeling that in the Early Iron Age the Israelites – whatever their distinctive religious beliefs – had no separate material culture that allows them to be distinguished from the Canaanites.

Not all archaeologists, however, even accept that the site's function was religious. Bill Dever remains sceptical upon the point. The most uncompromising rejection of Zertal's view, however, came from a distinguished archaeologist called Aharon Kempinski. He did not regard the site as cultic at all. He suggested that the central structure was nothing more than an ancient farmhouse, which was subsequently filled in to form the foundations of a watchtower. What Zertal described as the ramp leading up to the altar, he dismissed as a partially eroded wall. The other walls adjoining the ramp, which Zertal construes as enclosing two courtyards, Kempinski claimed were house walls.

Mount Ebal has become one of the conundrums of contemporary Near Eastern archaeology. The strange stone structure that Zertal has uncovered upon the broad shoulder of mount Ebal has an undeniable sense of power and mystery. It seems to have a secret to tell, but, like all stones, it cannot speak. The archaeologists must try and elucidate its purpose and the guesses that they make, perhaps inevitably, tend to reflect the widely differing views they hold about the very nature of the Israelite settlement in Canaan.

CHAPTER 4

King David

K ing David is one of the stars of the Old Testament. The slayer of Goliath, the singer of the Psalms, the friend of Jonathan, the lover of Bathsheba and, in the Christian tradition, the forefather of Jesus: he is despite, or perhaps because of, his occasional faults, one of the most colourful and attractive characters in the whole biblical narrative. Although his name occurs throughout the books of the Old Testament, his story is told principally in the two books of Samuel and in the opening chapters of the first book of Kings.

It is a rags-to-riches saga in the best tradition. David is first shown to us as a poor shepherd boy in the land of Judah, the youngest of eight sons of a Bethlehem farmer. He grows up at a time when the scattered tribes of Israel are struggling against an array of more powerful foes – particularly the Philistines. In an effort to provide some united leadership against these common enemies, Saul – from the tribe of Benjamin – is chosen by the prophet Samuel as the first king of the Israelites, very much against the prophet's wishes and better judgement. Samuel's misgivings are soon justified. He falls out with Saul, and is told by Yahweh to seek out David and to anoint him, too, as a possible future king.

David presents himself at Saul's court where he wins general favour as a royal attendant. He is particularly well regarded on account of his skill as a musician; his harp playing is said to be able to soothe the famously cantankerous Saul during his recurrent bouts of ill temper.

But even this accomplishment pales before his first intervention in the nation's military affairs.

While delivering some home-cooked provisions to his elder brothers on the front line, he hears the Philistine champion, Goliath, taunting the Israelites and their god. The champion is a giant of a man – 'six cubits and a span' (or 9 ft 9 in) tall, with a brass helmet, a coat of mail, 'greaves of brass upon his legs and a target of brass upon his shoulders'. His spear is the size of a weaver's beam and its head – in a rather un-aerodynamic piece of design – weighs over fifteen pounds. Goliath's taunts provoke panic. The Israelites are all 'sore afraid'. Apart from David. To the general amazement of the Israelite army – and to the decided irritation of his older brothers – David volunteers to take up the Philistine's challenge. It is a mismatch of almost grotesque proportions: the seasoned warrior against the untried youth. David moreover is not only untried but also unarmed. Saul offers to kit him out in a full suit of armour, but David prefers to put his trust in his sling and 'five smooth stones out of the brook'. In the event he only needs one of them. His first shot scores a direct hit on Goliath's forehead. The Philistine champion crashes to the ground, and the Philistine army turns and flees.

In the wake of this surprise victory, David is taken up at court. He enjoys an exalted position as one of Saul's trusted commanders; he becomes the friend of Saul's son Jonathan, he marries one of Saul's daughters. The king is unaware that he has welcomed his Yahweh-chosen successor and rival into his own house. Nonetheless he does gradually become jealous and mistrustful of his protégé. Eventually he tries to kill him and David is forced to flee. He takes up arms against Saul and, allied with the Philistines, leads a sort of guerrilla group in the Judean hills. Despite this bitter enmity, David twice spares the old king's life when he has him at his mercy.

After the death of Saul and Jonathan in battle against the Philistines on mount Gilboa, Saul's other son Ishbaal takes over the kingdom. But it is on the verge of collapse. He moves his centre of operations away from Saul's old capital at Gibeah, to Mahanaim on the eastern side of the Jordan, leaving the whole central hill-country unprotected. David steps into this vacuum, as Yahweh's chosen candidate. He occupies Hebron, and is proclaimed king – not over the whole of Israel – but of Judah, the land in the southern highlands south of Jerusalem.

Over the course of the next seven years, however, he expands his territory and completes the task of uniting the kingdom, drawing the northern tribes of Israel together with the southern tribes of Judah, into what is now known as the United Monarchy. He proclaims the recently captured city of Jerusalem as the new capital of this nation.

This is, in some ways, presented as the high point of his reign. Even at the moment of achievement the first seeds of self-destruction are sown. David develops an unfortunate passion for Bathsheba, the wife of Uriah the Hittite. He engineers Uriah's death so that he can carry on his liaison with Bathsheba. This sin brings, according to the biblical narrator, its inevitable retribution. David's house is soon riven by revolt, incest and murder. One son rapes his own half-sister and is duly murdered by her brother, Absalom. Absalom then rebels against David, his own father, and is forced into exile. Such internecine strife continues until David's death, when he hands over the reins of power to Solomon, his son by Bathsheba.

Although the David of the biblical story clearly had his weaknesses, an undoubted glamour attaches to him as a man and a leader. And it is a glamour that has grown rather than dimmed with the years. For the Jews David stands as the true founder of the first unified state of Israel – and the founder, too, of its capital: Jerusalem. But how true is this picture? Did he really found a powerful and unified state? Or a great capital city? In an attempt to answer such questions archaeologists in the past have, inevitably enough, started by looking at Jerusalem.

Saul, as has been noted, had his capital at Gibeah in the heart of his own tribal homeland. The site of Gibeah had been tentatively identified at the Tell el-Ful, to the north of Jerusalem. David, in the early stages of his reign, seems to have ruled from Hebron. But it was his establishment of the capital at Jerusalem, in the heart of the Judean hills, that — according to the biblical author — confirmed the success of his kingdom. In the book of Samuel the city is described as belonging, at this period, to the Jebusites — a people whom it seems were related either to the Canaanites or, perhaps more probably, to the Hittites. As such Jerusalem stood outside the traditional territory not only of the tribe of Judah (David's tribe) but of all the other tribes of Israel. Some biblical commentators consider this to be one of the marks of David's strategic brilliance. They argue that David's choice of a capital from outside the established tribal framework made it more readily acceptable to all the tribes, so that it could become a focus for unity.

David, it is claimed, captured Jerusalem — or the stronghold of Zion as it is also referred to — by leading a surprise attack up a water pipe into the heart of the city. By the standards of the time the conquest seems to have been a mild one, as it is mentioned that the defeated Jebusites continued to live on in the city even after David made it his capital.

Little is known from historical records about the Jebusite city that David is said to have captured. Jerusalem certainly had a long history before David ever arrived there. It is first mentioned in Egyptian texts dating from the nineteenth and eighteenth centuries BCE. Its name is thought to mean the foundation of the god Shalem (Shalem was an early Canaanite god of the night, who was usually twinned with 'Saha, the deity of the day.) Among the famous cache of el-Amarna correspondence (letters sent in the fourteenth century BCE by various Canaanite sub-kings to their Egyptian overlords, Amenhotep III and his successor Akhenaten), there are several from 'Abdu-Heba, the Canaanite ruler of Jerusalem. Just when the Jebusites took control of the city is not known, but references to them in the Bible occur only shortly before the coming of David, which would seem to suggest that the biblical authors considered them fairly recent arrivals on the scene.

Although the modern city of Jerusalem spreads out over several hills, archaeology has established that the oldest part of the city is the southern spur of what is now the eastern hill of the city. The whole of this narrow eastern ridge was, from an early period, known as Zion: it is bounded by the Kidron valley to the east, the Hinnom valley to the south, and the Valley of the Cheesemakers to the west. The northern spur of this long ridge is, in early texts, designated as mount Zion, while the southern outcrop – a small area no more than 200×600 yards – is referred to as the hill of Ophel. And it is on this southern spur that scholars suppose the stronghold of the Jebusites stood. The Bible describes how David, having captured it, 'dwelt in the stronghold, and called it the City of David'. It is a name that it still bears today.

The City of David may have been the heart of David's Jerusalem but, according to the biblical account, the king did much to extend and glorify his new capital. It is said that he made the city part of his royal estate, thus establishing a lasting bond between Jerusalem and the Davidic dynasty, that he brought the Ark of the Covenant to Jerusalem as a symbol of the unity of the twelve tribes of Israel and of their bond with Yahweh, and that he instituted a building programme appropriate to a capital city. The Bible describes how he built a magnificent 'House of Cedar', employing a team of craftsmen sent from Lebanon by Hiram, king of Tyre (II Samuel v, 11). Other imposing sounding new edifices also mentioned include 'the house of the mighty men' and the 'Tower of David'. It is suggested by some scholars that King David must also have extended the town's fortifications northwards to include mount Zion, the area immediately to the north of the City of David proper, as there is a reference later in the book of Kings to Solomon completing such a project.

According to the book of Samuel it was on mount Zion that David bought a large threshing floor from an old Jebusite nobleman, as a location for an altar. The whole area became the planned site for a new acropolis. And it is David who is credited with having begun the plans for this first temple – the temple that was eventually completed by his successor, Solomon – and which gave the area its other designation: Temple Mount. This is a key moment in the biblical narrative – and in the mythology of the Western world. It is David's choice of the site that inaugurates Jerusalem as a great religious centre. For over 2500 years the connection has endured. Jerusalem has come to hold an exalted position among the great spiritual sites of the world through centuries of change. Not that the changes have left it unaffected. Indeed as a result of them Jerusalem has become the holy city not only of the Jews, but also of the Christians and (along with Mecca and Medina) of the Muslims. Mediaeval maps of the world took Jerusalem as their centre and showed the known continents radiating out to form a clover-leaf shape. And a large part of the world's population still regards the city as a sacred site, a place of central importance.

So much holiness – or so many different claims to holiness – confined in such a small area have, perhaps inevitably, proved difficult to accommodate. Popular tradition, ignoring the claims of 'the god Shalem', asserts that the name Jerusalem is derived from the Hebrew phrase, *Ir Shalom*, meaning City of Peace. The derivation, if it were true, could not be more ironic. Few cities can boast such a legacy of strife. And it is a legacy that lives on. For many Jews there remains a strong feeling that their claims to the city are pre-eminent. They were there first. The other religions came later and, in some respects, considered Jerusalem sacred because of the traditions established there, according to the account in the Old Testament, by King David and King Solomon.

Under the 1947 United Nations Partition Plan, which divided the former territory of Palestine between the Jews and the Arabs, Jerusalem – in acknowledgement of its unique status – was designated as a separate entity, outside the control of either party and open to both. This, however, was a diplomatic ideal doomed to speedy failure. Even as British troops began to withdraw, the two sides were battling for control of 'their' sacred city. By the end of the 1948 war, the city was split down

The medieval Psalter
map showing Jerusalem
at the centre of the world

Modern-day Jerusalem,
the skyline dominated by
the Dome of the Rock on
Temple Mount

Professor John Garstang's
photograph of the Jericho mound,
taken in the 1930s

John McCarthy with Bill
Dever at Jericho

Bull-El, an early Canaanite god

John McCarthy and
Amnon Ben-Tor examine
a reconstructed olive press
at Hazor

An aerial view of the site
on Mt Ebal that some
claim to be Joshua's altar

'The art of surveying… is to concentrate on the ground and to look for little tiny pieces of pottery…' Adam Zertal shows John McCarthy the way

Caravaggio's depiction of David with the head of Goliath

John McCarthy tries out one of Larry Stager's most recent finds: a large, carved chalk basin which probably served as a Philistine bathtub

John McCarthy in
deep discussion with
Israel Finkelstein at
Megiddo

The stele of
King Mesha of Moab

A painting by the
Italian artist
Giorgione of the
Judgement of
Solomon

A detail of the Black
Obelisk probably showing
King Jehu prostrate
before Assyrian
King Shalmaneser

Baruch Halpern explaining his
theory that the troughs in the
foreground – previously thought
to be for watering Solomon's
horses – were in fact receptacles
for producing opium

The Tel Rehov trench

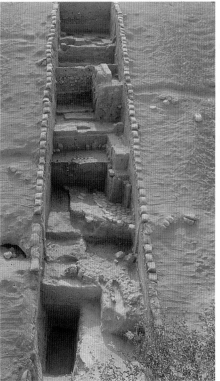

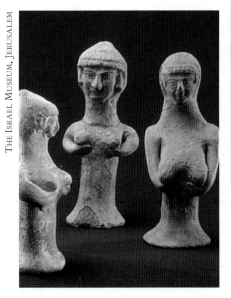

Asherah figurines

The Isiah scroll from
the Dead Sea Scrolls

A relief showing the
siege and
capture of Lachish
by the Assyrian
King Sennacherib.
A siege engine is
battering the walls

the middle, with the Jews occupying the western suburbs and the Arabs controlling the rest, including the old walled city and the City of David in the east. Between the two areas a United Nations controlled buffer zone was established, to maintain an uneasy peace. It was a peace that could not last. During the Six Day War of 1967 the Israelis swept into eastern Jerusalem and the Old City, and claimed it as their own. They pronounced the city 'the eternal united capital of Israel'. It was a conquest made in the name of the biblical tradition: the capital of King David's United Monarchy was once again the capital of a united Israel. The conjunction of the military and the religious is everywhere apparent in accounts and memorials of the event. Archive photographs record the young Israeli soldiers breaking down and weeping as they reached the Western – or Wailing – Wall. On the Temple Mount a large marble plaque commemorates the name of Major General Shlomo Goren, 'First Chief Rabbi of the Israel Defence Forces and Chief Rabbi of Israel . . . Outstanding Torah Scholar and Leader of the Liberators of the Temple Mount and Western Wall.'

Israel's claim to control East Jerusalem is still hotly contested; it is not recognised by most of the international community, although President Bush has announced that the US Embassy will now move to Jerusalem, recognising it as the capital of Israel. But the chances of reaching any sort of compromise on the matter remain elusive. For many Jews, King David's royal city has been reborn. Certainly David's name has been reborn. It is everywhere in the modern Jerusalem: King David Street, King David Court, the King David Café, the King David Beauty Parlour, even the King David Video Store. But what of the fantastic city that he is said to have created? Do any traces of all the building activity – secular, military and religious – described in the Old Testament survive to inspire and comfort the new Zionists? Archaeology, of course, faces a major challenge in Jerusalem. The site is not a long-deserted tell that can be excavated at will. It is a crowded, bustling, living city. Much of the ground is simply ineligible for excavation. There are people living on top of it. Not, however, that some enthusiasts don't go to extraordinary lengths to carry on their investigations even in the face of such constraints.

One group of Zionists has recently established a settlement on mount Ophel, the site shown on many maps as, they believe, the original City of David. For them it is a place rich in vivid associations. 'We are standing on the actual ground where the palace of King David once stood,' explains Rabbi David Marcus, a young man of eager enthusiasm, and imagination, as he conjures up the biblical past from the ancient ramparts. 'I can comfortably look down on the city and see the boundaries of the city from the perspective of King David. I can imagine him writing the book of Psalms, understanding the passages he is describing. But,' he adds, 'there is so much that we don't understand in terms of how the city functioned and how the people lived here.'

The Zionist settlers, anxious to pass on something of their vision of how the city did perhaps function, applied to establish a Visitor Centre on the site. In the sort of quid-pro-quo arrangement familiar to many planning applicants, they have been granted permission on condition that they finance an excavation of the site by the Israel Antiquities Authority. The settlers' hopes for the dig are high and clearly defined. As David Marcus explains: 'Every time you put a shovel in the ground here and lift it up, more evidence comes up, and more passages of the Bible come to life.'

Such a belief, however, seems more optimistic than true in regard to King David. It is a belief that has not been confirmed through the excavations carried out by Ronnie Reich, the archaeologist leading the IAA dig. At least, not thus far. His discoveries have tended to fall either side of the mark. They are either several centuries too early, or several centuries too late. The massive blocks of the main fortified wall date in origin to the early Canaanite period of the Middle Bronze Age. If David did capture the city his achievement, as Reich points out, was certainly very impressive; he had to get into a very well defended stronghold. A spur of outer wall projecting from the City of David is later in date. But it is almost certainly too late to be ascribed to King David. 'It cannot date from the time of David and Solomon,' Reich explains, 'because our digging inside the wall produced only finds from the eighth century BCE, two centuries after the time of David and Solomon.'

Elsewhere, in the immediate vicinity, it has proved curiously difficult to forge a clear connection between David and his eponymous city. In 1867 the British explorer Charles Warren, while investigating the area immediately below the City of David was excited to discover a vertical shaft running up into the city from the Gihon spring. He at once leapt to the conclusion that it must be the water pipe up which David is said to have led his surprise attack. The attribution – a classic piece of biblical archaeology – is now contested. Although it does have to be admitted that there is no agreement among Warren's modern critics. Some archaeologists are convinced that the tunnel is relatively recent, dating from the ninth century BCE, over a hundred years after the supposed time of David. Others claim that it is very early indeed. They date it to the eighteenth century BCE. As such they admit it would certainly have existed at the time David is supposed to have conquered the city. But, they point out, there is absolutely nothing to indicate that the tunnel was either used or known in the tenth century BCE. No artefact from that period has ever been found in or near the shaft. A third body of opinion holds that the shaft is in fact a natural fissure in the rock, and has nothing to do with the city's water system, King David's surprise attack or anything else.

'If we go by the pottery,' explains Reich, 'and that is the only evidence there is, then we have a problem. We don't have a single sherd in the close vicinity of the spring dating to the tenth century BCE, the days of David.' There is a huge gap in the archaeological record: 'We have only the Canaanites in the eighteenth century BCE and the Israelites in the eighth century BCE, a millennium later, but in between we don't have anything. That nobody, during the tenth century [BCE] broke a bucket or a water jar or anything made of pottery near the site is very difficult to accept.' If archaeology teaches one thing it is that people in ancient times broke pottery in huge quantities. It is a bizarre anomaly. Reich describes it as 'a confrontation between texts and archaeological finds'.

It is a story that has been repeated throughout the city. After a century and a half of surveying, digging and sifting, almost no clear archaeological evidence for King David's capital has come to light. Even remains that were once thought to date from his period have recently been questioned, if not conclusively re-ascribed.

A certain amount of hope was held out for the curious stepped stone structure that rises up one side of mount Ophel. When Kathleen Kenyon excavated the site in the 1960s, she suggested that this might be the so-called *millo*, which David is described as having built at the heart of his new capital. *Millo* is the Hebrew word for fill, and the terraced stone blocks appear to have been some sort of infill, a restraining buttress reinforcing the steep eastern slope of the hill. The structure provides a firm foundation for the buildings erected at the top of the slope. Potsherds discovered within the terracing by Kenyon and by Yigal Shiloh, the archaeologist who worked on the site during the 1970s, suggested to them that the thing had indeed been built in the tenth century BCE.

Further encouragement for such a dating was provided by Kenyon's discovery, in a layer at the south-eastern summit of the site, of a carved palmette capital, similar to ones found at other supposedly royal – and supposedly tenth-century – sites, such as Hazor. Was this perhaps a remnant of David's royal palace? If so it was the only trace of it to survive. Reich suggests that this in itself need not be surprising. 'When people hear the word palace,' he remarks, 'they have something like Buckingham Palace in mind. But I don't think David's palace would have been like that. It would have been probably only a little bit larger than a private house in modern Jerusalem.'

Nevertheless some archaeologists remain unconvinced about some of these datings and ascriptions. They are inclined to date both the construction of the stepped terracing and the site of David's palace to preceding periods. To some scholars the absence of any clear evidence for David's city has called into question the very fact of its existence. The few scattered objects and remains dating from the tenth century that have been recovered from the site appear to suggest – at least to some – that Jerusalem at this time can only have been a minor settlement, not any sort of royal capital. 'There is almost no evidence for the tenth century,' says Israel Finkelstein. 'There is almost no evidence for Solomon. Jerusalem at this time was probably a very small village, or a very poor town.' According to such arguments, Jerusalem's emergence as an important urban centre only occurred in the ninth century, a century after King David, and well after the United Monarchy had split back into its two constituent parts. As such, Jerusalem was never the capital of Israel; it was the capital of Judah, as the southern kingdom was known. The distinction means that, if one were asked when, in biblical times, Jerusalem became the capital of Israel, the correct answer would be that it never did.

These arguments are, of course, considered highly contentious and highly dangerous by many modern Israelis. As Tomy Lapid, leader of the secular Shinui party, remarks with barely concealed exasperation, 'I don't think that they [the archaeologists] are actually trying to threaten the existence of the state, but they are supplying armaments to those who want to de-legitimise the Israelis.' It is not, however, just the Zionists who rankle at the extreme claims made by some of the archaeologists of the new school.

Many archaeologists and scholars consider that the case for Jerusalem's establishment under King David is still open. The more extreme sceptics, after all, have based much of their argument on the 'absence of evidence' for King David's city, and that – as their less hardline colleagues argue – is a very limited and suspect basis for argument.

Seymour Gitin, the genial director of the W. F. Albright Institute in Jerusalem, remains unimpressed with the arguments of the hardliners. 'If you look at all the excavations that have gone on for over a hundred years, in Jerusalem – a very heavily excavated site – you can barely find a handful or two of sherds that you can date to the tenth century – that is to the so-called Solomonic period,' admits Gitin. 'Based on this evidence it seems likely there wasn't a city here. However, to speak about the absence of evidence as proof is ridiculous. There are current excavations in Jerusalem and I don't think I'm misquoting the excavator if I say that in all of his excavations, even in his dumps, digging down from the top to the bottom, he has never found *one* Byzantine sherd. Now we know that Jerusalem was a big city in the Byzantine period. Because he has not found any Byzantine evidence in his excavations does that mean there wasn't a Byzantine city?' The question is well asked and the answer is, obviously not. But, then, there are other traces of Byzantine Jerusalem readily to hand.

Scholars wishing to conjure up David's tenth-century city have a harder time. Carol Myers, the Professor of Biblical Studies and Archaeology at Duke University in America, presents an argument to explain the absent evidence. She considers that David's Jerusalem was probably a victim of its own success. The great and enduring importance of the city over the coming decades, centuries and – indeed – millennia, ensured that all of David's original building work was totally obliterated by new construction projects. During the frequent redevelopment of the site, builders often returned to the bedrock to establish their foundations, brushing aside all previous remains. Each new regime in Jerusalem, whether succeeding to power from within or sweeping to power from without, wished to confirm its status by creating its own, new public buildings.

Added to these years of demolition and rebuilding there is the fact that many of the key sites are off-limits. They are clustered on what was mount Zion, or the Temple Mount, now also the site of the Dome of the Rock. The location is both too sacred and too disputed to allow for the possibility of a full-scale excavation. During previous decades archaeologists have unearthed some evidence to suggest that the summit of mount Zion already had a long tradition of sacredness well before the Israelites ever came to Jerusalem. But that is all they have discovered and all they are likely to discover for some time.

The site is under the control of the Jerusalem Waqf, the Jordan-based charitable institution that oversees the Muslim holy sites on the Temple Mount. They are not about to allow archaeologists – especially Israeli archaeologists – to search for traces of King David's city under their own sacred ground. Ironically they have been carrying out some excavations of their own – but not archaeological excavations. In an effort to improve safe access to the site for Muslim pilgrims they have been redesigning the area, and using earth shifting equipment to do it. It is a move that has dismayed many archaeologists, who fear that vital evidence is being lost or destroyed in the process. Whatever mysteries relating to David's establishment of an altar and an acropolis upon mount Zion might lie under the ground, they will, it seems – for the time being – remain mysteries.

In the absence of tangible evidence of building remains at Jerusalem, Myers has been obliged to look elsewhere, in an attempt to build up a picture of the city's power and importance at the time of King David. She has gathered together evidence of what appear to be new settlements, established in the Judean hills during the course of the tenth century (or Iron Age IIA, as archaeologists refer to it). To her mind the pattern of settlement suggests that these new villages were focused upon – and related to – some larger urban centre in their midst. And she believes that all the circumstantial evidence points to the fact that this large urban centre was Jerusalem – the City of David.

There is, too, the reference in the book of Kings to pharaoh

Shishak who, it is said, sacked Jerusalem shortly after the reign of Solomon (David's successor). It is a reference, however, that is only partly corroborated by an Egyptian inscription at Karnak which lists the victories achieved by Shoshenq I (generally considered to be the biblical Shishak). The inscription confirms that the Egyptians campaigned in the area, but the list fails to mention Jerusalem specifically as one of the cities sacked. The reasons for this omission are debated and the arguments of the apologists hold little sway with the sceptics. The doubters point out that not only is archaeology silent about David's achievements but so, too, is literature. None of the contemporary narrative sources from the Near East so much as mentions a mighty David (or Saul, or Solomon). This, the sceptics contend, is a very surprising fact if these kings really were establishing a great new empire in the region.

Once again this is an argument based upon the absence of evidence, and – as such – is met with the usual counter-thrust. Nevertheless, rather than merely claiming that literary evidence of David and his kingdom probably did once exist but is now lost, some scholars adopt a more positive approach. They counter the doubters, and explain the absence of literary references to the new regime, by suggesting that the United Monarchy of Israel emerged under David at a particularly troubled time for the rest of the Near East. Israel's mighty (and literary) neighbours were, it is suggested, all too busy worrying about internal strife or external threats to take any note of a new balance of power in Canaan.

The dynasty in Egypt throughout the second half of the eleventh and the first part of the tenth century BCE was a particularly weak and ineffectual one. The Tanite pharaohs won few victories and inscribed fewer monuments. During this period Egyptian pretensions to control in Canaan all but ceased, a fact that might well have hastened the emergence of the new kingdom of Israel, but not one that the pharaohs would have been likely to boast about in carved stone. Assyria and Babylon were, apparently, suffering from similar dips in their fortunes during the crucial years of the tenth century BCE; there were weak rulers and vexed successions. Neither power was launching campaigns of conquest nor looking much beyond its own borders.

There is an ingenuity about such arguments. But, once again, it is an ingenuity that does not convince opponents. For them the wall of silence that envelops David's kingdom is just too thick. Where there is no smoke, they argue, perhaps there is no fire. There is, moreover, the doubters suggest, another side to the equation. If there is no hard evidence for David, what about the evidence for his old enemy, Goliath? Are the early Philistines as elusive as the early Israelites? Is the lack of evidence for David's kingdom merely part of a general lack of evidence for the whole period throughout the region?

Not, it would seem, at all. David's detractors are delighted to point out that the Philistines can very probably be glimpsed – albeit as shadowy figures – in some contemporary Near Eastern texts outside the Bible. There are what seem to be references to them in Egyptian documents and pictures of them in Egyptian reliefs. They perhaps appear too in early Ugaritic inscriptions and Akkadian sources. And from all this information a picture of their origins begins to take shape.

They were, it seems, part of a whole group of so-called 'Sea Peoples' who began arriving on the south-eastern Mediterranean littoral early in the twelfth century BCE. Historians have linked their advent with the more general upheaval that occurred in the world of the eastern Mediterranean at the end of the thirteenth century BCE. It is to this period that the conflict between the Achean and Hittite civilisations – a conflict that perhaps stands behind the myth and legend of Homer's Trojan War – belongs. The defeat and displacement of the Hittites produced a series of ripples across the region. Many peoples were obliged to seek new territories.

In about 1180BCE waves of invaders began to arrive on the coast of Canaan and Egypt. From Egypt itself they seem to have been repelled. The great pharaoh, Ramases III (1184–53BCE), claimed several important victories over them. In Canaan, however, the story was different. Although the whole area was ostensibly controlled by the Egyptian colonial administration, the newcomers managed to gain a foothold. They encountered opposition both from the Egyptian regime and from the local Canaanite population, but they overcame it. There is archaeological evidence that they destroyed several existing Canaanite cities on the coastal plain and built their own settlements upon the ruins. According to the biblical narrative they soon established a pentapolis, a state based on the league of five great cities – which are named as Ashkelon, Ashdod, Gezer, Ekron and Gath.

The sites of all these cities have been identified with a good degree of certainty. And excavation work at them has begun to reveal some of the details of Philistine life and culture. At Ashkelon at the southern end of Israel's Mediterranean coast, just north of the Gaza strip, Larry Stager (an impressively bearded figure, even among the generally hirsute ranks of biblical archaeologists) has been directing work for some fifteen years, uncovering the extent of the Philistines' great seaport. It was a city that they had taken from the Canaanites. They rebuilt it on a grand – or at least a large – scale. The Philistine town covered 150 acres (sixty hectares) and ran for almost half a mile (1 km) along the coast. It was protected on the landward side by the curve of a great earth rampart which, at some quite early period of Philistine control, was surmounted by an additional mud-brick wall running between two mud-brick towers.

Within the boundaries of this wall Stager has uncovered evidence of a thriving civilisation, distinct in many ways from that of the neighbouring Canaanites and Israelites. 'This is a cosmopolitan world compared to the agrarian world [of the Israelites and/or Canaanites] in the hills,' he explains. 'We have new elements that have never been seen before.' At least not in Canaan. Some of the new elements do, however, have strong echoes of other early cultures. 'The Philistines were somehow related to the Greeks,' explains Stager. Many of the apparently novel features of Philistine material culture have their echoes and origins in the Greek world: their distinctive loom weights, the arrangement of their houses, and – not least – their pottery.

'We have painted pottery that relates to Greek Mycenaean proto-types,' Stager says. And, indeed, the simple elegance of many of his finds, decorated with monochrome motifs such as stylised birds and geometric patterns, is at once recognisable as Greek in inspiration, and as entirely different from the simple Canaanite ware.

And although, over the years, the Philistine potters clearly absorbed something of the Canaanite ceramic tradition, their work continued to have a distinctive grace and flavour. In contrast to the unadorned pots of the Canaanites, Philistine work can seem positively stylish. The forms too were entirely different. While the traditional Canaanite cooking pot was a broad, shallow casserole-type dish with a slightly pointed base, which allowed it to rest in the chimney hole on the top of a typical beehive-shaped Canaanite fireplace, the Philistines favoured a tall, one-handled design, more 'cooking jug' than cooking pot. It had a flat ring base, so that it could stand directly in the ashes of the fire.

These different forms of casserole suggest different approaches to cooking, eating and life. Philistine life seems to have been focused upon a central hearth. This was a new concept in Canaan, where cooking had always been carried out in a separate kitchen area. The Philistine arrangement seems to belong more to the Aegean world of social living and discourse. It is just about possible to imagine a symposium – as described by Plato – taking place around a Philistine hearth, the talkers sustained by the contents of a Philistine cooking-jug.

Stager, throughout his work, has been confronted repeatedly by the essentially ancient Greek, or Mycenaean, nature of Philistine culture. It is everywhere apparent and clearly affected every aspect of life. 'We have found in Cyprus and here, and in other parts of the Greek world, "scapula",' he explains. 'A "scapula" – in this instance – is the shoulder blade of a cow, that has been incised with maybe twenty or forty incisions, and it would have been used as a musical instrument. Again this is something that we find among the Philistines but not among the surrounding cultures.'

This connection between the world of the biblical Philistines and the world of Homer's Greeks makes sense, according to Stager, of some of the more improbable sounding Bible stories. 'If you look at the story of David and Goliath,' he says, 'David is not dressed in armour; Goliath is. David does not have a helmet; Goliath does. We know that the Canaanites and Israelites didn't have helmets, but the Greeks did. Goliath is essentially a Mycenaean warrior. He wears something that a Canaanite or an Israelite would never wear: shin guards, or greaves. And these are made of metal. We have some warriors from this period depicted on the so-called "Warrior Vase" from Mycenae. And the warriors all have helmets and wear shin guards.'

This close match between the contemporary image of the Mycenaean warriors and the description of Goliath in the Bible seems not only to confirm the connection between the Philistines and the Greeks but also suggests something more. It is generally agreed by archaeologists and scholars that Philistine culture had ceased to be distinctive by the ninth century BCE, well before the time the Bible was probably written down. By that time it would have been indistinguishable in its physical remains from Israelite culture. The author of the book of Samuel – writing in, say, the sixth century BCE – would have had no first-hand knowledge of the armour of an early Philistine warrior. But he must, it seems clear, have had an early and authentic source or tradition to work from. What this source might have been remains unknown. Some have suggested that it might have been, not an early Israelite history, but a now-lost Philistine epic poem, a sort of *Iliad* for the conquest of Canaan, which was then adapted to the purposes of the Israelites.

The accuracy of the description of Goliath's armour does not, of course, confirm the historical truth of the whole David and Goliath story. And indeed some biblical scholars have long harboured doubts about its veracity. They point out that later in the book of Samuel (II Samuel xxi, 19) there is a reference to Goliath having been killed, not by David at all, but by a warrior called Elhanan. The English translation of the passage ingeniously tries to gloss over the discrepancy by declaring that 'Elhanan, the son of Jaare-oregim, a Beth-lehemite, slew the *brother* of Goliath'. But, despite such ploys, many commentators suspect that this passage represents an earlier tradition, and that Elhanan is the more likely vanquisher of the giant whose spear-staff was like a weaver's beam.

As with many biblical stories, however, there is plenty of room for alternative readings and explanations. *El-hanan* translates as 'God being merciful' and might not be a name at all, but rather a gloss on the deed carried out by the unnamed weaver's son from Bethlehem who could – after all – be David.

The word Philistine has crept into the English lexicon as a term used to denote an uncultured and uncultivated bore. And something of this unfortunate association seems to have tinged early research into the Philistines of Canaan. One distinctive form of Philistine drinking vessel was, on first being categorised in the late nineteenth century, labelled as a beer jug. Stager's discoveries at Ashkelon show, however, that the Philistines, far from being beer swilling yobs, were wine sipping sophisticates. He has uncovered several shallow, plastered vats that were almost certainly used in wine production.

And one of his most spectacular recent finds has been a large, carved chalk basin, which would have served as a bathtub. It was another Philistine innovation. 'Bathtubs are known from the Mycenaean world and from Cyprus,' Stager explains. 'But never from this area until the Philistines arrive.' The evidence of archaeology suggests that the Philistines had a cosmopolitan culture.

If the Philistines distinguished themselves from the local population by the form of their cooking pots, there was an even more marked difference about the content. The newcomers were keen pork eaters.

The absence of pig bones noted in the Early Iron Age highland settlements is reversed among the Philistine cities of the coastal plain, where pig bones abound. The Philistines seem to have arrived in the land complete with their herds of swine. Indeed it has been suggested that the apparent taboo on pork consumption instituted in the highland settlements may initially have had less to do with religious scruple than with a desire by the early Israelites to create a clear outward distinction between themselves and the Philistines.

Although the material differences between the early Israelites and the Philistines must have been striking, and may well have been pointed up by both sides, the distinction is sometimes obscured in the biblical account by the fact that its author lumps the Philistines together with the Canaanites, the Hivites and all the other '-ites' who are opposed to Israel. Nevertheless, during the early years of Israel's development, it is the Philistines who are most often described as posing a threat. The two peoples did not, it seems, get on. There are frequent references to war and conflict. The Philistines are, in many respects, presented as the arch villains during this period. From the book of Judges through to the book of Kings they are the Israelites' most persistent and dangerous foes.

A close reading of the text does reveal occasional hints of coop-eration, or – at least – contact between the two peoples, but it was often uneasy. There is the account in the first book of Samuel (xiii, 19–21) of how the Philistines maintained a local monopoly on iron smithing, so that the Israelites were obliged to take their ploughshares and other agricultural implements down to the Philistine towns to get them sharpened. And although Samson's Delilah was a Philistine, the Bible story shows just where that liaison landed him.

The broad picture built up from the biblical narrative is that of the Philistines expanding from their cities on the coastal plain and pushing up into the central hill district. This was a movement that inevitably caused friction – or worse – with the Israelite settlers established there. Quite early on in this process, it is said that the tribe of Dan (to which

Samson belonged) was obliged to leave its traditional lands on the coast and resettle in the far north of the country, beyond the Sea of Galilee. The Philistines are presented as ruthless and devious. They destroy the sacred shrine at Shiloh and, at one awful moment, even capture the Ark of the Covenant.

According to the biblical narrative, it is in direct response to this threat of Philistine expansion that the Israelites decide to ask the ageing judge, Samuel, to establish a kingship for them. The disparate tribes of Israel are shown as believing that this greater political cohesion will give them a better chance to counter the Philistine incursions. The ploy did not pay immediate dividends. The Philistines defeated Saul, the Israelites' first king, at mount Gilboa. But King David was more successful. He 'smote the Philistines and subdued them'. He recovered some towns that had fallen under their control and effectively pushed them back, out of the hill-country. By the end of his reign the Philistines are back within the bounds of the Pentapolis.

The clear evidence of the Philistine presence, and the rich details about their material culture that have been uncovered, not only at Ashkelon but at other sites, contrasts strangely with the vestigial remains associated with David's kingdom. It is a discrepancy that has led some commentators to doubt the very existence of King David. They have suggested that he was perhaps a complete and late fabrication. Or, at best, a mythical figure like King Arthur, blown up to magnificent proportions from very modest beginnings, an heroic champion created by later generations as the symbol of a long-vanished golden age that never actually existed.

Such theories enjoy considerable support, but they received a decided jolt in 1993. That was when the veteran Israeli archaeologist Avraham Biran made an extraordinary discovery when digging at Tel Dan, a site in the richly fertile lands at the foot of mount Hermon, north of Galilee, near the source of the river Jordan.

It is now confidently thought that Tel Dan is indeed the site of the biblical city of Dan, established by the eponymous tribe after they migrated north. It has the distinction of being Israel's longest continuous archaeological dig. Modern excavations began here in 1966 and have continued every season since then. Over the years it has yielded many intriguing finds and not a few inscriptions. Even in the year before excavations officially began, a ninth-century BCE pottery bowl was turned up by chance on the surface of the mound. Its base was inscribed in Aramaic with the legend 'of the butchers'. It is a phrase that suggested to the archaeologist Nahman Avigad that the bowl had belonged to the butchers of the royal household at Dan.

Another early find was a potsherd marked with the words 'belonging to Amotz' in an eighth-century BCE form of Hebrew script. This briefly conjured up some exciting possibilities, as an Amotz is mentioned in the Bible as the father of the prophet Isaiah; but, then, it was realised that Amotz was really rather a common name during the period. But these early and interesting finds paled besides Biran's discovery.

During the 1993 season Biran was working on the outer walls of the ancient city. He had uncovered evidence of an elaborate gateway structure, with significant ninth-century elements. Set in the outer part of this gateway he even found a niche containing a row of five small standing stones – a sacred shrine that perhaps corresponded with the *massebot* mentioned in the Old Testament. Continuing his excavations out from this gateway Biran and his team began to uncover a large paved area bounded – they discovered – by a low wall on its eastern edge. And it was in this wall that they made their amazing discovery.

'Our surveyor was mapping the walls,' he recalls, 'and as we were walking by this low wall, suddenly she yells, and says, "I think we have an inscription!" So I walked over and I looked down, and yes, there it was.' The rays of the sun were illuminating a flat basalt stone, protruding out of the ground. Letters were clearly visible on it. It was at once apparent that the stone was only a fragment, and that it was not in its original setting. It had been broken up and used in the construction of the old wall. The stone, as Biran recalls, was easily removed. When he turned it towards the sun, the letters leapt into life. And what letters they were. 'I said, "You see the word *melech* – king, and *melech beth dawid* – king of the house of David." It was an unforgettable moment. You see, in the first place one doesn't find inscriptions. And in the second place one doesn't find inscriptions with the name David on them. And here was one.'

The discovery was amazing indeed. No previous reference to David had ever been found outside the Bible. Not surprisingly the news created much excitement, and not just in archaeological circles. The find was reported on the front page not only of the Israeli papers but also of the *New York Times*, and it made the cover of *Time* magazine.

Not that there weren't some doubters. A few archaeologists just could not believe the neatness of the find. They suggested that the inscription might be a fake. There was no thought that Biran himself might have faked the find, but there have been cases – throughout the history of archaeology – of pranksters 'salting' objects in the ground, in order to confuse, surprise or fool future archaeologists. And certainly there are forgers competent to make an inscription that might take in even an expert. The antiquities market is littered with fakes. Nevertheless many experts have scrutinised Biran's discovery, and all the evidence points to it being an early and authentic artefact.

The language of the inscription is early Aramaic, but it is written in a distinctive form of Aramaic script, which relates to the Hebrew form used in the years before the Babylonian captivity. (In exile the Jews adopted the square-formed Aramaic script which is the basis of modern Hebrew epigraphy.) The style of the lettering (and also the fact that the stone was discovered under a layer of destruction debris dating from the late eighth century BCE, when Dan was sacked by the Assyrians) convinced Biran and his colleague, the palaeographer, Joseph Naveh, that the inscription dated from early in the ninth century. This put it only about a hundred years after David's supposed time. Although the stone mentions David – or, rather, 'the house of David' – it is not *about* the King. Indeed it was clearly set up by an enemy of the house of David.

Of the thirteen preserved lines of the inscription, none is complete. They present a tantalising puzzle:

> . . .
> . . . my father went up
> . . . and my father died, he went to [his fate . . . Is⁄]
> rael formerly in my father's land . . .
> I [fought against Israel?] and Hadad went in front of me
> . . . my king. And I slew of [them X footmen, Y cha⁄]
> riots and two thousand horsemen . . .
> the king of Israel. And [I] slew [. . . the kin⁄]
> g of the House of David. And I put . . .
> their land . . .
> other . . . [. . . ru⁄]
> led over Is[rael . . .]
> siege upon . . .

Fortunately the phrases 'house of David' and 'king of Israel' can both be read without resort to filling in gaps. But elsewhere Biran and Naveh have had to guess at possible word formations.

On the basis of only a single letter, they have suggested that the word preceding 'house of David' might be *melech* or king, an echo of the reference to the king of Israel in the line above. Their theory is that the stone commemorates the victory of some Aramean king over the kingdoms of both Israel and Judah, the two halves of what had once been the United Monarchy. Biran has even suggested a possible connection between the stone and the war described in I Kings (xv, 16–22) involving Ben Hadad I of Aram and King Baasha of Israel in 885BCE.

Biran's reading, however, is not uncontested. In early Hebrew inscriptions each word as a rule is separated by a dot. In the line where the reference to the house of David appears, however, there is no dot between the two words for house and David. Biran and Naveh argue that the elision is not significant. It merely confirms that 'house of David' was well established as a descriptive phrase that could be used to denote the southern kingdom of Judah.

But to 'Minimalists' like Philip R. Davies all these biblical associations seem like so much wishful thinking. In an article that came out soon after Biran published his views upon the find, Davies contended that Biran and Naveh had been much too overeager in their readings. The six letters of the inscription – *bet yad tet daled vav daled* – which are transliterated as *bytdvd* – can, he points out, be read in many ways besides *Beth David*/house of David. Although the word for 'house' is certainly *byt* (pronounced 'beyt', as in Beyt Lechem, or Bethlehem, meaning House of Bread), in Hebrew *vav* can be pronounced 'vee' (as in David), 'va' (as in *va-yomer*, he said), 'o' (as in Sime-o-n) or 'u' (as in Yeh-u-dah, Judah). So *dvd* could be read as *dah-veed, de-vad, dod* or *dood*. It might, Davies suggests, in the instance of the inscription, more plausibly be a placename, such as Beth-Dod. Certainly, even in the Bible, as he points out, the configuration *dvd* does not always signify 'David'. It can mean beloved, uncle and even kettle. The desire to read the letters *bytdvd* as house of David is, he asserts, a classic example of scholars working backwards from the Bible, rather than forwards from the evidence.

Davies has also criticised Biran's suggestion that the inscription might in some way relate to Ben-Hadad's victory over King Baasha of Israel. He points out that in that particular conflict Ben-Hadad was – according to the biblical sources – allied to the king of Judah, not opposed to him. While the inscription – in Biran's own reading of it – links the kingdoms of Israel and Judah as enemies of the Aramean king.

Despite the pertinence of this last point, on the more general question of whether the stone can be interpreted as saying house of David, the tide of critical opinion seems to be with Biran and against Davies and the more extreme 'Minimalists'.

The former camp has received much support from what appears to be another early inscription mentioning the house of David. This is contained in the so-called Moabite stone, a basalt stela erected by the ninth-century BCE Moabite king, Mesha, to commemorate a victory over the Israelites. The stone, which was discovered way back in 1868 in the ruins at Dhiban (the biblical city of Dibon), east of the Jordan, has been in the Louvre since 1875. Nevertheless it was only in 1994 that a full and authoritative version of the text was pieced together and translated, by the French scholar, André Lemaire.

Lemaire's work was complicated considerably by the stela's troubled history. It is a history that is worth retelling, if only to reveal the complex way in which evidence sometimes comes down to us. The stone was discovered, if that is the correct term, by a French born, German affiliated, Anglican missionary called F. A. Klein. He, at least, was the first European to see it. He was led to where it lay, amid the ruins of Dibon, east of the Jordan, by a bedouin tribesman, who quite rightly suspected that Klein might be prepared to pay for it. Klein was amazed to be shown a monumental tablet some three feet high with a flat base and rounded top, like a small gravestone, inscribed with thirty-four lines of text, lying face up on the surface of the tell. It was clearly of major importance. He offered to buy it at once, and for a considerable sum. A deal was struck, but Klein first had to find a way of raising the money.

Initially he offered the German consul the chance to acquire the stela, but this deal soon became entangled, as representatives from other European powers threatened to take an interest. Charles Clermont-Ganneau, a young French diplomat attached to the consulate in

Jerusalem, determined to secure the stone for France. To gain a fuller understanding of its contents he went behind Klein's back and sent a man called Ya'qub Karavaca out to Dhiban to take what is called a 'paper squeeze' of the inscription. A paper squeeze is made by laying sheets of soft, wet paper onto an inscribed surface and then pressing the paper down into the incisions; once the paper has dried, it can be peeled off, retaining a facsimile of the text in raised, reversed letters on the back.

Karavaca, together with two attendants, rode out to Dhiban and managed to persuade the bedouins to let him make a paper squeeze of it. While he was waiting for the squeeze to dry, however, a fight broke out and he was forced to flee. One of his attendants just had time to rip the still-damp paper off the stone. It tore into seven pieces, but these he stuffed into his robe. The other attendant was less lucky: he got speared in the leg.

Clemont-Ganneau received the fragments of the squeeze, with their faint impressions of the letters, and began vainly to try and decipher the intricacies of the text. Meanwhile the German authorities were still negotiating to buy the stone itself. The deal, however, was proving very difficult to conclude. In desperation they sought the help of the Ottoman pasha, who was supposed to have control of the region. In fact he had almost no influence in what was pretty much a no-man's land east of the Jordan. His pretensions to power served only to incur the hatred and distrust of the local tribesmen. When the bedouin learnt that the Ottoman authorities had opinions on the matter of the disposal of the stone, they decided to destroy their find rather than hand it over. They apparently heated up the stela and then doused it with cold water; it broke into over fifty pieces. They then distributed these fragments among themselves and dispersed.

At this point the Germans seem to have given up the chase. But Clermont-Ganneau remained determined. He set out to acquire as many of the fragments as he could. Over the next few years he managed to track down and buy some thirty-eight pieces of the stone, bearing 613 of the thousand or so letters of the original inscription. Charles Warren, of the Palestine Exploration Fund, over the same period managed to acquire a further eighteen fragments (bearing fifty-six characters). In 1873 Clermont-Ganneau presented his collection to the Louvre, and the following year, in an all-too-rare gesture of international scholarly cooperation, Warren's fragments were presented to the museum as well.

Clermont-Ganneau, working with the tattered paper squeeze, managed to piece together the collection of basalt fragments. About two-thirds of the stone and the inscription were recovered; the remaining third he had to recreate from the squeeze. So that the stone could be exhibited as an apparent whole, the missing portions were modelled in plaster. Although Clermont-Ganneau did publish an edition and translation of the text, neither, he felt, was definitive. Although he planned to produce an *editio princeps*, the work was still incomplete at his death. It is a lack that obliged André Lemaire to return to the original, to carry out his own close investigation of the stone fragments and of the paper squeeze.

The inscription, the longest found in the Holy Land, is taken up with the details of Mesha's various victories over the king of Israel: '. . . And the men of Gad had dwelt in the land of Atarot from of old, and the king of Israel built/ Atarot for himself; but I fought against the town and took it, and I slew all the people . . .' and so on. Much of the text can be clearly deciphered by using the fragments of the inscription together with the paper squeeze, but down towards the bottom of the stone the task is much more difficult.

One line in particular – line 31 – has long baffled scholars. It begins, 'As for Horonen, dwelt there . . .' but then the fragmentary nature of the text makes the next word, the subject, unclear. By referring to the paper squeeze, scholars have established that the spoilt word is almost certainly *bt[-]wd*. Lemaire's careful scrutiny both of the stone and of the paper squeeze has convinced him that the missing letter in the midst of this partially reconstructed word, is a *d*. Thus the word is rendered *btdwd* or house of David.

Lemaire's interpretation certainly makes sense. The text of the stela now runs: 'And the house [of Da]vid dwelt in Horonen./[. . .] and Karosh said to me: 'Go down! Fight against Horonen.' And I went down, and [. . .].' Once again *Beth David* appears as one word – *bt[d]wd*. The spelling, it must be admitted, is slightly different from that of the Tel Dan inscription, house is rendered *bt* rather than *byt* but this, according to Lemaire, was a common Moabite variation.

Lemaire's reading has provoked the expected scepticism of the 'Minimalist' camp. There is, they claim, a wishful element in his guesswork. But many scholars are convinced. With two mentions of his name, dating from the ninth century, King David has emerged from the shadows, if only slightly. Perhaps he did exist. Perhaps he was a king. But a king of what? That question is still hotly contested. The existence of his kingdom might be admitted but its scale and character remain open to question. David is presented in the Bible as a great military leader: certainly he would have relished the battle that rages over his reputation.

CHAPTER 5

Solomon

In the far south of Israel, only a little above where the country tapers to a point at Eilat on the Red Sea, lies the crater-like valley of Timna. It is an alien terrain: a red tinged moonscape peppered with bizarre rock formations; vast boulders perch on improbably small columns of rock, curiously eroded outcrops stand out against the blue sky, and dramatic shifts in plane fracture the level run of the land. A curtain of wind eroded cliffs hems in the valley, lending it an air of almost oppressive seclusion and even mystery. At the entrance to this strange and wonderful landscape a signpost announces that you have arrived at King Solomon's mines.

Here, it is claimed, was the source of King Solomon's fabled wealth – the wealth with which he glorified his name, his kingdom and his god. The claim is only too believable. The very landscape seems to echo the grandeur of his royal vision. Two vast buttresses of rock, sculpted from the cliff face by millennia of wind and rain, are known still as King Solomon's pillars. And even now the minerals seem to spring unbidden out of the ground; vast green stains of copper blossom on the red rocks.

King Solomon's mines are not, it must be said, mentioned in the Bible, at least not specifically. But they are part of the myth that has built up around his name and his reputation. It is a potent and enduring story, and one that certainly has its origins in the biblical account. It is in the pages of the Old Testament – and particularly the first book of Kings – that Solomon's name is set as a byword for wealth, wisdom, glory and splendour. If David rose from rags to riches, the career of his son, Solomon, was from riches to still greater riches.

Solomon was not David's only son, nor was he the eldest. According to the biblical account his succession was far from clear. An older half-brother – Adonijah – made an attempt to claim the kingdom even as David was on his deathbed. But Solomon, supported by his mother, Bathsheba, by the prophet Nathan and by Benaiah, a particularly loyal and ruthless hatchet man, outmanoeuvred his sibling and secured the throne for himself. Then, with an almost Machiavellian lack of sentiment, he had Adonijah killed along with every other real or potential opponent.

Having established a firm foundation for rule, Solomon proceeded to flourish. His reign is portrayed as a rising tide of prosperity and power, marked by luxurious imports, grandiose building projects and wide-ranging political reforms. His kingdom is said to have stretched from the Euphrates in the north to the borders of Egypt in the south.

He governed it wisely. When Yahweh appeared to him in a dream and asked him what gift he might like, Solomon asked for wisdom: 'that I may discern between good and bad'. The efficacy of his gift was soon revealed in his famous judgement in the dispute between two prostitutes over which of them was the true mother of a child. He suggested cutting the baby in two and giving each woman half. When only one of the harlots protested at this solution and offered to relinquish her claims to the child so that it might live, he realised that she must be the real mother (I Kings iii, 16–22). His wisdom, however, was not exercised solely in the affairs of the family court; it was apparent too in the governmental reforms that the Bible describes him carrying out.

The Bible details how he divided the country into twelve new administrative regions, each one under its own royal-appointed officer who was responsible for collecting revenues for the crown. Some biblical scholars have suggested that this reorganisation was probably an ingenious ploy to weaken the traditional but disparate allegiances of the various tribes. Certainly the author of the book of Kings thought that his policy of centralisation greatly increased royal wealth and, with it, royal prestige.

The world's rulers, according to the Bible, sought alliances with Solomon. And he seems to have been expert at turning the needs of diplomacy towards the pursuit of pleasure. His reputed assemblage of 700 wives and 300 concubines bound him to the affections of many of his powerful neighbours. His principal consort was the daughter of pharaoh. He enjoyed another important, if rather less intimate, alliance with the Phoenician ruler, King Hiram of Tyre, who helped him to establish a merchant navy on the Red Sea. It was this navy that opened up the possibilities of lucrative trade with distant Ophir, bringing in all the necessary luxuries of regal housekeeping: 'gold and silver, ivory, and apes and peacocks' (I Kings ix, 26–7; x, 22).

Solomon's international reputation also prompted the famous visit of the Queen of Sheba, who had travelled from the wealthy lands of south-western Arabia (roughly equivalent to modern Yemen). She came partly to test Solomon's wisdom and partly to see if the reports of his wealth were true. She was not disappointed on either count. (The legend that she went away with more than just her curiosity satisfied, and that she bore Solomon a son, who became, in time, the founder of the Ethiopian royal house, is not included in the Bible.)

Though Solomon was endowed with gold, silver, ivory, apes, peacocks and concubines, the real measure of his glory seems to have been his building works. The Bible devotes much space to listing and describing them. Foremost among these arrangements was his temple – the first temple built to Yahweh at Jerusalem. This was –

and, to many Jews, remains – Solomon's great claim to glory. And, certainly, as described in the book of Kings, it must have been pretty glorious.

> And the house which King Solomon built for the Lord, the length thereof was three-score cubits, and the breadth thereof was twenty cubits, and the height thereof thirty cubits. And the porch before the temple of the house, twenty cubits was the length thereof, according to the breadth of the house; and ten cubits was the breadth thereof before the house. And for the house he made windows of narrow lights. And against the wall of the house he built chambers round about . . . And the house, when it was in building, was built of stone made ready before it was brought thither: so that there was neither hammer nor axe nor any tool of iron heard in the house, while it was in building. (I Kings vi, 2–7)

At sixty cubits long by twenty cubits wide the structure was not particularly large. (A cubit was supposedly the length of a man's arm from his elbow to the second knuckle of his middle finger; it is reckoned at about twenty inches or fifty centimetres.) But then the temple didn't have to be very big as, according to tradition, almost no one was allowed inside it. The building itself was not a place of public worship; it was reserved for the priests. The sacrifices and other ceremonies which the public might be allowed to witness were performed in the courtyard in front of the temple.

The glory of the temple in the biblical description lay in its decoration. Two magnificent, decorative columns of hollow bronze flanked the doorway and the whole interior of the edifice was panelled with cedar and then gilded. Inside the Holy of Holies – a perfect cube room, twenty cubits by twenty – two gilded 'cherubs' stood sentinel over the kingdom's most sacred object – the Ark of the

Covenant, the golden chest containing the tablets inscribed with the Ten Commandments.

The building stood in a huge colonnaded courtyard and then, encircling that, was an even larger space – a great court – which seems to have included the royal palace. Every detail of the interior and the furniture was embellished with all that wealth and skill could offer. The temple is presented as standing at the heart of Solomon's kingdom both literally and figuratively.

It was not, however, his only building project. At Jerusalem he is also reported to have continued David's plans to expand and improve the city. The Bible describes how he extended and completed the city wall, and laid out a whole palace complex including a residence for his Egyptian queen and a magnificent 'House of the Forest of Lebanon' which seems to have served as a sort of armoury (I Kings, vii, 1–12). And he is credited with carrying out numerous other important schemes of construction throughout his kingdom.

They were schemes that seem to have taken their toll on the local population. Frequent levies had to be raised, and the non-Israelite population – 'all the people left that were left of the Amorites, Hittites, Perizzites, Hivites, and Jebusites' – were conscripted into 'bondservice' and put to work. There is mention of building work at 'Beth-horon the nether, and Baalath, and Tadmor in the wilderness . . . and cities for his chariots, and cities for his horsemen'. And there is a particular focus on his grand projects at three cities: Hazor, Megiddo and Gezer (I Kings ix, 15–21).

All this rich and specific physical detail about his building schemes – placenames, dimensions, materials – serves to make Solomon and his kingdom seem very real. It fixes the more transitory and fantastical elements of his story – his boundless wisdom, his boundless wealth, his boundless harem – in a seemly tangible world of bricks and mortar. But just how tangible is Solomon's world? Where are the bricks and where is the mortar?

These are questions that, perhaps more than any others, have divided archaeologists and scholars – and divided them with an often uncompromising sharpness. When Benno Rothenberg, as a young archaeologist in the 1950s, went to excavate the mines at Timna he had no reason to believe that they might not indeed be connected with King Solomon. Popular traditions and placenames often do preserve historical truths over hundreds, even thousands, of years. But they can also create and foster myths.

At Timna, Rothenberg uncovered many things – and much evidence of early mining activity – but no trace of Solomon. 'These were mines,' he explains wryly, 'but they were not King Solomon's mines. They were not here and not anywhere in the region. We found stone altars and temples but they were built by Egyptian mining expeditions. The pottery that we found was not tenth century [BCE] – meaning Solomonic – it was late thirteenth to twelfth century BCE – Late Bronze Age pottery. And that,' as Rothenberg recalls, 'was when my troubles started. Because I was then saying, directly or indirectly, that there was no King Solomon in the area.'

It was not a message that anyone wanted to hear – not the general public certainly, but not the Israeli academic community either. There was an extremely nationalistic flavour to Israel's archaeological endeavour during this period. For many of the country's archaeologists national identity and the historical truth of the biblical story were closely entwined. Any perceived attack on a biblical hero or a biblical story represented almost an attack on the modern state. It did not seem to matter that King Solomon's mines were not actually mentioned in the Bible; King Solomon was and that was enough.

'There was a conference in Eilat in 1962,' Rothenberg recalls. 'All the archaeologists were there and I was not allowed to lecture.' His theories were against the whole prevailing concept of biblical archaeology. 'And then they hated me because I was successful – because I could prove my claims by thousands of finds – including inscriptions, so that there could be no argument.' He found one rock carving depicting the twelfth-century BCE pharaoh, Ramases III, presenting a lump of copper to the goddess Hathor. 'Everything dated from hundreds of years before Solomon.' Resistance to Rothenberg's finds was fierce and often took on a note of a personal animosity. 'I had actually to leave Israel's universities and go abroad,' he says, 'because of this impossible, personal situation.'

Solomon, at the time, was regarded as one of the triumphal figures of biblical archaeology. It was a position he had achieved several decades earlier, when a team from the University of Chicago began excavating the great mound at Megiddo in the valley of Jezreel in northern Israel. The arrestingly initialled expedition leader, P.L.O. Guy, uncovered evidence of a monumental city wall made of dressed stone and crowned by a magnificent fortified gateway with six chambers. There were also traces of other monumental buildings within the city wall, made from similar materials. The method of construction seemed to be exactly that which Solomon is described as having used at Jerusalem: 'hewed stones, sawed with saws, within and without, even from the foundation unto the coping'.

And there was more. In another part of the site, Guy and his team found the remains of a large building of a type they had not encountered before. It was subdivided into aisles by two rows of pillars. There was a narrow unpaved central aisle, flanked by two broader ones with cobbled floors. Between the pillars, running the length of the building, were two lines of what appeared to be stone troughs. Guy considered the curious shape of the layout of the building and the presence of the troughs and concluded that this must have been a large stable complex, perhaps the headquarters of a cavalry regiment. For Guy the evidence was too compelling to be ignored. 'And if we ask ourselves,' he wrote in his official report, 'who, at Megiddo, shortly after the defeat of the Philistines by King David, but with the help of skilled foreign masons built a city with many stables: I believe that we shall find our answer in the Bible.' Everything pointed to Solomon. 'If one reads the history of Solomon, whether in Kings or in Chronicles,' Guy continued, 'one is struck by the frequency with which chariots and horses crop up.' Surely this was one of those 'cities for his chariots, and cities for his horsemen' that Solomon is described as having built. The power and might of Solomon's kingdom came sharply into focus. The chapter and verse of the book of Kings seemed to be bodied forth in stone.

In the 1950s and 1960s, excavations at Hazor, carried out by the great Israeli archaeologist Yigael Yadin revealed traces of another monumental six-chambered gateway. He dated it to the tenth century BCE, the time of Solomon. Re-examining an old account of an early excavation at Gezer, he worked out that there was, in fact, a third such gateway there. It seemed all but impossible not to conclude that these three structures were part of Solomon's great reconstruction plan for the cities of Gezer, Megiddo and Hazor, mentioned in the book of Kings. The gateways were of exactly the same six-chambered design, and were almost identical in their proportions. The same royal architect, he conjectured, must have been used for all three. Here, it seemed, was the proof of Solomon's centralised and far-reaching authority, his close control of the nation's wealth and human resources.

Other fragments of evidence from elsewhere also appeared to reflect, if only tangentially, the truth of the biblical description of Solomon. A pottery sherd found at Tell Quisle was inked with the phrase 'gold of Ophir', a reference to the very place from where Solomon was said to have shipped his precious metals. At Bethel a distinctive ninth-century stamp seal from southern Arabia was dug up. To archaeologists eager to find traces of the biblical Solomon it seemed to be evidence that perhaps the biblical Queen of Sheba really had made her visit, and that it had led to the opening up of trade between Israel and her wealthy kingdom to the south.

It was against the prevailing tide of such ideas that Rothenberg had to struggle to voice his theories and to have them taken seriously. At first no one would listen. But in recent years the climate of opinion has shifted, and shifted dramatically. Solomon's grandeur and reputation are no longer so assured and Benno Rothenberg is back in Israel and has been able to return to a post.

The change has been brought about on two fronts. Some scholars have focused attention on the fact that Solomon's story is entirely uncorroborated by sources outside the Bible. He is presented as a king with widespread international contacts and influence. And yet not a single mention of his name occurs in any contemporary Near Eastern text. He is said to have been married to the daughter of an Egyptian pharaoh, presumably Pharaoh Siamun, whose reign is believed to be roughly contemporaneous with the early part of Solomon's rule, but no reference to this dynastic alliance has yet been found in any of the Egyptian records of the period.

This silence is at the very least curious. Solomon from the biblical account would seem to have been the most famous king of Israel, one who self-consciously reached beyond the borders of the realm to establish relations with foreign powers; of all the Old Testament rulers he is the one you would most expect to be mentioned in other sources. Nevertheless the silence that surrounds his name would be drowned out by the archaeological evidence for his glorious kingdom, if that could be clearly established.

But, of course, almost nothing in the world of biblical archaeology is ever clearly established. In recent years the younger generations of Israel's archaeologists, many of them based at Tel Aviv University, have begun to question the certainty of some of the accepted datings and interpretations of the great Solomonic sites.

At the heart of any search for the archaeological remains of Solomon's kingdom there stands a great void: Jerusalem. The absence of archaeological evidence in the city for the reign of King David, which has already been noted, is even more marked and even more surprising in the case of King Solomon. His buildings are supposed to have been many and monumental, and yet no trace of them has ever been found. It is true that his famous temple is said to have been destroyed by the Babylonian king, Nebuchadrezzar in 587/6BCE, but many other buildings in Jerusalem and elsewhere have been sacked and yet leave some vestige. But, as Jonathan Tubb, the curator of the Syro-Palestinian collections at the British Museum, remarks with an unsentimental candour, 'We do not have a single stone of Solomon's temple.' This fact is, at the very least, curious. It remains, however, only a negative argument against the actual existence of the temple. Absence of evidence, as rival archaeologists never tire of reiterating, is not evidence of absence.

Any continued search, however, for a single stone of Solomon's temple is made complicated – or, rather, is rendered impossible – by the fact that mount Zion, its supposed location, is now the site of the Dome of the Rock and the Aqsa mosque. The religious significance of the place for Muslims, combined with the fraught relations between the Muslim and Jewish populations, provides a double barrier to the possibility of any dig being made. There is little chance of uncovering a set of foundations, sixty cubits by twenty cubits; little chance of discovering a preserved panel of cedar wood that could be placed by carbon 14 dating to the middle years of the tenth century. Little chance of coming across an inscription commemorating the dedication of the temple in the eighth year of the reign of King Solomon. These things, alas, will probably be found only in the fevered dreams of archaeologists. In the absence of either materials or opportunities in Jerusalem, archaeologists have had to carry on their work elsewhere.

In 1994, Israel Finkelstein and David Ussishkin, together with Baruch Halpern of the Pennsylvania State University, went back to Megiddo, to carry out new excavations at the site. Their findings – and their interpretations of what they found – have been startling. At least they have startled the curiously entwined worlds of Near Eastern archaeology and modern Israeli public opinion. Megiddo, the place of the first named battle in recorded history, the scene of numerous sieges and sackings over millennia, the site (according to the Bible) of the coming Armageddon, is now the locus of fierce scholarly conflict.

As their work progressed many preconceptions and long-held opinions about the site and its development were called into question, if not completely exploded. It is a process that has had a drastic effect on the reputation of King Solomon, as well as upon the traditionally accepted chronology of the whole period. The two, it should be said, are intimately connected.

The chronology of the United Monarchy was really established at Megiddo in the 1930s. The correlation between the ashlar constructed buildings discovered in stratum VA-IVB of the site and the biblical description of King Solomon's building techniques convinced archaeologists that here was indeed the archaeological proof of a biblical story. The buildings were duly dated to the accepted time of Solomon: the tenth century BCE. By extension it was argued that the distinctive assemblage of pottery associated with stratum VA-IVB at Megiddo should also be dated to the tenth century BCE and could be used in dating the levels of other sites to the same era. This assessment seemed to be confirmed when, in the 1970s, this same distinctive type of pottery was discovered in a destruction layer at Tel Arad in the south of modern Israel. Archaeologists were quick to relate the evidence of destruction to the campaign of Pharaoh Shoshenq in c925BCE. Arad was one of the cities mentioned as having been subdued by the pharaoh in a monumental inscription at Karnak.

Finkelstein's doubts about this accepted pottery chronology were supported by the discovery of what appeared to be a ninth-century BCE destruction level at Jezreel, a site near Megiddo. The excavators noted that it contained pottery of the same type as had been discovered among the debris at Tel Jezreel and in stratum VA-IVB at Megiddo, supposedly the early tenth-century Solomonic level. If the destruction level at Jezreel really did belong to the ninth century then all the accepted levels at Megiddo – and elsewhere – needed to be re-dated by 100 years to be brought into line. According to this new reckoning, the Solomonic era at Megiddo should be looked for not among the impressive masonry of stratum VA-IVB, but among the less sophisticated remains uncovered two strata below. Ironically Finkelstein – who has tended to adopt a 'Rejectionist' stance – has sought to confirm his ninth-century dating of the Jezreel site by reference to the Bible. He has – following Ussishkin's lead – suggested that the town was very probably destroyed by Jehu, whose bloody coup d'état is described in the second book of Kings (and later on in this chapter).

Although Finkelstein's proposed revision of the entire chronology has had a profound effect upon the interpretation of the Megiddo site, it must be admitted that some doubt had already been cast on the dating of 'King Solomon's stables'. Yigael Yadin himself had suggested that they might date from the century after Solomon. Finkelstein and his co-directors were happy to confirm such a reading and carry it further. From their re-dating of that whole level of the site they concluded that the structure definitely belonged not to the mid-tenth century, but to the ninth century, or perhaps even slightly later. It probably had its origins in the time – not of Solomon – but of King Ahab.

They queried too whether the building really had been used for stabling horses. It is a query that Halpern has taken up with enthusiasm. 'We have a problem with these "stables",' he announces. 'There's no drainage under them. There's no way to bring the requisite hay, the requisite water up to the horses without intense investment of labour. And most of the troughs are incomplete. They're broken at the ends. They have channels cut through them. Some have weights associated with them.' Also many of the things that one might reasonably expect to find among the ruins of a stable are missing. 'We don't find tools,' he explains, warming to his argument. 'We don't find pottery. We don't find horse bones; not a single horse bone has come out of this site so far.'

These do appear to be significant gaps in the archaeological record, even allowing for the usual caveat about the limited weight that can be placed on absence of evidence. But what alternative use might the site have been put to? 'What we're looking for,' suggests Halpern, with an exemplary precision that can't quite conceal his keen sense of intellectual mischief, 'is some sort of industry that was worth investing twenty per cent of the most valuable real estate in northern Israel in, that leaves no real residue in the form of artefacts, that leaves no bones, no tools.'

Halpern makes his deductions from the available evidence with the neatness of a Sherlock Holmes. The peculiar arrangement of the broken ended troughs suggests to Halpern that they must have been used to hold 'a non-viscous liquid that would not leak out ... presumably something that could be pressed into patties or cut into cakes. And could then be removed for export without clay vessels.' He pauses to consider the options, before venturing, 'Something in the order of opium comes to mind.' It is a startling conclusion – though one that might have appealed to Sherlock Holmes. Others, however, are unlikely to find the notion that the early Israelite monarchy might have owed its wealth to drug trafficking so appealing.

'It's my wish-fulfilment scenario,' laughs Halpern. As yet his exposition of the known facts of the site remains only one theory among many. 'But,' as he points out, 'we do have evidence for the export of drugs from this area during the heyday of the Assyrian empire [in the eighth century BCE], so perhaps it's not entirely fantasy.' Although other scholars may be reluctant to follow Halpern into these exciting realms of speculation, the theory is at least intriguing. The medicinal use of drugs was well known in the Ancient World. Poppies clearly did grow in the region, as they are depicted on later Jewish coins. And what look very like ornately carved stone pipes have been found at several ninth-century sites.

Finkelstein and Ussishkin did not confine their own doubts to the stable block. Their reinterpretation of the pottery chronology at the site suggested several other revisions. At the site there is a major destruction layer immediately beneath the phase of the great stone-built palaces, walls and gates: clear evidence that the city was sacked and burnt. Archaeologists have long debated when Megiddo might have been destroyed and by whom. The orthodox theory was that the destruction occurred at the very end of the eleventh century and perhaps represents King David's suppression of the Canaanite city. Upon the ruins of this settlement King Solomon then erected his magnificent buildings.

According to Finkelstein's reckoning, however, Megiddo was destroyed in the late tenth century, probably by Pharaoh Shoshenq. The 925BCE campaign of Shoshenq I – as has been mentioned – is documented in a monumental inscription at Karnak, where a list of conquered cities is given; it includes Megiddo. If further confirmation of the pharaoh's presence were needed, the fragment of a victory stele erected by the pharaoh was discovered at the town. Unfortunately the fragment was found in the dump, among the debris of the dig, so it is impossible to determine which layer of the site it belonged to, but it provides a rare piece of extra-biblical corroboration. If Finkelstein's contention is right, and the major destruction layer at Megiddo can be set down to Shoshenq, then the fine stone buildings that rose upon the ruins belong to the ninth century BCE, not the tenth. They, like so much else once attributed to Solomon, can be ascribed to King Ahab.

Finkelstein and Ussishkin looked again at the great six-chambered gateway that Yadin had excavated, and which even now is marked with a large blue sign, describing it as King Solomon's gate. 'There is a problem here,' explains David Ussishkin, in his characteristically clear and precise tones, 'because the gate is built together with – and is connected to – a city wall which is later in date. The wall dates from the later period of the Israelite monarchy, to the end of the ninth century [BCE], or even the eighth century [BCE]. It is quite clear that the gate is built together with the wall, and that the wall is late in date. I feel that King Solomon probably turns in his grave whenever he hears the gate ascribed to him.' The tenth-century palace has suffered a similar fate: it has become a ninth-century palace, built – Finkelstein suggests – 'probably in the time of King Ahab'.

All this re-dating has not destroyed the notion of a tenth-century city at Megiddo, but it has drastically altered its size, its character and even its allegiance. The Megiddo that Shoshenq sacked in 925BCE was, according to Finkelstein, a relatively modest foundation. It was built of mud bricks not ashlar stones. It was not, moreover, an Israelite city at all, but a Canaanite one. That, at least, is Finkelstein's theory. Sitting in his camp chair under the flapping black awnings that shade the dig from the strength of the afternoon sun, Finkelstein seems to take a pleasure in making the most startling new claims in the mildest possible manner. 'It was a city,' he explains, 'from the period of David and Solomon, but – as I understand it – it was not a city *of* David and Solomon. We are here in the last breath of the Canaanite world, in the early and mid-tenth century [BCE]. The pottery is a continuation of the second millennium [BCE].' From the physical evidence uncovered at the site he can see nothing to suggest that the traditional Canaanite way of life had been interrupted before this point. According to his reading, there is no trace at Megiddo of an Israelite conquest by David or by Solomon. There are no signs of centralised control being exercised from Jerusalem (or, indeed, from anywhere else). There is only an uninterrupted line of traditional Canaanite pottery. It is a picture into which the biblical King Solomon and his magnificent kingdom just do not fit. 'We don't really have states here,' Finkelstein says, 'in the tenth century [BCE], although it's always possible to argue that there is one state centred on Jerusalem – it's hard.'

It is only in the ninth century, Finkelstein maintains, that the situation at Megiddo alters. The city was rebuilt; the mud bricks were replaced with cut stones. Monumental buildings and elaborate gatehouses were erected. And the pottery style advanced into something recognisably different. This, Finkelstein and Ussishkin consider, was the city of King Ahab.

So who was this Ahab to whom so much is being ascribed? How did he rise to power? And when did he rule? In the biblical account, Solomon, despite his great wisdom, manages to offend Yahweh at the end of his reign. As is so often the case with those in power, it was his libido that led him astray: 'But King Solomon loved many strange women, together with the daughter of Pharaoh, women of the Moabites, Ammonites, Edomites, Sidonians, and Hittites', all nations which Yahweh had warned the Children of Israel against getting romantically entangled with 'for surely they will turn your heart away after their gods' (I Kings xi, 1–2). Unfortunately Solomon failed to heed the warning. And to please at least some of these 'strange women' he erected temples or 'high places' to their particular deities – to Ashtoreth the goddess of the Sidonians, to Milcom 'the abomination of the Ammonites' and to Chemosh the god of the Moabites.

This, according to the biblical narrative, troubled Yahweh. He had promised David that his descendants should rule the land for all time, but he felt that he could not let Solomon's transgression go unpunished. As a compromise he decreed that the kingdom should be divided: the house of David should indeed continue to rule, but only over the territory of Judah.

At the king's death dissension does indeed break out. Jeroboam leads a rebellion against Solomon's son and heir, Rehoboam, and manages to wrest the northern part of the kingdom from his control. Rehoboam is left with a greatly diminished territory, centred on Jerusalem, and based on the old lands traditionally ascribed to the tribe of Judah. This becomes the southern kingdom of Judah or, as it seems also to have been called from an early date, the kingdom of the house of David. Jeroboam's northern territory was known, rather confusingly, as the kingdom of Israel, or the kingdom of Samaria.

Scholars are almost universally agreed that the Old Testament, as it stands, was compiled in Jerusalem or by people from Jerusalem. Certainly it has a thoroughly Judean bias. The kings of the northern territory get a very bad press. They are viewed as traitors and apostates. They are all denounced as rebels against the true succession of the house of David, and most of them are condemned too for not being exclusive in their veneration of the one true god, Yahweh. As a result the history of the northern kingdom is presented as one well merited disaster after another.

Five years after the division of Solomon's kingdom, the Bible – as has been mentioned – describes how the Egyptian pharaoh invaded the land and sacked Jerusalem. The account of Shoshenq's campaign inscribed at Karnak, however, although it records over 150 cities in the region sacked or subdued by the Egyptian force makes no mention of Jerusalem. From that list it appears that Shoshenq's energies were mainly concentrated in the northern kingdom of Israel. And certainly in the biblical account these were troubled times for the northern kingdom. Jeroboam's reign was followed by a succession of disputes and civil war. From this period of internecine chaos a victor finally emerged: Omri.

According to the rather terse account in the book of Kings, Omri re-established order in the kingdom and built a new capital city at Samaria, on a greenfield site he acquired for two talents of silver from a local landowner. After twelve years, he was succeeded by his son, Ahab. The positive achievements of Ahab's rule are also lightly treated in the book of Kings. There is only a cursory mention at the end of the biblical account of 'the ivory house which he made, and all the cities that he built' (I Kings xxii, 39).

Despite the reticence of the biblical author, other sources hint at the possible power and prestige of Omri and Ahab. Both kings are mentioned on the Mesha stele, or Moabite stone, as oppressors of Moab, who brought the northern part of the land east of Jordan under their control. In Assyrian documents Israel became known as 'the land of Omri', and was referred to as such well into the next century, long after Omri's actual dynasty had expired. Ahab himself is mentioned specifically in an Assyrian inscription erected by Shalmaneser III. He is listed as one of the twelve kings who allied against Shalmaneser and halted his advance in a battle at Qarqar on the river Orontes, in 853BCE. Nevertheless, if Ahab was famous in the Near East during the ninth century BCE, today — if he is remembered at all — it is as the husband of his more famous — or more infamous — wife, Jezebel.

Jezebel was a Sidonian (i.e. Phoenician) princess. According to some early genealogies she would have been the great-aunt of Dido, queen of Carthage. She was, the book of Kings notes disapprovingly, a devout worshipper of Baal, and she persuaded her husband to establish an altar to the god at Samaria. This apostasy provoked the ire of the prophets Elijah and Elisha and led to several heated confrontations. But Baal-worship was not — according to the biblical account — the limit of Jezebel's iniquity. The story of her great crime is told with relish in the Bible.

Close to the wall of the royal palace at Jezreel, the city from which the beautiful Jezreel valley takes its name, there was a vineyard owned by a man called Naboth. Ahab thought that this plot, given its close proximity to the palace, would make an excellent royal herb garden. So he approached Naboth and offered to give him another, better, vineyard, in exchange. Or, if Naboth preferred, he would pay cash for it. Naboth, however, seems to have had a pious dread of parting with 'the inheritance of [his] fathers'. He refused to consider selling or swapping the vineyard. This cast Ahab into a terrible sulk: 'he laid him down upon his bed, and turned his face, and would eat no bread' (I Kings xxi, 4).

When Jezebel discovered him in this sorry state, and found out the cause of it, she was not impressed. She told him to buck up, and assured him that she would see to it that he got the vineyard.

She then wrote a series of letters, in the king's name, to the elders of Jezreel, denouncing Naboth, claiming that he had 'blasphemed God and the King'. She commanded them to arrange a trial at which she produced two witnesses – 'sons of Belial' – who swore that they had indeed heard Naboth blaspheme both his God and his king. The unfortunate man was duly found guilty, dragged out into the street and, according to the law, stoned to death. On account of some legal nicety, all his property – including the conveniently located vineyard – reverted to the crown. Ahab was delighted by his wife's ruthless efficiency.

Not everyone, however, was taken in by Jezebel's ploy. The prophet Elijah, tipped off by Yahweh, was waiting for the king when he came to take possession of the vineyard. He denounced the crime and prophesied a speedy end to Ahab and his queen. The dogs of the street, he announced, would eat their carcasses.

Elijah's prophecy was not instant but it was accurate. Three years later, while campaigning against the king of Syria, at Ramoth-gilead east of the Jordan, the second book of Kings records that Ahab caught a stray arrow in the back. He managed to make it home to Samaria but died a lingering death. When his attendants were washing down his gore-bespattered chariot, the local dogs lapped up the spilt blood, thus fulfilling part of Elijah's prediction (I Kings xxii, 38).

Fate took rather longer to catch up with Jezebel. Indeed she had the satisfaction of seeing her son, Joram, on the throne of Israel, and her daughter Athaliah married to the king of Judah. The years immediately following Ahab's death were not, however, without their troubles. King Mesha of Moab rebelled in an effort to throw off the yoke of Israelite oppression imposed by Omri and Ahab. In the biblical account, Joram allied with the Judean king, leads a successful campaign into Moab, beating down cities, cutting down trees and stopping up wells (II Kings iii, 25). But the story has a dramatic and curious ending.

During the siege of the Moabite town Kir-hareseth, King Mesha, feeling that the battle is going against him, sacrifices his eldest son on the city walls. 'And,' the chapter concludes, 'there was great indignation against Israel: and they departed from him, and returned to their own land.' Exactly from where, or from whom, this 'great indignation' descended upon Israel is left unclear: from the Moabite god, Chemosh; from Yahweh; from King Mesha and his troops? But it seems to have resulted in the termination, if not the defeat, of the Israelite expedition. It was, perhaps, these events that lay behind the creation of the Moabite stone discussed in the last chapter.

Despite such setbacks, the Omride dynasty — as described in the second book of Kings — continued in power, and Jezebel — as the mother of the king — seems to have maintained an important and influential position. Her nemesis finally arrived, however, in the shape of Jehu, the commander of Joram's army. Inspired by Elijah, he led a coup d'état. He had himself proclaimed king of Israel, and then turned his troops upon their former sovereign. The Bible describes how Jehu killed both Joram, and Ahazia king of Judah, before marching into Jezreel to confront the dowager-queen herself.

When Jezebel heard of his approach, she dressed herself in all her finery, put on her make-up, and denounced Jehu from the palace window. Her splendid defiance was cut short, however, when she was unceremoniously defenestrated by a couple of renegade eunuchs. Perhaps she died in the fall; the Bible says, 'some of her blood was sprinkled on the wall'. But, for good measure, Jehu then trampled her under his horse's hooves, before going into the palace for a celebratory dinner. As the plates were being cleared away he gave orders to his men that they should go and retrieve Jezebel's body and bury it, 'for she is a king's daughter'. But when they got outside they discovered that, as Elijah had prophesied, the dogs of Jezreel had eaten her. There was nothing left except for her skull, her feet and her hands. 'This,' the chapter concludes, 'is Jezebel' (II Kings ix, 30–7).

And that, too, it seems, was Jezreel. Certainly it seems the city was destroyed at about this time and in the Bible the prophet Hosea denounced Jehu as having the blood of the town upon his head (Hosea i, 4). The cataclysm – though condemned by Hosea – has been welcomed by archaeologists. If true, it is thoroughly convenient: it fixes a whole and known phase of the city. A careful examination of the destruction layer, left it is to be supposed by Jehu's action, can reveal the city of Ahab and Jezebel. It can also establish the range of artefacts and pottery types then current, and this can be used in identifying other sites and fixing them to the same period.

The picture that archaeologists have managed to draw from the ruins of Jezreel is one that in many respects confirms, or at least coincides with, the biblical narrative. Although David Ussishkin, who carried out work at the site, did not quite find Naboth's vineyard, clearly marked out and labelled, he did uncover indications of viticulture close to the city walls: evidence of a winepress and even a subterranean storage cellar filled with wine jars.

The city itself, although built on the site of earlier small-scale habitations, appears to have been essentially a ninth-century BCE foundation. There has always been some debate among historians as to the exact character and purpose of Jezreel. Why, it has been asked, would Ahab build such a large new city only ten miles (15 km) from the existing centre at Megiddo? Some have suggested that Jezreel served as a winter capital for the kingdom, others that it – rather than Samaria – was established as a centre for the cult of Baal.

The recent excavations carried out by John Woodhead of the British School of Archaeology in Jerusalem together with David Ussishkin have uncovered evidence of a large, well fortified central enclosure, surrounded by an imposing wall with towers projecting at the corners. Access to the enclosure was, it seems, through a six-chambered gateway, of the type found at Hazor, Megiddo and elsewhere. The town's layout, its massive defences, its position on a spur overlooking the valley, all point to the conclusion that it was essentially a military foundation – perhaps, as Ussishkin suggests, the central base for Omri and Ahab's chariot troops.

Chariot troops do seem to have been at the heart of Ahab's military might. In the Bible he is shown in his chariot at the last and, in the Assyrian inscription listing the enemies of Shalmaneser III, he is credited with bringing 2,000 chariots to the great force that met on the banks of the Orontes. Even allowing for the fact that figures in ancient sources are often more symbolic than real, Ahab's force was clearly significant. It added up to ninety chariots more than the total supplied by all the other eleven allies put together.

The pottery finds at Jezreel, as has been mentioned, were among the key factors in persuading Finkelstein to realign the chronology of the period, and to date the monumental building work at Megiddo to the ninth century BCE. And they have encouraged him to ascribe the monumental gates at Hazor and Gezer to the time of Ahab as well. Evidence of the might and prestige of the early Israelite monarchy has also been found at Tel Dan, where the buildings in the religious complex at the site appear to have been extended and improved in the mid-ninth century BCE.

Samaria, too, has yielded up clear evidence of its former glory under the Omride kings. The site was excavated in the 1930s by the apparently indefatigable Kathleen Kenyon; she uncovered the foundations of what might well be Omri's original citadel and traces of Ahab's subsequent extension and improvement of it. Certainly both phases of building work uncovered by Kenyon employed the distinctive ashlar blocks found at Megiddo and elsewhere. But the site also provides a caveat about accepting any too easy connection between the biblical text and the archaeological evidence. One of the few specific references in the book of Kings to Ahab's building schemes is the mention of his ivory house at Samaria. It was clearly a byword for luxury and sophistication. Its existence seemed to receive wonderful confirmation when Kenyon uncovered large quantities of ivory furniture inlay in one of the destruction layers at Samaria. She marked the area on her excavation plan as the ivory house and even if she did not ascribe it to Ahab, others were tempted to do so. A recent re-evaluation of Kenyon's field-notes and sketches, however, has suggested that these ivory fragments almost certainly belong to another, rather later, stratum of the site. They are probably the remains of Jeroboam II's ivory house, not Ahab's.

A different aspect of this all-too-often elusive connection between the biblical record and the archaeological evidence is revealed in the evidence relating to Jehu. In the book of Kings he is described as killing both King Joram and King Ahaziah while they were recuperating from their battle against King Hazael of Syria (II Kings ix). The fragmentary inscription found at Tel Dan by Avraham Biran (discussed in the previous chapter) mentions the victory of an Aramean (thus presumably Syrian) king over a king of Israel and a king of the house of David. None of the kings is named on the main chunk of the shattered stele, and various suggestions have been put forward as to their identity.

Recently, however, two smaller fragments of the stone have come to light, which reveal the last letters of the king of Israel's name (-ram) and the first letters of the name of the Judean king (Aha-). From these shreds scholars have suggested that the kings referred to must have been Joram and Ahazia, whose reigns coincided for a single year: 842BCE. The erector of the stele would thus seem to be their common enemy, King Hazael. This is a fresh discovery that appears to confirm the biblical account of Joram and Ahazia acting in concert against the king of Syria.

However, in the inscription Hazael claims the credit for having killed his two rivals. This would seem to undermine the accuracy of the biblical account, which names Jehu as the exterminator of Joram and Ahazia. If the inscription from Tel Dan accurately reflects events, then the biblical record seems to be a tantalising mixture of historical fact, confused details, and deliberate distortion. But inscriptions – like histories – are never entirely objective records. The demands of propaganda encourage exaggeration and overstatement.

Jehu himself, though presented in the Bible as being particularly ruthless in his pursuit of power – even by the standards of the Old Testament – seems to have presided over a declining state. According to the biblical account, he lost control of all lands east of the Jordan to his rival Hazael of Damascus. From other sources it is also known that he was obliged to pay tribute to the Assyrian king, Shalmaneser III, who launched a fresh campaign against Israel in 841BCE. A beautifully carved black obelisk, now in the British Museum, records the tribute transaction. It either depicts Yahweh prostrate before Ashua, the principal Assyrian deity, or – perhaps more probably – Jehu prostrate before Shalmaneser. If it is the latter, it represents the first contemporary portrait of a king of Israel. He is a grovelling figure with a tightly curled, short beard and a loose-fitting skullcap – a vestigial presence from the pages of the Old Testament made real.

The difference between the vivid, horizontal Jehu and the elusive, unsubstantiated figure of Solomon could not be greater. And it is perhaps not surprising that some archaeologists seem keen to drag themselves and their discoveries out of the shadowy world of the tenth century BCE and into the more clearly marked uplands of the ninth.

The process, however, has not all been in one direction. The arguments of Ussishkin and Finkelstein are not uncontested. Nadav Na'aman, an historian at Tel Aviv University, has suggested that Jezreel was destroyed not by Jehu, but by Hazael, the king of Syria, who boasts of defeating the king of Israel on the Tel Dan stela. This adjustment, although plausible enough, does little to affect the dating structure of the site. The objections of other archaeologists pose more of a challenge. Some of Finkelstein and Ussishkin's colleagues feel that the pair have tried to cram too much material into the ninth century BCE, to take too much away from Solomon and to give too much to Ahab. There is, after all, they point out, only a hundred years between the two kings according to the biblical archaeology. It is not a very long span. Can it really be established that the same pottery did not continue between both reigns?

Amihai Mazar, the head of the archaeology unit at Jerusalem's Hebrew University, is sceptical: 'I believe that this pottery [such as has been found at Jezreel and elsewhere] has a long life, that it started in the tenth century [BCE] and continued into the ninth. What is the difference between the tenth century and the ninth century? They are just numbers. And the people in 900BCE on the first of January – they didn't realise that they were moving from the tenth to the ninth century [BCE].' It is a plausible argument, but it has proved very difficult to substantiate.

In the absence of a clear historical context (such as exists at Jezreel), or inscriptions, or coins, found alongside the pottery, there is almost no way of establishing a date independently. Where organic material – grain, wood, leather, cloth – is found it allows for the radiocarbon dating process to be used. Carbon 14, a molecule which accumulates in all living things and stops accumulating when they die, loses its radioactivity at a standard rate. This decline can be measured, to reveal the age of the organic material. The process, though extremely helpful to archaeologists, is accurate – even at its best – only within a frame of several decades. This can prove to be a frustratingly broad span.

'We found a large heap of grain at Tel Rehov,' recalls Mazar. 'It was under a collapsed wall, a very sealed context. We analysed this grain in two different laboratories. They gave us a date between 900 and 830BCE. Unfortunately the span of carbon 14 goes all the way from Solomon to Ahab, exactly. So we are in trouble.'

Mazar has had to draw out other lines of argument to support his dating. At Tel Rehov he has discovered the same distinctive pottery in two different levels of one room. 'My good friend Israel Finkelstein,' he cheerfully admits, 'would probably claim that both these two levels are dated to the ninth century BCE. Because, in his view, all this pottery that appears in the lower level must be ninth century; it cannot be tenth century. In my view I cannot condense all these phases – all this stratigraphy – into a period of less than seventy years.' The earlier – lower – layer of pottery must, he argues, date from the tenth century BCE, from the time of Solomon.

Even though he is prepared to re-ascribe some pottery and some urban centres to the time – and even to the kingdom – of Solomon, Mazar remains sceptical about the details of the biblical portrait of the king and his empire, as something great and glorious. Drawing back from the minutiae of pottery sherds and the intricacies of dating, the broader picture of tenth-century life in Israel and Judah comes into focus. There is little or nothing about this picture to suggest that it was the backdrop for a great and powerful empire. A well-ordered centralised kingdom, such as Solomon's is depicted as being in the Bible, would have required a well-organised and literate civil service to administer it. Yet almost no trace of writing has been found in the lands of Israel or Judah from this period.

Despite a few finds apparently linking Israel to Ophir and southern Arabia there is no evidence of any widespread trade between Israel and the nations around it. Nor have any finds been made to conjure up a world of luxury and cultural sophistication such as might have tempted the biblical Queen of Sheba, or anyone else, to pay a visit to the area. No works of indigenous art or even craft can reliably be dated to anywhere near the tenth century BCE.

And, at the most basic level, there just don't seem to have been enough people to have established or maintained a great kingdom, especially not in Judah. While the northern part of the land – what became the kingdom of Israel – was relatively prosperous and well-settled from the Late Bronze Age through into the Iron

Age, in the south the story was very different. The place was almost deserted. Around Jerusalem only half a dozen settlements from this period have been identified, and life in them seems to have been harsh and rudimentary.

Some fortified outposts do appear to have been established briefly in the Negev desert in the extreme south of Judah. But just when they were built and by whom remains unclear. Solomon is only one possible candidate. The settlements, moreover, seem to have been more in the nature of military centres than urban ones.

For most scholars the compass and character of Solomon's kingdom has dwindled. For some it has vanished to nothingness. Israel Finkelstein considers that the very grandeur of the buildings at Megiddo – and elsewhere – undermines Solomon's claims to them. 'Is it possible,' he asks, 'that cities with monumental architecture like this were ruled from a city – Jerusalem – where there is almost no evidence for the tenth century [BCE], almost no evidence for Solomon? Jerusalem was probably a very small village or a very poor town at the time. And here – at Megiddo – we have this monumental architecture. It doesn't feel right.'

Solomon's grandeur remains stubbornly and disconcertingly mythical. But, if it is a myth, how did such a myth arise? And can it be resolved in any way with the known historical facts? One possible answer to these questions might lie with the Samaritans.

While Orthodox Jews insist that the Samaritans derive from settlers introduced by the Assyrians, the Samaritans themselves claim to be the descendants of Ahab and Jehu's northern kingdom of Samaria. When this kingdom fell to the Assyrians in 721BCE many of the inhabitants apparently fled south from Samaria to the kingdom of Judah to seek refuge and they were absorbed into the population of Jerusalem. But a few, it is claimed, remained on the land and continued their own traditions. Although these Samaritans belonged to the broad spectrum of Judaism, their traditions were distinct from those observed in Judah. For them only the Pentateuch, the first five books of the Old Testament, have become holy scripture – and even then only in their own special version of the text.

Their place on the margins of Jewish society at the time of Christ is pointed up in the parable of the Good Samaritan. And their status among Orthodox Jews has not risen very much higher since then. Nevertheless they still maintain their traditions and festivals. For them the sacred mountain is still mount Gerizim. And they still gather there in their white robes to celebrate the Passover with feasting and prayer.

Orthodox Jewish tradition makes Jerusalem the centre of Israelite history. Mount Zion, the mountain where Solomon built his temple – not mount Gerizim – is regarded as the site of Abraham's sacrifice and it was there that the great Passover celebrations were held. The Samaritans, however, consider this a late innovation. They believe that Jerusalem did not become an important centre until well after the time of Solomon. It was only after Samaria was destroyed by the Assyrians, and the refugees poured south, that Jerusalem's population swelled and its importance increased.

In 587/6BCE Judah was conquered by the Babylonians. Jerusalem was destroyed and the Jews (together with the Samaritans) were dispersed. Not until 538BCE were they allowed to return to Jerusalem to build a second temple there. The Samaritans still maintain that when this happened the traditions associated with their own sacred site at mount Gerizim were transferred in their entirety to Jerusalem. It is a belief that has received some academic support. Biblical scholars – particularly 'Minimalists' who argue for a late date of composition – consider that it might provide a real insight into how the Bible was written and compiled. 'The people composing the biblical stories in – let us say – the period of the Babylonian exile, would have seen Jerusalem in its heyday, in its golden age, as being the capital city,' explains Jonathan Tubb. 'And I'm sure that's where the tradition comes from.'

And it was perhaps at this time, too, that some of the traditions associated with Solomon were also invented. It has been pointed out that, in the biblical account, the reign of Solomon is presented as a golden period of peace. His name in Hebrew – Shlomo – is written *slm*, the same three letters as also would have been used to spell *shalom* or peace. It is at least possible that he is a story figure – an idealised version of an historical personage.

Such theories are contentious. They carry the biblical Solomon off into the realms of myth. But they do not completely deny the possibility of a real Solomon, out there among the rough unhewn stones and rustic potsherds of tenth-century BCE Judah. The search for him must continue.

CHAPTER 6

Asherah

A dispute has broken out in the shadow of the Wailing Wall. Voices are raised in anger. Stones are thrown. Scuffles erupt. The police move in. Jerusalem is a city of tension. It is used to conflict and the Wailing Wall – the most holy site in Judaism – has seen its share of strife. A vast cliff face of massive finely cut stone blocks, it is thought to be the last surviving remnant of the so-called Second Temple. According to tradition this was the building erected on the site of Solomon's temple by the small band of Jews who returned to Jerusalem from the Babylonian exile at the end of the sixth century BCE. It was destroyed by the Romans in 70CE following the first unsuccessful Jewish Revolt. It is the memory of this destruction, and the lamentation that it still calls forth, that have given the Wall its popular name.

Even here, it should be said, the archaeologists have raised the spectre of doubt. They do not dispute that the Romans destroyed the Second Temple; they think, however, that they did it completely. Nothing remained, or remains, of the sacred building itself. The Wall, they are convinced, was not, in fact, part of the temple at all. It was a retaining bulwark erected by King Herod the Great in about 20BCE, to support the western side of the Temple Mount as part of his general overhaul of the temple and its precincts. Nevertheless this morning's row has been sparked not by a confrontation between radical archaeologists and religious fundamentalists, or between Muslims and Jews, or Jews and Christians, but by a division between Jews: male Jews and female Jews.

The plaza in front of the wall is designated as a synagogue. It is divided into two distinct spaces. To the right, women are allowed to pray. In the larger left-hand area the men worship: there they gather, wrapped in their black and white prayer-shawls, rocking back and forth in the intensity of devotion as they recite from the scriptures. Traditionally the men are allowed to pray out loud, but the women are expected to commune with God in silence. It is a tradition that many modern Jewish women feel increasingly unhappy with. This is the source of the friction. Groups of women have started to come to the Western Wall and to pray out loud. They read from the Bible and sing. To the more orthodox of their male coreligionists, on the other side of the low dividing wall, this is a shocking affront to the sanctity of the place and the sanctity of tradition. As one irate old ultra-Orthodox man exclaims, with more anger than logic, 'These women are not Jews; they are lesbians!' At a more formal – and more alarming – level, there have been moves in the Knesset to pass a law against women worshipping out loud before the Western Wall. It would become an imprisonable offence.

These are attitudes that Anat Hoffman, a leading member of a reformist Women of the Wall group that regularly conducts services in the plaza, finds frustrating and deluding. 'If we look at Miriam, the prophet,' she says, 'she would be in administrative detention if she were alive today, for what she did. She took the drum. She started dancing. What?' she exclaims in mock horror. 'Dancing and singing in a holy place? God forbid! We don't even try to do that at our services. There's no doubt Miriam would have been in gaol today.'

Miriam, the sister of Moses, who led the celebrations after pharaoh's army had been swallowed up by the Red Sea, is just one of the many exuberant and powerful women in the Old Testament. And several of them seem to have been the singers of triumphal hymns – and the leaders of triumphal dances. There is Deborah who sings of the defeat of the Canaanites (and of Sisera's grisly death by tent peg), and Hannah who bursts into song to thank God for sending her a child (Samuel), and Jephthah's daughter who celebrates her father's God-given victory over the Ammonites 'with timbrels and with dances'.

Nevertheless it is hard to ignore the fact that such women tend to get moved to the margins of the story. The general tone of the Bible is male-centred and patriarchal and over the centuries this bias has been amplified by generations of male critics and commentators. It is a bias that makes itself clear from the very beginning. God, the creator of heaven and earth, is traditionally represented as a male figure. And, in that famous exchange in the Garden of Eden, Adam blames Eve for telling him to eat the forbidden fruit.

It is an imbalance that feminists, in recent times, have struggled to address – and redress. Some have tried to piece together a fuller picture of women's lives in the biblical era in order to provide a proper context for understanding the stories about them. Others have sought to recover some of the pro-female strands of the biblical narrative, and to bring them into a new focus. They have scoured the text for examples of God being compared to a woman (as in Psalm 22 when he is alluded to as a midwife: 'thou art he that took me out of the womb'). They have hunted out overlooked incidents relating to females (such as the account – given in the book of Numbers – of how the daughters of Zelophehad were allowed to inherit their father's possessions). They have reassessed many of the traditional interpretations of specific incidents (they argue, for instance, that Adam is just as responsible as Eve for eating the forbidden fruit). And they have even made new translations of the Bible, in an effort to reduce the gender imbalance of the traditional text; (in the most extreme cases God is designated as 'She' throughout).

Such critical initiatives are, in their different ways, interesting enough. But would the anxiety of these modern critics and modern

Jews over the male domination of religious practice have been shared by their sisters in the first millennium BCE? Perhaps not. There is, it appears, a possibility that the feminine element was rather more prominent in the spiritual life of the early Israelites than is immediately apparent from the Bible. That, at least, is what some archaeologists are now suggesting.

It is a little known fact that the commonest distinct items discovered in excavations throughout Israel have been small clay figurines of large-breasted females; a few of them appear to be pregnant, others are nursing children. In recent years over 3000 of these statuettes have been recovered by archaeologists. They may be abundant, but they remain mysterious. Debate rages as to who or what these figurines might be. A few archaeologists have tried to suggest that they are no more than toys or children's dolls. But this explanation is thought unlikely. The prevailing view is that they had some religious significance. The figure's generous embonpoint – as well as her other attributes – would seem to mark her out as a fertility deity. And – given the large number of finds – her cult would seem to have been both widespread and sincere.

But can this really be true? The notion of an Israelite fertility goddess is certainly startling. The whole point of Israelite religion, at least as presented in the Bible, is that it was monotheistic. That is what makes the Children of Israel separate and special. While their neighbours bow down before graven images, strange gods and stranger goddesses, the Israelites worship the one true and jealous god, Yahweh. And they worship him without the aid of idols or images. The relationship between Yahweh and his chosen people runs back in the biblical narrative to the time of Abraham. It is presented as a matter of unique revelation, and it was traditionally accepted as such.

So what are all these large-breasted figurines doing? They conjure up a very different religious world – a world that was both polytheistic and iconographic. It is not a world that springs from the pages of the Old Testament at first glance. Biblical scholars have not been able to discover any direct and specific references to these figurines, or the role they played, in the Bible. They have had to search for their explanations between the lines and they have made some interesting discoveries.

Throughout the text of the Bible they have discovered hints of a more mixed and pluralist approach to religion among the early Israelites than is usually acknowledged. The fact, often buried in the original, tends to become even more obscured in English translations of the Bible, where a certain degree of standardisation has occurred. The English word God, for instance, is used as a translation for a whole variety of different Hebrew terms. The proper name of the Israelites' god, as recorded in the Bible, was *YHWH*. In the original Hebrew text the name is written without vowels and there has long been debate as to how the missing sounds should be filled in. It was a sixteenth-century European convention that rendered the word Jehovah. Most modern biblical scholars, however, favour Yahweh, which they suggest might relate to the Hebrew verb to be, perhaps having a meaning close to He who causes to be.

Nevertheless, Yahweh is not the only designation given to the god of the Old Testament. One strand of the narrative refers to God as Elohim, at least until the moment when he reveals himself to Moses in the burning bush. This, strictly speaking, is not so much a name as a descriptive epithet. Other variants, such as El and Eloha, are also used. Rather confusingly Elohim is a plural form that can sometimes be used to mean gods. While, no less confusingly, El was both the general word for god in all Semitic languages, and, more specifically, the leading god in the Canaanite pantheon. In the Bible it is often combined with other words to create divine designations such as El Elyon (God Most High), El Olam (Everlasting God) and El Shaddai (God Almighty). It seems likely that some of these epithets were originally used for gods in the Canaanite religion.

Suddenly the notion of a single, inviolable deity begins to look less assured. The opening words of the book of Genesis take on a curious look if we imagine them to read – as, indeed, they can be read – 'In the beginning gods created the earth'. Rabbi Professor Jonathan Magonet, the Principal of Leo Beck College, considers this confusion of names to lead back to the Bible's origins. 'The names used for God in the Bible are a strange mixture of things,' he explains. 'It's as if the biblical authors tried to assimilate all the different names from the local Canaanite culture and translate them into Jewish terms.'

The notion of a close connection between Israelite and Canaanite religion is not perhaps as surprising as it first appears, given what we now know of the Israelites' probable origins among the indigenous Canaanite population. It has already been noted that the very name Israel means defenders of El. But what about Yahweh? There was no Yahweh among the Canaanite deities. So, where did he come from?

That is something of a mystery. Some scholars have suggested that he might have had his origins among the Midianites, the tribesmen of northern Arabia. It was to Midian that Moses is said to have fled from pharaoh's court after he had killed a man. He married the daughter of the Midianite priest, Jethro. And it was among the rose-red mountains of Midian that he is supposed to have heard God speaking from the burning bush. Although much of the Moses story is regarded as mythic by modern commentators, and there is little hope that archaeology can provide any useful corroboration of the burning bush story, there are suggestions from Egyptian records that the land of Midian was associated with Yahweh. The territory lists of Pharaoh Amenhotep III refer to the area bordering the north-eastern end of the Red Sea as 'the Land of Shasu: Yhw3' (as the Egyptologists transliterate it), which might well be a reference to Yahweh. And archaeology does reveal the existence of trade links between the early Israelites and the Midianites, with painted Midianite pottery cropping up at several early Israelite sites.

Nevertheless even if the Israelites did derive their cult of Yahweh from the tribesmen of Midian, this is not to say that the cult was monotheistic at first. Some scholars see the mixture of bibilical references to El and to Yahweh as the faint echo of what was once a polytheistic pairing – very similar to the pairing of the gods El and Baal in Canaanite religion. It has been suggested that El was gradually subsumed by Yahweh: the two gods became one.

The Israelites certainly did develop a religious system which, in the end, became monotheistic and developed into Judaism. But when did this happen? When did Yahweh emerge as the sole, true God? Most scholars now seem to be agreed that it was not a matter of sudden revelation and instant conversion, but a slow process, neither continuous nor inevitable. The theory of the moment is that the Israelites moved from polytheism (the worship of many gods), to something called henotheism or monolotry (the worship of one god whom they regarded as the special protector of their tribe, and superior to all the other competing, rival gods of their neighbours). And only in time did this evolve into monotheism (the worship of one god as the sole recognised and universal deity). Nevertheless although this outline enjoys wide support there is no consensus as to the time scale or the detail of the process.

There is surprisingly little direct evidence outside the Bible to expand our understanding of the worship of Yahweh. The earliest known extra-biblical reference to Yahweh is on the ninth-century BCE Moabite stone. King Mesha boasts of having dragged the sacred things from Yahweh's temple before the altar of the Moabite chief god Chemosh. The inscription seems to depict the conflict almost as a clash between rival national deities – Yahweh loyal to the Israelites and Chemosh loyal to the Moabites. But the inscription also makes passing mention of another Moabite deity – Ashtar, suggesting that Moab was polytheistic at this time. And if Moabite religion still accommodated more than one god it is at the very least possible that Israelite religion did too.

Archaeology has uncovered very few early references to Yahweh at Israelite sites. At Jerusalem only one object has ever been discovered with Yahweh's name on it. A relatively late seventh-century BCE silver amulet was found bearing the inscription, 'Yahweh bless you and grant you peace', a priestly blessing from the book of Leviticus. In 1984, however, a Jerusalem antiquities dealer came across a small, carved ivory pomegranate that had probably been the head of a ceremonial sceptre. Several such sceptres – some with pomegranate heads – have been discovered at other sites. Around the shoulder of this new find was an inscription in early Hebrew. The writing, dated by experts to the eighth century BCE, was clear but tantalisingly broken in the middle section. It read: 'Belonging to the temple . . . —h, holy to the priests'. Several prominent scholars were quick to fill in the gap so that it read, 'Belonging to the temple [of Yahwe]h'. Here, it seemed, might be an object from the religious paraphernalia of the First Temple at Jerusalem, the only such relic ever found. The Israel Museum paid over half a million dollars for it in 1988.

But have they really got what they think they have? Some scholars have questioned the interpretation of the inscription. They have proposed a new reading; and it is one that has profoundly shocked many of the established guardians of Israel's history and culture. They believe that the pomegranate might not come from the temple in Jerusalem, and that it might not be dedicated to Yahweh at all. The missing letters of the inscription, they point out, could just as well be filled in: 'Belonging to the temple [of Ashera]h'. It is a reading that is hotly disputed. To understand the heat of the dispute it is necessary to know something about Asherah.

Asherah is identified as another Canaanite deity. She was a fertility goddess and the recognised consort of the chief god El (and, later, of Baal). Many small figurines representing her have been found at early Canaanite sites. The statuettes, with their large breasts and well-defined sexual organs, are closely related to those found at the slightly later Israelite sites. It is a relationship that has led scholars to suggest that Israelite fertility figurines may represent Asherah too.

This was a connection, however, that has proved hard to establish — until recently.

In the late 1960s, Bill Dever, then at the outset of his distinguished career, was carrying out excavations at Khirbet el-Kom near Hebron. On the wall of a Late Iron Age tomb, dating from the mid to late eighth century BCE, he discovered a bold drawing of what appeared to be a hand together with an inscription that ran, 'Blessed ... by Yahweh ... and his Asherah'. It was wonderful enough to come across an early reference to Yahweh, but it was even more extraordinary to discover the god of the Israelites linked by name with Asherah, the great fertility goddess.

'When I first discovered it,' Dever recalls, 'I really didn't want to publish it, as a young scholar. It was too controversial. But then in the 1970s a second site was found by Israeli archaeologists — also eighth century — in the Sinai. And you have the same expression again: "May X be blessed by Yahweh and his Asherah". The reference to Asherah is to the great goddess herself.' The discovery was made at Kuntillet Ajrud, in the north-eastern Sinai. The inscription, written in ink on an old storage jar, was accompanied by a drawing of two curious figures, one apparently male, the other female, and both crowned. It is hard to escape the conclusion that this little sketch represents Yahweh and Asherah, and that they are linked as consorts.

As Dever remarks, 'It seems that Yahweh did have a consort, like all the other gods of the ancient Near East — at least in the minds of many Israelites.' A Mrs God? The idea is oddly shocking. 'I think for modern Jews and Christians it sounds like a huge shock,' says Diana Edelman, an archaeologist from the Department of Biblical Studies at Sheffield University, and one of the relatively few women working in the field of ancient Near Eastern research. 'We have always thought that this religion was monotheistic right back to Abraham. But, in fact, it's almost ridiculous to suggest that you could have had a male god without a wife.'

The comparative study of other early religions suggests that one of their principal concerns was with ensuring harvests. As Edelman asks, 'How could you possibly guarantee fertility of crops and fertility of the land with a single deity without a female partner? In many ways it's more ridiculous to assume that, than not to accept that the early Israelites had the same structure of belief as everyone else did.'

In the 1920s, as Freudian ideas filtered into the study of early cultures, and particularly early religions, it was suggested by some scholars, on rather scant literary evidence, that the worship of El and Asherah was focused on two main sacred objects: a masculine element represented by an erected stone or 'pillar', and a feminine element represented by a sacred tree, either real or symbolic. These two objects when combined together in a place of worship, it was claimed, realised the idea of fertility, both in its human and in its agricultural sense. The Freudian derivation of this picture is only too apparent: the phallic standing stone and the tree-like nature goddess. Direct archaeological evidence to support the theory was, however, hard to come by. And, if it could not be shown that the early Canaanites worshipped in this way, there was even less reason to suppose that the early Israelites adapted, or adopted, similar practices.

But at Tel Rehov, a vast tell set on the rich alluvial plain where the Jordan valley meets the valley of Jezreel, they have recently made an interesting discovery. In a ninth-century BCE layer of the dig, archaeologists have uncovered a sacred site that fits remarkably well with such a pattern of worship. To untutored eyes it is not obviously impressive. Diana Edelman brings it vividly to life, and is persuasive about the place's sacredness.

Standing beside the construction she has identified as the central altar Edelman points out that it has been set on a low mud-brick platform, which itself has been erected in the middle of an open courtyard. The altar looks like little more than a pile of small stones. This, as it turns out, is unsurprising: it is nothing more than a pile of small stones. But, as Edelman explains, this fact is significant. Some ancient Near Eastern cultures insisted that altars should be made only of unworked stones. The books of the Old Testament reiterate this prescription several times (eg Exodus xx, 25). Standing beside this altar, however, Edelman points out something that certainly is not prescribed by any of the books of the Old Testament: a row of three upright stones.

The exact significance of these stones, Edelman admits, is open to debate. But she puts forward two theories. They could be something called *yod* or *yad*, that is a sort of memorial or proxy set up by an important worshipper to represent himself or herself before the deity at all times. Or – and this Edelman believes is the more likely explanation – the stones could represent deities themselves. To one side of the altar the excavators uncovered a round hole bored into the platform. In the hole they found fragmentary traces of wood. It has been too tempting not to suggest that here might be a fixing bracket for a wooden pole – or symbolic sacred tree – dedicated to Asherah, as is frequently described and frequently condemned in the Bible.

The arrangement of the site – at least as interpreted by Edelman and her colleagues – chimes almost exactly with that put forward by the Freudian theorists to describe early Canaanite religious practice. But the date of the find is ninth century BCE – a time when Tel Rehov was definitely and distinctly Israelite. This site clearly reflects the pattern of Israelite worship at this period. It certainly looks polytheistic and the cult of Asherah seems to have held a prominent place in proceedings.

It is a curious fact that during the early years of archaeological investigation in the Holy Land, when digs were sponsored by religious groups or Zionist organisations, very little evidence was found for Israelite polytheism. Now, however, sponsorship comes from diverse quarters. The dig at Tel Rehov has been funded by an American mystery writer. And some of the discoveries made certainly add new twists to the plot of Israelite religion. Among the finds made at the site recently was a beautiful tenth-century figurine of a goddess, probably representing not Asherah, but Astarte, another Near Eastern deity, roughly equivalent to the Greek goddess Aphrodite. Although it predates the altar by a hundred years, it too is from an Israelite, rather than a Canaanite, level of the site.

Having encountered the names of two female deities, both beginning with 'A' and both associated with fertility, it is not surprising to learn that many scholars think that Asherah and Astarte became conflated in the religious imagination of the Israelites – rather as El and Yahweh may also have done.

It is, of course, true that the Bible does refer to the Israelites, on occasion, worshipping other gods apart from Yahweh. Indeed it is one of the constant themes of the books running from Joshua to Kings. The Israelites are always 'doing that which is wrong in the eyes of the Lord', and being punished for it. Solomon himself is rebuked for erecting altars to strange gods at the end of his reign. And, following his death, when the kingdom splits into two parts – Israel and Judah – the whole history of the northern kingdom of Israel is defined by the fact that the first king, Jeroboam, set up a pair of golden bulls – the sacred symbols of El – at the northern and southern borders of his territory.

Such behaviour is roundly condemned by the biblical authors, as apostasy and backsliding. But was this the contemporary view? The Bible, it is generally agreed, was written up in its final form many years after the period associated with the figures of Solomon and Jeroboam. The authors, if they weren't monotheistic, were certainly Yahwistic. For them Yahweh was the only god worth worshipping. And it seems they had definite views about how and where he should be worshipped too. Anything else was simply wrong. Did they, perhaps, project these firmly held beliefs back through the long history of their people, making post-facto judgements on religious arrangements that had once seemed perfectly normal and acceptable? The Bible paints a picture of the northern kingdom of Israel relapsing into idolatry while the southern kingdom of Judah remains true to Yahweh. The picture is graphically drawn, but is it true?

Sites such as the altar found at Tel Rehov seem to indicate how widespread polytheistic practices were among the northern Israelites well into the ninth century BCE. But were such altars and standing stones merely manifestations of an unofficial folk religion, and were they confined to the northern kingdom? What was the official line of the Judean south? Archaeologists have sought an answer to exactly this question at Tel Arad.

Tel Arad preserves the remains of a fortified outpost, perched high on the Judean plateau, dominating the white wastes along the northern fringes of the Negev desert, on what was once the south-eastern border of the kingdom of Judah. The citadel, it is believed, was established in the tenth century BCE, perhaps by Solomon, to guard the routes south into Edom. It was rebuilt several times over the next four centuries. But it remained an important military and administrative centre for the kings of Judah.

Excavations at the site have uncovered the well-preserved remains of a temple complex in the north-western corner of the fortress. It was clearly an important structure within the settlement. Although it was remodelled as the citadel itself developed, its basic three-part layout remained constant. It provides a rare glimpse of an official religious site. It opens with a paved courtyard, surrounded by a low wall. In the middle of this open space stand the remains of a large sacrificial altar. Animals were slaughtered here and offerings were then burnt on top of the altar. Running along the far side of the courtyard was the main hall (or holy place). Archaeologists have characterised it as a broad-room because the doorway is on the long, rather than the short, wall of the building. Opposite the doorway, set into the back wall of the broad-room, was a little niche-like space, which represented the most sacred part of the temple, the holy of holies.

The basic layout was slightly different from that of Solomon's temple, at least as described in the book of Kings. The main hall of Solomon's building was long rather than broad, an arrangement that some have seen as a reflection of sophisticated Assyrian models. The ground plan of the Arad temple, by contrast, seems almost to echo that of the traditional four-room house. While the typical four-room house had a large broad-room and three long rooms running off from it at right angles, the Arad temple had a broad-room with a courtyard which is almost square running off from it at right angles. The courtyard space was divided lengthwise, partly by the altar and, along the northern edge, by a long storage room. Nevertheless the builders of the Arad temple do seem to have been thoroughly conversant with conventional religious design prescriptions. The sacrificial altar in the centre of the courtyard was not only built out of unhewn stone, it was also found to be exactly 'five cubits long by five cubits broad', the very measurements of the tabernacle altar as described in Exodus xxvii, 1.

The holy of holies was set slightly higher than the great hall and had to be approached up two steps. Standing sentinel either side of this entrance were two low, square-cut limestone incense altars, while at the back of the niche were set two, smoothed, plain standing stones. The overall effect of the reconstruction that has been made at the site is one of uncluttered simplicity.

For some scholars this sense of simplicity is the key fact about the site. As Zvi Lederman, an archaeologist from the University of Tel Aviv and a colleague of Ze'ev Herzog who excavated the site, puts it: 'No idols, no figurines were found here. It seems to have been a culture, or religion, without icons.' This, as he points out, is an arrangement that fits closely with the biblical proscription against setting up 'graven images'. And certainly it stands in marked distinction to the surviving shrines of some other Near Eastern cultures of this period. Just across the Beersheba valley in Edom the picture seems to have been very different. Biblical tradition describes the Edomites as kin to the Israelites: they are supposed to trace their ancestry back to Isaac's brother Esau. And yet, despite their shared heritage and their shared border, they seem to have developed a very different attitude to their gods. They loved depicting them. Archaeologists working at Edomite sites in what is now Jordan have uncovered numerous bulbous ceramic figures representing what is believed to be the Edomite tribal god, Qos, and his fellow deities.

Set against this profusion of images, it is tempting to view the simplicity of the temple at Arad as evidence of a monotheistic, aniconic culture and religion. And some – like Zvi Lederman – argue this case eloquently. But the bare facts of an archaeological site are rarely open to only one interpretation. The temple at Arad is no exception. Other archaeologists have taken exactly opposite views based on exactly the same material. The lack of obvious and representational idols is considered by some scholars to be deceptive. According to Bill Dever's reading of the site, 'There were two – if not three – standing stones in the holy of holies, carefully smoothed and dressed. They are clearly what the Bible means when it refers to "standing stones". They represent the presiding deity of a place. And the fact that you have two, or maybe three, here, suggests polytheism.'

The apparent simplicity of the Arad temple, moreover, is almost certainly uncharacteristic. The biblical descriptions of Solomon's temple at Jerusalem make clear that even if the Israelites stopped short of representing Yahweh or setting up idols there were plenty of other iconographic excitements on view. There was the curious 'molten sea' made of bronze, standing upon the backs of twelve bronze oxen, the panels of brass decorated with 'lions, oxen and cherubim', the bronze serpent supposedly made by Moses to protect the children of Israel from snakebite while they were travelling through the wilderness.

And then, within the holy of holies, there was the Ark of the Covenant itself, an oblong box containing the tablets carved with the Ten Commandments. The Ark was covered with an ornate lid, known as the Mercy Seat, surmounted by two cherubs, their wings spread out over the box, wingtips touching.

To the modern mind the word cherub might conjure up the image of some plump, winged infant decorating an Italian church or an English Christmas card, but archaeologists have discovered that Solomon's cherubs – or cherubim – were of a rather different order. They were more like sphinxes: human faced lions or bulls with finely pointed wings. Nor were they exclusive to the temples of the Israelites. They seem to have been symbols of majesty and power for most of the main civilisations of the ancient Near East. At Megiddo archaeologists found a Canaanite ivory relief, dating from 1200BCE, of a king seated upon a throne flanked by two such sphinx-like cherubim. And the same motif has also been found on the beautifully carved, late tenth-century Phoenician sarcophagus of King Ahram of Biblos.

Although the Bible describes God as being seated above the cherubim that guarded the Ark of the Covenant, his presence was invisible. Within Solomon's temple – as described in the Bible – Yahweh himself was not depicted. And although the cherubim and the Ark and the other sacred objects were physical manifestations of Yahweh's presence, they were not themselves idols, or substitutes for God. As a result of this distinction it seems that the authors of the Bible were not shy of mentioning the prominent positioning of such items within the temple and the other places of worship. They displayed rather more circumspection, however, when discussing some of the other pieces of devotional paraphernalia – particularly those relating to Asherah.

'There are almost forty references to Asherah in the Bible,' explains Diana Edelman. 'And yet when you look at those references you don't really know that they are talking about a goddess. The later Bible scribes have systematically written Asherah out as a goddess. They disguised her presence in the text.' This disguising seems to have been a matter of subtle but significant additions and adjustments. For example when Gideon is told to destroy his family's shrine, the original instruction would, apparently, have been: 'Throw down the altar of Baal, and chop up Asherah'. But the scribe writing the book of Judges amended this to: 'Throw down the altar of Baal and chop up *the* asherah.' By the addition of the single word – the – Asherah ceases to be recognisable as a deity, and becomes a thing.

This process of deliberate obfuscation was inadvertently carried on by the English translators of the Bible. When they encountered the word asherah they did not recognise it as a proper name, and they did not know what it might mean as a noun. So it simply disappeared. They either excised the reference, or – given the not infrequent descriptions of asherah being chopped down, chopped up and even burnt – they translated the word as grove. Thus in the King James Version of the Bible, Gideon is instructed to 'Throw down the altar of Baal and cut down the grove that is by it' (Judges vi, 26).

Nevertheless, despite the extent to which mention of Asherah has been disguised and obscured in the Bible, scholars have been able to piece together enough fragments of evidence to suggest something of her importance, and the manner in which she was venerated. As has been mentioned, there are no obvious biblical references to the small Asherah figurines so often found by archaeologists; but this, apparently, is not surprising. The Bible has remarkably little to say about the rituals and practice of private, domestic worship. It is more concerned with charting the formal, public religious arrangements sanctioned by the state, and Asherah seems to have received such sanction.

Although many of the references in the Bible concern the removal of Asherah – or the asherah – from the established places of worship; the fact that she had to be removed at all, and removed so often, testifies to the enduring strength of her cult – and her place at the heart of the public temples, next to the main altar. There are references to Asherah being venerated at Jerusalem, Samaria, Ophrah and Bethel.

The recurrent biblical allusions to Asherah being chopped down and burnt (coupled with other references to her being made, set up and planted), seem to confirm the notion that the goddess was often worshipped, not as a life-like effigy, but in the symbolic form of a tree, or a carved pole. (Such references can be found at Judges vi, 25–6, I Kings xv, 13, xvi, 33, xviii, 19, II Kings xiii, 6, xvii, 16, xviii, 4 and elsewhere.) Reading between the deliberately fudged lines of the Old Testament account, it is clear that, just such a stylised tree stood in the temple at Jerusalem. Before it were set specially consecrated vessels and within the temple compound there was a building given over to the women whose duty it was to weave garments for the goddess and/or her symbolic effigy.

Sometimes the very silences about Asherah seem significant. When Elijah arranges a contest of faith on mount Carmel with the priests of Baal, he initially includes the 450 'priests of the Grove' in his challenge as well (I Kings xviii, 19). But, although there is a full description of him defeating the priests of Baal and putting them to death, there is no further reference to the priests of Asherah. It has to be supposed that he did not destroy them or their goddess. A similarly pregnant silence hangs over the account of Jehu's religious reforms. Following the death of Ahab, Jehu razed the temple of Baal at Samaria and had it turned into a latrine (II Kings x, 27). But there is no mention that he attempted any parallel attack on the worship of Asherah. None of the early prophets specifically condemn the cult of the goddess.

From such evidence it would seem that Asherah was an important and officially sanctioned element of Israelite religion throughout much of the period of the divided monarchy (927–722 BCE). And yet only the barest trace of her presence remains in the biblical account.

So, when and why was Asherah comprehensively expunged from the record? Perhaps the answer – or the beginnings of the answer – lie at Tel Arad. The remains of the temple complex there are intriguing. 'The temple was put out of use deliberately,' according to Zvi Lederman, 'at some time in the eighth century BCE. It was not burnt, it was not destroyed. The standing stones were laid on their sides, the incense burners were laid on their sides. It was all covered up with dust and sand. It all went out of use, deliberately, slowly, with no big event, as though there has been an order: stop worshipping Yahweh in Tel Arad.' The clear evidence of pre-planning and care suggests that the temple was dismantled as part of a well-directed programme of religious reform.

The book of Kings records two such major reform programmes, one in the reign of King Hezekiah (721–694BCE), the other, half a century later, in the reign of King Josiah (639–609BCE). Both of them took place against the background of the ever increasing domination of the Assyrian empire throughout the region – a background that will be explored in more detail in the next chapter.

Hezekiah is described as doing 'that which was right in the sight of the Lord'. There was a strong iconoclastic flavour to his reforms. He 'brake down the images, and cut down the groves' – or representations of Asherah. He is also described as smashing into pieces Moses' brazen serpent – or the Nehushtan as it was called – because people burnt incense in front of it (II Kings xviii, 4).

One of the key facts of his reforms, however, seems to have been its insistence upon the pre-eminence of Jerusalem and its temple. Hezekiah is shown dismantling the high places and altars outside the capital, and commanding all Judah to worship only before 'this altar in Jerusalem' (II Kings xviii, 22). Mordechai Cogan, a biblical scholar at the University of Beersheba, considers this to have been an important and defining moment: 'Hezekiah undertook to centralise religion on Jerusalem,' he explains. 'He was the first king to attempt to do so. So it seems to have been a pretty major reform.'

If so, it was a major reform for what was rapidly becoming a major city. In 722BCE the northern kingdom of Israel, or Samaria, was conquered by the Assyrian king, Shalmaneser V. Many of the country's leading citizens were taken to Assyria, and conquered peoples from elsewhere were settled on the land. The territory became an Assyrian controlled province. This cataclysm marked the end of the northern kingdom as a distinct entity.

In the aftermath of this catastrophe many of the inhabitants who had not been deported fled south into the bordering kingdom of Judah. There they were welcomed by the newly established King Hezekiah. To accommodate the numbers of refugees who arrived at Jerusalem he was obliged to carry out a series of major public works. 'The city extended itself to the west and the north-west tremendously,' explains Ronny Reich, who, as an archaeologist working under the auspices of the Israel Antiquities Authority, has carried out extensive investigations into Jerusalem's early growth and development. 'It expanded to include what is today called the Jewish quarter inside the old city of Jerusalem.'

It was, perhaps, as part of this process of expansion and resettlement – as well as part of the process of making Jerusalem the hub of the nation's religious life – that Hezekiah instituted a major new religious event. He invited all the peoples of Israel, even those from the further reaches of the old kingdom of Samaria, to come to Jerusalem to celebrate the Passover on the Temple Mount. It seems as if he was staking a claim for the religious importance of his capital, and attempting to supersede the established northern tradition of celebrating the Passover on mount Gerizim.

It is difficult not to see the dismantling of the temple at Arad as part of this programme of centralisation, or Jerusalemisation. Indeed there is other archaeological evidence that hints at the impact of Hezekiah's religious reforms outside the capital. Archaeologists working at Beersheba, in the south of Judah, discovered an ancient limestone altar that had been deliberately dismantled, probably at this time, and reused as building material.

The second key element of the reformist programme appears to have been the attempt to focus all the worship carried out in the temple at Jerusalem exclusively on Yahweh. All the other previously acknowledged gods of the pantheon were obliterated or banished. Hezekiah's reforms, at least on the evidence of the Bible, were the first concerted attack on the status of Asherah. And the reformists seem to have pursued that attack with brio.

Nevertheless, despite the enthusiasm of both the king and his biblical chronicler, the process of reform appears to have been fraught. There is at least a suggestion that it was prosecuted in the face of both popular and informed opposition. Certainly Hezekiah's successor, Manasseh, reversed the reformist measures. The Bible gives a graphic account of his volte-face. 'He did that which was evil in the sight of the Lord, after the abominations of the heathen . . . He built up again the high places which Hezekiah his father had destroyed; and he reared up altars for Baal, and made a grove, as did Ahab king of Israel; and worshipped all the host of heaven and served them. And he built altars in the house of the Lord . . . And he made his son pass through the fire, and observed times, and used enchantments, and dealt with familiar spirits and wizards . . . And he set a graven image of the grove that he had made in the house [of the Lord]' (II Kings xxi, 1–7).

It was left to Josiah (who succeeded after the short-lived Amon) to reintroduce and reiterate his great-grandfather's reforms. At the centre of Josiah's reformist project – at least as described in the book of Kings – was a remarkable 'discovery'. While carrying out some repairs to the temple in Jerusalem, Hilkiah, the high priest, claimed to have come across a previously unknown 'book of the law', full of stern admonitions against the religious backsliding of the Israelites and their promiscuous worship of foreign gods. It is generally considered that this conveniently discovered scroll formed – and still forms – the basis of the book of Deuteronomy in the Bible. The core of this book purports to be a collection of laws given by God to Moses to supplement the commandments passed down on mount Sinai. It is a full and thorough code of practice. All aspects of life, both secular and religious, are brought under the divine purview.

Most biblical scholars are convinced that, although the book of Deuteronomy may draw on earlier traditions, it was first written up either by a single author or by a circle of reformist scribes during the reign of Josiah. And it seems that it is not just modern scholars who hold this view. The prophet Jeremiah, who was at Josiah's court, perhaps reflected contemporary opinion when he remarked, probably of this newly found book of the law, 'God's Bible? Look at it – it was made as a lie by the false pen of scribes' (Jeremiah viii, 8). Certainly the book of Deuteronomy's insistent emphasis on the Israelites as one people, under one god, whom they worship in one temple, chimes with the temper of Josiah's reforms.

Armed with his newly discovered text, Josiah threw himself into the work of purifying the nation's religious practices with great zeal. He purged all the idolatrous priests who worshipped Baal, the sun, the moon, and the planets; he destroyed (once again) the shrines and altars and 'high places'. But he seems to have preserved a particular animosity towards Asherah and her devotees: 'And he brought out the grove [i.e. Asherah] from the house of the Lord, without Jerusalem, unto the brook Kidron, and burnt it at the brook Kidron, and stamped it small to powder, and cast the powder thereof upon the graves of the children of the people. And he brake down the houses of the sodomites, that were by the house of the Lord, where the women wove hangings for the grove [i.e. Asherah]' (II Kings xxiii, 6–7).

Some scholars have argued that it was probably also under Josiah that the so-called Deuteronomic history (the books of the Bible from Joshua, via Judges and Samuel, up to Kings) was first compiled. It is a theory that is examined in more detail in the next chapter. But it is certainly possible that the same circle of scribes and teachers who supported Josiah and his reforms might have decided this was the time to survey the whole history of the Israelites in the land, from the time of Joshua up to the time of Josiah himself. And if they did attempt to write up a coherent history of the people of Israel it is only to be expected that – as religious reformers – they would present a version of that history that confirmed and reinforced the message of those reforms.

The specific ideals of the late seventh-century reformers were, perhaps, projected back through six confused turbulent centuries of settlement, division and war. The exclusive worship of Yahweh and the pre-eminence of Jerusalem were two of those ideals, and anything that ran counter to them would, very properly, have been condemned or excised. The reign of Josiah was, perhaps, not only the moment when Asherah got dragged out of the temple and incinerated, but also the point at which the process of editing her out of the religious history of the Israelites began.

Nevertheless, if the first Deuteronomic writers and editors were able to obliterate Asherah with a dash of the pen or the insertion of the definite article, it seems to have been more difficult to edit her out of the hearts of the commonality of Israelites.

Josiah's own exclusive devotion to Yahweh seems to have had only a limited practical effect. He met an abrupt end at Megiddo in 609BCE, when he rashly tried to block the advance of Pharaoh Neco who was marching north with his army, to join forces with the Assyrians against the newly emerging might of Babylon. Josiah's successors, while they preserved his nationalist political vision, abandoned most of his religious reforms. Neither ploy brought him much fortune. When Babylon superseded Assyria as the dominant power in the Near East, after the battle of Carchemish in 605BCE, the Judeans ill-advisedly allied themselves with the Egyptians against this new threat.

Nebuchadrezzar,* the Babylonian king, marched into Judah and besieged Jerusalem. The city fell in 597BCE, and the leading men of the kingdom were taken off into exile.

Many of Judah's less prominent inhabitants, however, were not taken away to Babylonia. The poorest peasants remained on the land.

---

* Nebuchadrezzar's name is sometimes rendered 'Nebuchadnezza', but the former spelling is now generally preferred as being a closer equivalent to the original Babylonian, 'Nabu-kudurri-usur', meaning 'the [god] Nabu has protected the succession'.

But others, the prophet Jeremiah among them, after submitting briefly to the rule of a Babylonian-appointed governor, made their way to Egypt, where they lived in self-imposed exile.

Although Jeremiah's prophecies about the doom of Jerusalem had proved only too accurate, there seems to have been some division of opinion among his fellow exiles over the true cause of the cataclysm. While Jeremiah was convinced that the worship of Asherah and other foreign gods had provoked Yahweh to punish the Israelites, it appears that others thought the disaster might have been brought about by their failure to worship Asherah and her co-deities enough. Many of the exiles in Egypt continued to lament for their lost gods, and not least for the goddess who had so often sustained them in the past.

They protested against Jeremiah's words, announcing:

we will certainly do whatsoever thing goeth forth out of our own mouth, to burn incense unto the queen of heaven, and to pour out drink offerings unto her, as we have done, we, and our fathers, our kings, and our princes, in the cities of Judah, and in the streets of Jerusalem: for then had we plenty of victuals, and were well, and saw no evil. But since we left off to burn incense to the queen of heaven and to pour out drink offerings unto her, we have wanted all things, and have been consumed by the sword and by the famine. And when we burned incense to the queen of heaven, and poured out drink offerings unto her, did we make her cakes to worship her, and pour out drink offerings unto her, without our men? (Jeremiah xliv, 17–19).

This, however, seems to have been a last burst of defiance, as they sought to make sense of the disaster that had overtaken them. Away in Babylon the mood was different. The exiles there seem to have refined and amplified the vision of the Deuteronomists. According to some scholars they continued to rework and re-edit the so-called

Deuteronomic history of the people of Israel throughout this period. They sought to explain all the vicissitudes of the past in terms of their fluctuating fidelity. They sought to emphasise their exclusive worship of Yahweh, and they all but denied the existence of Asherah. And when, after some sixty years they returned from exile, and began rebuilding the temple at Jerusalem, and with it the religious life of the place, their vision prevailed. The worship – and the name – of Asherah did not make the return journey.

Although some scholars have suggested that a trace of the Asherah cult might live on in the female figure of Wisdom described in the book of Proverbs (xvii, 9), the echo is a faint one. The female element – once so important a part of Israelite spiritual life – seems to have been quietly removed from the religious landscape. And to judge from the scenes at the Wailing Wall it is a loss that is still felt in many quarters.

CHAPTER 7

Ezra

I n 1947, in the arid hills of Qumran on the north-western shore of the Dead Sea, when a young bedouin shepherd was searching for a lost goat, he came upon a narrow opening in the rock. He threw a stone down into it and was surprised to hear what sounded like breaking pottery. Intrigued, he clambered down to investigate. He found a cave stocked with cylindrical storage jars. Some were broken, others contained scrolls wrapped carefully in linen. Together with two friends, he returned and gathered up seven scrolls. To their excitement they discovered that the scrolls were written on parchment which was made from hides and would thus be suitable for making sandals . . .

The story of the discovery of the Dead Sea Scrolls is quite worthy of the Old Testament itself. Shepherd boys, lost goats, mysterious caves: it has many of the classic ingredients of the biblical genre.

Luckily, before embarking on full-scale footwear production, the excited bedouin boys showed their find to a local antiquities dealer in Bethlehem. The man was unable to decipher the writing on the scrolls but, thinking that it might by Syriac, he sent four of the parchments to the Archimandrite of the Syrian Orthodox Monastery in Jerusalem. The Archimandrite recognised the script as Aramaic – the early precursor to Hebrew – but was unable to make out the content. Nevertheless he bought the four scrolls and began to tout them around among scholars in Jerusalem, seeking an opinion on their meaning and significance.

At the same time, rumours of the bedouin boy's discovery filtered through to other archaeologists in Jerusalem. One of them, Eleizar Sukenik, Professor at the Hebrew University in Jerusalem, decided to check on the report. It was a risky business: in 1947 Palestine was in the throes of partition. The land was being divided and tensions between the Jewish settlers and the Palestinians were rapidly escalating towards war. Bethlehem, like Qumran itself, was on the Palestinian side of the Green Line; Sukenik was a Jewish settler. Despite this background, and against the advice of the military authorities, Sukenik crossed the border and succeeded in buying the remaining three scrolls from the antiquities dealer. He at once recognised the extraordinary nature of his purchase.

Scholarly assessment of the script suggested that the earliest scrolls dated back to around the beginning of the middle of the third century BCE. The dryness of the air in the caves as well as the careful wrapping had ensured their almost incredible survival. Written on the scrolls – in Aramaic – were books from the Old Testament, writings now included in the Apocrypha, and several secular works relating apparently to the group that had copied and preserved the scrolls.

Sukenik tried to bring his three scrolls together with the four in the possession of the Syrian monastery. But his efforts were overtaken by war when the British mandate came to an end on 15 May 1948. Jerusalem became divided. The monastery, located in the Arab zone, was cut off from the Hebrew University in the Jewish zone. The Archimandrite smuggled his four scrolls out of the country and took them to America. After several abortive attempts, he finally sold them in 1954. They were subsequently presented to the new state of Israel and re-united with Sukenik's collection.

In the meantime the local bedouin, alerted to the value of their discovery, had been scouring the barren hills of Qumran and had discovered further caves, and more scrolls. In all, over 500 documents were recovered – some no more than tiny fragments, others complete texts. At least partial copies were found of every book in the Old Testament, except for the book of Esther.

The scrolls were clearly related to a large archaeological site nearby, at Khirbet Qumran. The early excavators, French Dominican friars from the École Biblique in Jerusalem, thought that the site must be the remains of a community of Essenes, a radical Jewish sect, to which it is sometimes suggested that John the Baptist belonged. The sect, which flourished between the first century BCE and the first century CE was opposed to the orthodoxy proclaimed by the priests who controlled the temple in Jerusalem. The community appears to have been wiped out at the time of the Jewish Revolt in 70CE. Perhaps it was in preparation for this cataclysm that they hid the scrolls so carefully in the caves around Qumran.

Although the identification of Khirbet Qumran as an Essene community remains the established line, some archaeologists have recently suggested that the group that lived at the site was perhaps less marginalised and ascetic than has been generally understood. The place may have been more of a prosperous villa than a monastic encampment. Perhaps the monastic excavators of the École Biblique had unconsciously projected their own, monastic, values on to the silent remains that they had uncovered. It is a possibility that haunts every archaeological excavation: the evidence is always silent and needs interpretation. And interpretations often follow the lines of unconscious prejudice. Nevertheless the exact character of the Khirbet Qumran community does little to alter the key fact about the scrolls: their antiquity.

The texts predate all other existing manuscripts of the Old Testament by over a thousand years. It has taken years of scholarship to sort through, edit and assess this extraordinary cache. As so often with archaeological finds in the Near East there is a political dimension to the equation: the scrolls found after 1947, coming as they did from Palestinian territory, fell under Jordanian control. They were housed initially in the Arab – or eastern – half of Jerusalem, at the Palestinian Archaeological Museum (now the Rockefeller Museum), an imposing neo-gothic block built by the British in the 1920s. During the war of 1967, as the Israelis threatened to take East Jerusalem, the Jordanians planned to move the scrolls to safety in Jordan, but they were too slow. East Jerusalem – and the Palestinian Archaeological Museum – fell to the Israeli advance. The scrolls were removed to the new, specially designed, building – the Shrine of the Book – at the Israel Museum, on the western edge of the city. There they joined the scrolls already assembled by Sukenik and his successors.

Set in spacious, well-tended grounds, the modern, circular building is surmounted by a vast, white, tapering dome. The dome is modelled on the tapering lids of the storage jars in which the scrolls were originally found. The site is magnificent, the building impressive. And beneath the distinctive roof some of the choicest scrolls are kept on public display; precious scraps of parchment, suspended behind glass with muted lighting. The very name of the building – the Shrine of the Book – emphasises the extent to which, for many Israelis, the place is more than a mere museum. The Palestinians continue to demand the return of the scrolls. But there seems little chance that the Israelis will give them up. The scriptures continue to exert a power over the life of land that is more than just religious.

The information that scholars have been able to glean from careful study of these ancient texts has revealed much about the composition and shaping of the Bible. It had long been recognised that the Bible was a work of compilation, editing and re-editing. As early as the seventeenth century scholars had noted the discrepancies, repetitions and contradictions littered through the biblical text. The first five books of the Bible – Genesis, Exodus, Leviticus, Numbers and Deuteronomy – were, for instance, traditionally ascribed to one author – Moses. But they are fraught with inconsistencies. They retell the same stories, twice, sometimes thrice, and often with contradictory details and messages.

As more and more discrepancies were pointed out it became harder to believe that all the books could really have come from the same hand. Nevertheless the notion that this large swathe of holy scripture might not have been written all at one time by a single author proved very difficult for many to accept.

At first the suggestion provoked outrage. But by the late nineteenth century the idea was well enough established for the great German biblical scholar, Julius Welhausen, to elucidate the theory without opposition. He contended that the first five books of the Bible (known in the Jewish tradition as the Torah, and to Christians as the Pentateuch) were derived from four main strands, composed at different periods and by different hands and only brought together and edited into their current form at a later date. He designated these four sources as the Yahwist, Eloist, Priestly and Deuteronomic strands on account of their particular prejudices of thought or vocabulary.

And if the first five books of the Bible had gone through a long drawn out editorial process, so, it might be assumed, had the others. At what date all the various strands and texts were brought together, re-edited and woven into the canonical form of the Old Testament or Hebrew Bible was – and remains – a matter of debate among biblical scholars. It is a debate that still stirs up strong passions. Many scholars believe that a major part of the editorial process took place in the immediate aftermath of the Babylonian captivity, others place the key period slightly earlier. But when the process was completed is uncertain.

Prior to the discoveries at Khirbet Qumran the earliest authoritative version of the Hebrew Bible or Old Testament was the so-called Masoretic text, an early mediaeval version developed by a school of scribes and scholars (the Masoretes) who first introduced vowels into the consonant-only script of the traditional Hebrew text. Of the thirty or so surviving early Masoretic manuscripts, ranging from the late ninth century to the twelfth century, the earliest complete text dates from 1009CE. This text still provides the template for modern rabbinic Bibles. Over the centuries it has remained fixed, if not in stone, then in ink.

A tradition of careful copying has striven to maintain the purity and accuracy of the text. In an effort to prevent scribal errors – errors that might have unlooked-for religious implications – copyists are obliged to sound each letter and each word as they copy it. Rather than reading over their work to check its accuracy, the scribes count up the letters of each chapter to ensure that they have reached the right total. Every aspect of the work is regulated by detailed prescriptions. The types of material to be used – parchment from a kosher animal, ink made to an ancient recipe and applied with a quill pen – are all specially designated. Before even writing the name of God a scribe is obliged to purify himself in a ritual bath. It has been tempting to read this tradition back in an unbroken chain – via the Dead Sea Scrolls – to the time of the Bible's first composition.

The biblical texts preserved among the scrolls at Khirbet Qumran often do confirm the readings of the so-called Masoretic text. But not always. There are not infrequent divergencies and alternate versions. Sometimes these are mere matters of spelling and copying, but they can also be more substantial. Of course some of the discrepancies may lie behind the community's separation from the mainstream Judaism of the Pharisees in Jerusalem, but they do also seem to suggest that scribes continued to reshape and enlarge upon the text, often to address the particular concerns of a particular place or period.

The Dead Sea Scrolls include several subtly different editions of the books of Exodus and Numbers, as well as variant versions of Psalms and Deuteronomy. The Bible, it appears, for these early scribes and their readers, was not yet a rigidly fixed text, but one that was open to constant adjustment and tuning in order to point up its relevance to the concerns of the present.

If contemporary concerns crept into the copying of the text, how much more did they affect the initial composition – and early editing

– of the work? If we are looking for the historical truth behind the books of Deuteronomic history (Joshua, Judges, I & II Samuel, I & II Kings), should we be looking not at the events they describe, so much as anxieties and prejudices of the people who composed them? So, what were the great contemporary events that dominated the minds of the first authors (and early editors) of the Deuteronomic history, and coloured the story they chose to tell? And what effect does this colouring have on the historical reliability of the narrative?

To try and answer these questions we must make some attempt to uncover when and how the books of the Deuteronomic history came to be written. Needless to say, as with the composition of the books of the Pentateuch, there is no agreement (and much heated disagreement) on the point. Estimates range from the twelfth to the third century BCE. Nevertheless many scholars would recognise that some trace of the books' origins might be found in the seventh century BCE during the heyday of the Assyrian empire. There is a good case for taking Judah and Israel's relations with that great power as the starting context for the development of the so-called Deuteronomic history.

In 1853 a British funded archaeological expedition to the ruins of Nineveh, led by Henry Layard, discovered the Assyrian royal library. Numerous clay tablets were unearthed, each inscribed in cuneiform – an early form of geometric writing. Among the tablets were the annals of several Assyrian kings. They gave detailed accounts of campaigns undertaken, battles won and tribute acquired. Other collections of Assyrian royal annals were subsequently found at other sites. These early texts, together with the other elements of the archaeological record, provide a remarkably full and contemporary record of events relating to the kingdoms of Israel and Judah, independent of the Bible. This is not to say that this record is itself unbiased. The compilers of the royal annals were intent on aggrandising their kings, recording victories not defeats, exaggerating achievements, putting the best interpretation upon events. Nevertheless the annals, inscriptions, official letters and pictorial reliefs, do allow us to compare the stories told in these sources with the ones preserved in the Bible. At one level they can help confirm (or refute) the facts of the biblical narrative, at another the discrepancies of detail and tone evident in the two sources help to point exactly what sort of history the Bible was seeking to record.

Among the treasures of the British Museum are the huge, beautifully carved panels recovered from the royal palaces of Nineveh and Nimrud. The great, pale grey stone slabs are covered with vivid scenes and captioned with cuneiform script: they are comic strips that lead us back to the eighth century BCE and beyond. They depict in graphic detail the claims to glory of the late Assyrian dynasties of Tiglath-pileser III and Sennacherib. There are royal lion hunts, royal building projects and – above all – royal campaigns. At its height the Assyrian empire spread from its base on the river Tigris (in modern day Iraq) to lake Van in the north and Egypt in the south. The scenes of conquest are many and bloody – very bloody.

The Assyrians seem to have introduced a new note of ruthlessness into the political life of the Near East. The panels depict a whole catalogue of horrors. Defeated enemies are beheaded, impaled or skinned alive. In their original form the panels were probably painted, heightening the vividness of these grisly images. Even in monochrome grey they have the power to shock the modern viewer. Such scenes, however, do not seem to have disturbed the equanimity of the Assyrian rulers; they frequently appear on the relief-panels, implacable and unmoved.

They are awesome, hieratic figures, shown always in profile. Their spade-like beards are ornately curled, their eyes stare intently from beneath strong curved brows. The fact that they wear hats like upturned flowerpots only seems to add to their imposing might. Often they are flanked by guardian deities, towering presences with human bodies and the heads of birds or beasts. The world conjured up by these reliefs still – across the distance of over 2500 years – has the power to impress. How great the impact of the real Assyrians must have been upon the people they intimidated, fought and subjugated can only be guessed at.

The first great period of Assyrian expansion had been the ninth century BCE under the leadership of Ashurnasirpal II and his successor Shalmaneser III. But after that era the empire had been weakened by internal strife and rebellion. It was in the mid-eighth century BCE, that Tiglath-pileser III revived Assyrian fortunes and began a fresh campaign of conquest and expansion that would last for almost 150 years.

Standing amid the glass-fronted cases of the British Museum, Jonathan Tubb, the curator of the Near Eastern collections, conveys something of the effect upon the various peoples of the Near East – not only the Israelites and the Judahites, but also the Syrians, Phoenicians, Philistines, Edomites, Ammonites and Moabites, even the Egyptians – as the Assyrians sought to bring the area under control. 'The effect on the region was absolutely devastating,' he explains. 'Neither Israel nor Judah had seen anything like it before. This was an empire on a new and unique scale – with completely different policies. When you are dealing with the Egyptian empire you were talking about paying tribute and taxation. The Assyrians were completely different. They came into this area and dominated it. If you opposed them in the slightest they came down on you like a ton of bricks. The levels of taxation, booty, tribute, that they demanded were absolutely crippling. And they also took the area over. They removed vassal kings who opposed them and put in their own governors. And, as we know, when they conquered an area, they actually deported whole sections of the population.'

When Tiglath-pileser III first marched south into Canaan he met with little opposition. The regime in the northern kingdom of Israel submitted to Assyrian demands. According to Tiglath-pileser's own account, King Menahem at first fled, but was then reinstated on his throne by the Assyrian force and obliged to pay tribute. Although not specifically mentioned it is to be supposed that the king of Judah also submitted voluntarily to a similar arrangement.

The burden of such taxation was certainly heavy, and at some time around 734BCE, Rezin, the Syrian king of Damascus, persuaded the new ruler of Israel, Pekah, to join in a rebellion against Assyrian rule. They tried to enlist the support of the Judahites, but the new ruler of the southern kingdom, Ahaz, refused to participate. The rebels promptly turned on him and launched an attack on Jerusalem. As a counter measure, King Ahaz despatched an advance tribute to Tiglath-pileser III together with a begging request for assistance.

The Assyrian king was only too happy to intervene. Indeed he would certainly have intervened anyway. He marched south, crushed the rebels, executed the leaders, deported the populations and set up his own centrally controlled government. The northern part of the kingdom of Israel was partitioned into the new Assyrian provinces of Dor, Gilead, and Megiddo. The lands east of the Jordan were also brought under direct Assyrian control at this time.

Samaria, the capital of Israel, and the lands to the south of it, were only saved from a similar fate when the rebellious King Pekah was assassinated by his disgruntled subjects. Tiglath-pileser III allowed the new king, Hoshea, to rule as an Assyrian appointee. The respite, however, was brief. After paying tribute for a few years, Hoshea sought to throw off the Assyrian yoke by entering into an alliance with the Egyptians. It was an ill-judged move. In 722BCE the new Assyrian king, Shalmaneser V, marched west and laid siege to Samaria. Although the account in the Assyrian sources is slightly unclear as to the details, it seems that Shalmaneser captured the city, and then his successor Sargon II completed the conquest. Many of the leading inhabitants were deported. Peoples from other parts of the Assyrian empire were settled on the land and a new Assyrian province of Samarina was established to control the territory. The kingdom of Israel – one half of the old United Monarchy – was no more.

There can be little doubt that the impact of this event upon the people of the kingdom of Judah was very great. On a psychological level the possibilities of defeat, exile and extinction must have been made horribly real and brought horribly close. The archaeological record suggests that thousands of refugees fled south from Samaria and settled in and around Jerusalem. The city, as we have seen, grew rapidly in size at this period. The people of Israel shared a common language, common traditions, and – to a large extent – common religious practices with the people of Judah.

According to some scholars it was at this point that the two earliest strands of the Bible – the so-called J (or Yahwist) and E (Eloist) sources – were brought together. The fleeing Israelites brought with them their own account of their origins and heroic beginnings (the E source). The J source, with its similar but separate traditions of the creation and the patriarchs, was – it is suggested – already preserved at Jerusalem. For some reason, and despite the many differences of tone and detail between the two, it was decided to combine them into a single work.

Although the kingdom of Judah continued to pay tribute to Assyria it maintained its semi-independent status as a vassal state, while all around the local territories were being transformed into Assyrian provinces under direct imperial control. A new political map was being drawn. As Mordechai Cogan of the Hebrew University of Jerusalem explains, 'For the first time in ancient Near Eastern history, the whole Near East is one, under the single political control of the Assyrians. There is a blending of peoples. The Assyrians had a policy of exchanging populations.' There were certain benefits in this new arrangement. Trade could flourish, and Judah, situated on one of the major routes running from the Arabian desert to the Mediterranean coast, was well placed to prosper.

But the levies exacted by the Assyrians were heavy and the temptation to rebel was ever present. At the end of the eighth century, in 705BCE, King Hezekiah of Judah gave way to this temptation.

The conditions might have seemed propitious. The Assyrian king,

Sargon II, the eradicator of Samaria, had just been killed in battle while campaigning in Anatolia. It was the signal not only for rejoicing throughout the empire, but also for revolt. In the area just north of the Persian gulf, the Babylonians and their neighbours the Elamites launched a rebellion. And so did King Hezekiah. He rallied the coastal city states of Sidon, Ashkelon and Ekron to his cause and gained a valuable promise of help from the dynasty in Egypt. But even so it was a pitifully small confederation to set against the might of Assyria.

The foolhardiness of the uprising still amazes historians. 'They must have been complete idiots,' says Jonathan Tubb. 'To be honest I really don't understand why they opposed the Assyrians in the way that they did. They must have seen and understood what had happened before to Samaria and what was likely to happen to them.' And yet they went ahead. In an effort to explain the apparently suicidal nature of Hezekiah's actions, some scholars have suggested that he must have been motivated by some moral imperative, a belief that he represented something that was right and that must prevail over the essential evil of the Assyrians. And while there is little direct support for such a reading even in the pages of the Bible, there is – according to some commentators – a discernible sense, in the pronouncements of the Prophets, of a revulsion against Assyria and a promotion of a novel and growing insistence on a vigorous morality.

If the motivation of Hezekiah remains something of a mystery, the actual course of his rebellion is remarkably well documented. It is clear that the rebels at least had time to prepare themselves. The new Assyrian king, Sennacherib, devoted his energies initially to containing the revolt in Babylonia. Archaeological evidence suggests that Hezekiah was able to reinforce and extend the walls around Jerusalem. Traces have been found of a massive fortified wall some sixteen feet thick dating from this time. Apparently expecting a siege, he took pains to secure the city's water supply by digging the so-called Siloam tunnel through the limestone bedrock of the city of David to bring water from the Gihon spring in the Kidron valley up to a reservoir pool inside the city. Hezekiah's workmen cut a winding passage through almost half a mile of solid limestone to complete the task. It was an impressive feat of engineering. Two teams worked from opposite ends, and met in the middle. A remarkable Hebrew inscription recording the meeting of the two work parties was discovered inside the tunnel.

'While there were still three cubits to be [tunnelled, there was heard] a voice calling to his fellow, for there was a fissure in the rock on the right [and on the left]. And on the day when the tunnel was cut through, the stonecutters struck towards one another, axe against axe. The water flowed from the source to the pool for 1200 cubits, and the height of the rock was 100 cubits above the heads of the stonecutters.'

Hezekiah seems not only to have strengthened the physical defences of his city; he also reinforced its spiritual position. As described in the previous chapter he undertook a comprehensive reform of his people's religion. He banned the worship of all assimilated foreign gods (gods that were or had been subject to the presiding Assyrian deity, Ashua). He concentrated worship upon Yahweh alone. He closed down regional temples, shrines and 'high places', and focused all worship upon the temple in Jerusalem.

A few commentators think the P (or Priestly) source now found in the Pentateuch – the largest source, comprising most of Leviticus and Numbers – may well have been written down during the reign of Hezekiah by a circle of priests at the newly enhanced Jerusalem temple. Others believe that it belongs, more probably, to the period after the return from exile. There is general agreement, however, that it originated as a separate source, written in opposition to the combined J and E account, to which it offered an alternative version. As such it would certainly have provided both an inspiration and a justification for Hezekiah's reforms. It is the Priestly source, rather than any of the others, that stresses the need for centralisation of religious practice upon the temple at Jerusalem. This, it should be noted, was an arrangement that counted greatly to the benefit of the Jerusalem temple priesthood: officiating priests received a portion of every sacrifice that they made.

In 701BCE Sennacherib and his army, having dealt with matters in Babylonia, marched south along the coastal route that ran down through Canaan. The rebel alliance assembled by Hezekiah melted away before the Assyrian advance. The king of Sidon took to his ships and fled. Ashkelon was razed and an Egyptian force that advanced to meet the threat was comprehensively routed. Having crushed the Philistine cities of Ekron and Timna, Sennacherib finally turned his attention inland to Judah. One by one he picked off the fortified sites on its borders. In his official account he lists forty-six. Most of these were probably no more than villages, but one at least was a major centre. Lachish was the second city of the kingdom. An imposing walled town, it controlled the important trade routes across the fertile lowlands of the Shephelah, south-west of Jerusalem.

The site, at modern Tell ed-Duweir, still suggests something of the city's scale. On a summer's evening the massive grass-covered sides of the mound slope sharply up towards the golden sky. Little imagination is needed to envisage the circling walls and towers that once surmounted the incline. It would have been a difficult place to take. Indeed Sennacherib was so proud of his achievement that he had it recorded in one of the elaborate wall reliefs made for his palace at Nineveh now in the British Museum. It shows the desperate defenders raining arrows, stones and flaming brands down upon the implacable Assyrian troops. The attackers are assaulting the crenellated walls with their own volleys of stones and arrows and with specially constructed siege engines and battering rams. They are also building a giant ramp up against the city wall to provide a means of access.

David Ussishkin, who has carried out the most recent excavations at the site, has identified the remains of this massive earthwork, together with a counter-ramp that the defenders began constructing on the other side of the wall. He also uncovered numerous other traces of the conflict: arrowheads, pieces of chain mail, the crest of a helmet, and a chain apparently used by the defenders against the Assyrian battering-rams. This last item can only have had limited effectiveness. Ussishkin found a thick destruction layer within the city, datable to the end of the eighth century BCE, suggesting the devastation when the city fell. The discovery, in a nearby cistern, of the jumbled bones of over 1500 people, is another dark hint of the ruthlessness shown by the Assyrian victors. The exact details of their fate cannot be known, but the Nineveh wall relief does depict a line of captives being impaled outside the city wall.

With Lachish in the hands of the Assyrians, the kingdom of Judah effectively comprised the city of Jerusalem and not much more. Hezekiah began to sue for peace. Sennacherib demanded a huge tribute payment, and to back up the demand began to encircle Jerusalem. The net closed rapidly. As for Hezekiah, Sennacherib boasted in his official record of the campaign, 'I shut him up like a bird in a cage in the midst of Jerusalem, his royal city. I connected siegeworks against him so that it was unthinkable for him to go out by the city gate. I cut off the cities that I despoiled from the midst of his land, and I gave them to Mitinti, king of Ashdod, Padi, king of Ekron, and Silli-Bel, king of Gaza, so that I diminished his land.'

Nevertheless even if Hezekiah could not get out of his cage, Sennacherib could not get into it. The new walls held firm, and the water supply remained secure. All around destruction reigned. As Isaiah lamented, 'Your country lies desolate, your cities are burnt with fire; in your very presence aliens devour your land.' But Jerusalem continued to hold out.

Sennacherib sent a delegation to parley with Hezekiah and exact terms. They were met by Hezekiah's own envoys close to 'the upper pool, which is in the highway of the fuller's field' — a site reckoned to have been just outside the city walls to the north. The leader of the Assyrian delegation, instead of speaking, as Hezekiah's envoys expected, in Syrian, the lingua franca of the Near East, began in Hebrew. This was alarming, as his words could be clearly heard, and clearly understood, by the anxious conscripts manning the walls of the city.

And, indeed, after some brief preliminary comments to Hezekiah's envoys – in which he memorably described the Egyptian pharaoh as a 'broken reed' (Isaiah xxxvi, 6) – he launched a direct appeal to 'the men that sit on the wall'. He explained to them that all resistance against Assyria was useless, and urged them to surrender at once and be spared, rather than put their trust in their god and face certain death.

The exact details of the denouement of this struggle are difficult to untangle. Sennacherib alludes to the 'splendour of my majesty' overcoming Hezekiah, and mentions that Hezekiah's mercenary army went on strike. But there is no specific mention that Sennacherib actually managed to take Jerusalem. It is, however, clear from the Assyrian records that Hezekiah subsequently dispatched a large tribute payment to the Assyrian king at Nineveh: 'He sent a heavy tribute and his daughters and his harem and singers, together with thirty talents of gold, eight hundred talents of silver, choice antimony, blocks of stone, ivory couches, ivory armchairs, elephant hides, ivory, ebony, boxwood, and all sorts of things . . . and he sent his ambassadors for the giving of tribute and the performance of vassal service.' The absence of any archaeological evidence for a destruction of Jerusalem at this time amplifies the silence of the Assyrian records. It has been suggested that, for some reason – possibly an outbreak of plague in the camp – the Assyrians were obliged to raise the siege, but not before securing a limited form of surrender. Hezekiah, recognising the very narrow escape he had enjoyed, and seeking to prevent any further reprisals, agreed to pay a large indemnity, as well as resuming the annual tribute payments expected of a vassal king.

It had indeed been a close thing. If Jerusalem had fallen, Judah
– like Israel – might have been obliterated, its capital destroyed,
its people dispersed in exile. And, given the discrepancy between
all-powerful Assyria and little Judah, the escape was all the more
remarkable. Perhaps to some within the city it seemed to be nothing
short of miraculous. It was a certainly a key moment in the history of
Judah – and it is perhaps not too fanciful to call it a key moment in the
history of the world. If the Assyrians had razed Jerusalem and scattered
its inhabitants, some commentators argue, it is a moot point whether
Judaism could have survived and developed. And if Judaism had not
survived, Christianity and Islam could not have evolved from it. To
imagine the last two and a half millennia of human history without these
three great religions is to conjure up a very different world indeed.

It is possible that within Hezekiah's circle a direct connection was
made between the religious reforms instituted by the king, and the city's
miraculous deliverance from the hands of the Assyrians. If so, the
connection was by no means apparent to all. Hezekiah's successor,
Manasseh, while preserving allegiance to Assyria, reversed many of
his predecessor's religious and social reforms. According to the very
negative biblical account, he introduced a policy of assimilation with
his neighbours and masters, he re-established altars to foreign gods
in the temple, and introduced foreign customs and foreign fashions
into Jerusalem. The results – by most objective standards – were not
unsuccessful. He ruled for fifty-five years in relative peace and prosperity;
the longest reigning king in the history of Judah. He is reviled in the
Bible but the archaeological evidence attests to the recovery of rural life
and settlement in Judah during this period of stability.

It was only with the accession of Hezekiah's great-grandson, Josiah,
in the late seventh century BCE that a policy of exclusive Yahwistic
religious reform seems to have been taken up again in earnest. By this
time the political situation had changed. It was a period of flux, of
new allegiances and uneasy power struggles. Assyria's pre-eminence

was being challenged by the emergence of Babylon as a rival power. In a reversal of previous arrangements, Egypt, which had long been locked in conflict with Assyria, was now offering to assist her erstwhile enemy in stemming the rising might of the Babylonians. The smaller kingdoms of the Near East had to survive in this troubled climate and it is against this backdrop that the events of Josiah's reign were set.

Josiah had succeeded to the throne in 639BCE at the tender age of six, after his father – King Amon – was assassinated. There is no record of who exercised power during the king's minority, but it is at least possible that it was a priest. (During the childhood of Joash, an earlier Judahite monarch, who succeeded to the throne at the age of three, it is recorded that the high priest had acted as regent.) Some sort of early priestly connection might explain the strong religious flavour of Josiah's reign. Josiah seems to have introduced a series of religious reforms very similar to those of Hezekiah. All gods except for Yahweh were banned again. Local shrines were again destroyed and religion was once more concentrated upon the temple at Jerusalem.

These reforms – as has been mentioned briefly – seem to have been galvanised in part by a discovery. In the eighteenth year of Josiah's reign a book of the torah – or holy law – was found in the temple by Hilkiah the high priest who gave it to Shaphan the scribe. Shaphan read it to the king who, on hearing its message, tore his clothes and promptly set about destroying the 'high places' and shrines outside the capital. The writings found in the temple are generally considered to be, if not the book of Deuteronomy itself, the law code that stands at the heart of that work. This code purported to be a fuller supplement to the Ten Commandments given by Yahweh to Moses on mount Sinai. It was supposedly passed on by Moses shortly before his death, as he looked towards the Promised Land from mount Nebo.

The laws enshrined at the heart of the book of Deuteronomy emphasised the vital importance of worshipping no god but Yahweh and worshipping him at only one altar, 'the place that the Lord your

God will choose out of all your tribes as his habitation to put his name there' (Deuteronomy xii, 5). It also listed a whole table of other rules and regulations relating to everything from cross-dressing to scrumping. And it continually urged the Children of Israel to take special care of 'the stranger, the fatherless and the widow'. If they observed these laws they would prosper in their new home; if they did not they would be 'plucked from the land' and scattered among the nations (Deuteronomy xxxviii, 63).

Scholars debate whether Shaphan himself was the author of the code, or whether the code perhaps predated the reign of Josiah, if only slightly. Nevertheless the point remains that the text was almost certainly discovered at this time and that it was given an especial prominence. The story of how Moses came to deliver the code on his deathbed was, most commentators believe, almost certainly embroidered around the text, to give it a narrative frame and a more vivid authority. And this embroidery was, perhaps, part of a more general literary enterprise being carried forward at this time. As has been mentioned, many biblical scholars believe it was among the reformist elements at the court of King Josiah that the decision was taken to compile a complete history of the people of Israel, from the time of their arrival in the land up to the 'present day'. This great undertaking became the so-called Deuteronomic history. There is, according to the literary analysts, a strong stylistic unity running through the language of the books of Deuteronomy, Joshua, Judges, Samuel and Kings to suggest that they all share the same author — or school of authors.

Besides the linguistic unity, there is also a unity of purpose. This was a history with a message. It was written in — and by — the light of the recently found Deuteronomic law code. All the vicissitudes of the Israelites over the centuries were to be described in relation to the key factor of the people's obedience, or disobedience, to the dictates laid down by Yahweh to his servant Moses, as recorded in the book of Deuteronomy. The land, it said, was Yahweh's gift to the Israelites, sealed by the covenants with Abraham and Moses, and confirmed in numerous miracles from the destruction of the walls of Jericho onwards.

Some commentators believe that the Deuteronomic history – at least in its first version – was an undertaking that both reflected and conditioned the political and religious situation at the time of King Josiah. And even in the version of it that has come down to us this sense is still strong. To the members of Josiah's court the key events of the recent past were the fall of Israel and the survival of Judah. Both could very readily relate to the dictates of the Deuteronomic law code. The fall of Israel was ascribed to the people's failure to worship Yahweh either correctly or exclusively from the time of Jeroboam onwards. All the kings of Israel mentioned in the book of Kings are castigated for 'doing wrong in the eyes of the Lord' on this account.

There was one slight problem with this line of argument. Although Hezekiah's timely reforms might have persuaded Yahweh to spare Jerusalem from the wrath of Sennacherib, what about all those kings of Judah before him, who had – like their counterparts in the northern kingdom – 'done wrong in the eyes of the Lord'? They, too, had set up altars to Baal, Asherah, and other 'abominations'. Why had not Yahweh destroyed Judah too on account of their persistent failings long before Hezekiah came to the throne?

To explain this it seems that the author of the Deuteronomic history invoked – or perhaps created – the so-called 'Davidic covenant'. In II Samuel (vii, 16) Yahweh promises David that, on account of his great faithfulness, he and his descendants will hold the kingdom forever: 'And thine house and thy kingdom shall be established for ever before thee: thy throne shall be established for ever.' Unlike the covenant that God made with Moses, assuring the children of Israel a place in the Promised Land *if* they obeyed his commandments, the covenant with David is presented as being unconditional. Although Solomon's worship of foreign gods might lead to the division of the kingdom, and the loss of the lands of

Israel, the territory of Judah, so the author of the Deuteronomic history implied, could never be forfeit. No matter how often the kings of Judah 'did wrong in the eyes of the Lord', Yahweh would forgive the offence for David's sake.

Yahweh's patience, the Deuteronomist suggested, had now been rewarded with the arrival of King Josiah. Josiah certainly appears to be the hero of the whole history. He is presented as the king who will turn the torah – the law enshrined in the book of Deuteronomy – into the constitution of the state. Even King Hezekiah does not receive quite such a good press. Josiah is described as a second David.

The original authorship of the Deuteronomic history is not known. Some scholars have put forward the idea that there was a dedicated circle of reformist scribes centred upon the court, working on the great project. Others have posited that the entire work might be the composition of a single man. They have even gone as far as to suggest that the author might be the prophet Jeremiah – or perhaps his scribe Baruch, the son of Neriah. Such theories, based on arguments from close analysis of the text, are hard to confirm or deny through archaeology. One recent discovery did, however, bring this whole world of reform and literary endeavour tantalisingly close.

The back streets of Jerusalem are full of antiquities dealers, little shops crammed with shelves of dusty pottery and ancient artefacts. Over small cups of bitter coffee gracious, poker-faced dealers convince you of the genuineness and rarity of their stock and haggle with you over the prices to be paid. Much of the stuff is indeed genuine. It is here that many of the artefacts turned up by the ploughs of peasants and the spades of treasure seekers find their way. And it was in one such shop that a collector discovered a seventh-century BCE clay seal impression – or *bulla* – marked with the inscription: '[belonging to] Berechiah, son of Neriah, the scribe'. Berechiah, he realised, is the full form of the name Baruch. It was an extraordinary find. There is, of course, the possibility that this Baruch was not the friend and scribe of Jeremiah mentioned in the Bible, but another man of the same name and profession. But the coincidence is so great that it is hard not to believe that this is a relic of the biblical Baruch, that it is a mark made by the man who may possibly have first written out, or even composed, a substantial chunk of the Old Testament.

Although the theological intention of the Deuteronomic history soon reveals itself, the question remains: does this particular bias completely vitiate the work as an historical source? The account of events given in the early books of Joshua, Judges and Samuel is not always – or, even, often – supported by the archaeological evidence. And it is hard to make any claims for their factual accuracy. But what of the later books? The author of the Deuteronomic history seems to have had access to some written sources. Throughout the book of Kings he constantly refers his readers to the 'History of the Kings of Israel' and the 'History of the Kings of Judah' for fuller accounts of the various reigns. And if the work was first composed at the time of King Josiah, the latter chapters of the book of II Kings must have been recounting very recent, almost contemporaneous, events.

Nevertheless, despite this proximity to the events being described, the Deuteronomic historian just does not seem to have been concerned with objective historical truth, as conceived by modern historians. He always selected his material to point up the particular moral of his story. The theological vision coloured descriptions of even the most recent events and dictated which elements of a story were recorded and which left out.

In the biblical account of Sennacherib's campaign almost all extraneous details are edited out. No reason is given for Sennacherib's actions. The fact, alluded to in the Assyrian records, that Hezekiah had been conspiring with Egypt to throw off Assyrian control, is left unexplained, if not quite unstated. The fall of Lachish, although it can be inferred by the fact that Sennacherib is described as having his headquarters there, is not specifically mentioned, let alone described.

The raising of the siege of Jerusalem is given an explicitly miraculous twist. The biblical account claims that God himself intervened, sending an 'angel of the Lord' who 'slew a hundred and eighty-five thousand in the camp of the Assyrians' (II Kings ixx, 35), and forced Sennacherib to withdraw. And Sennacherib's death is set down to divine vengeance, even though it happened almost twenty years later.

God's original covenant with Abraham had promised all the land from Egypt to the Euphrates to Abraham's descendants. From the high point of the United Monarchy when, under David and Solomon, this ideal had – according to the doubtful testimony of the Deuteronomic historian – been achieved, the territory had been whittled down to the limits of Judah. And after Hezekiah's rebellion the territories of Judah had been reduced still further. Nevertheless, to the author of the first version of the Deuteronomic history, it seemed certain that Yahweh's unswerving loyalty to the house of David would ensure that the monarchy and its kingdom endured. Under King Josiah there was, it appeared, even a chance that the former lands of the kingdom of Israel might be won back. Josiah seems to have tried to extend his religious reforms into the northern lands. It is recorded that he destroyed the altar at Bethel, the site where Jeroboam had marked the border of his kingdom by setting up a golden calf.

The optimism of the Deuteronomist was misplaced. In 609BCE Josiah confronted the Egyptian forces at Megiddo and was killed. The biblical account is extremely laconic. It is hard to know what happened. No battle is recorded. But the king's untimely end is all too certain. Josiah's death was bad enough. What followed was worse. The Babylonians first defeated Assyria and then – in 605BCE – routed the Egyptian army at the battle of Carchemish. It was a victory that established their position as the undisputed superpower of the whole Near East.

The people of Judah soon found themselves having to submit to this new master. The punishing round of tribute payments began again.

When Jehoiakim, Josiah's son, prompted by the Egyptians, dared to rebel, he was crushed. Jerusalem was besieged and – this time – was taken. The temple was desecrated, thousands were deported, including most of the upper classes, the military elite and all skilled craftsmen.

Zedekiah, another of Josiah's sons, was set up by the Babylonians as a vassal king. But when he rebelled nine years later, Nebuchadrezza returned and completed the destruction of the city: he razed the walls, the temple was burnt to the ground and the Ark of the Covenant disappeared. Zedekiah himself fled and was captured. His children were put to death in front of him and then he was blinded and led away in chains. Despite the vaunted Davidic covenant, it was the end of the rule of the house of David.

A man named Gedaliah, who appears to have been the grandson of Shaphan (the scribe who reported the discovery of the scroll in the temple), was appointed as governor. But his rule was brief. A minor member of the house of David, affronted at his family's fall from power, assassinated the governor, perhaps hoping to spark a popular rebellion among the remaining inhabitants of Judah. No rebellion followed. Instead 'all the people' (including the prophet Jeremiah), perhaps fearing Babylonian reprisals, fled across the border into Egypt.

The community was scattered – either in Babylon or in Egypt. Only a few peasants remained on the land. Some explanation had to be attempted. Some biblical scholars, having scrutinised the text of Deuteronomy and the books that follow it, are convinced that the work, originally compiled in a spirit of optimism during the time of King Josiah, was revised to take into account the cataclysm that followed after him. The story was brought up to date with a perfunctory account of the reigns of his successors and the fall of Jerusalem, but – more importantly – the reviser went through the whole text of Deuteronomy and the history that followed on from it, and inserted references to the possibility of exile. It became a theme running through the text.

According to this reading, one of the main pillars of the book had to be moved. The unconditional Davidic covenant had to be toned down and the more conditional convenant made between Yahweh and Moses had to be emphasised. Nevertheless, despite the sad position that the people of Judah found themselves in following the sack of Jersualem, the author – or reviser – of the Deuteronomic history did manage to introduce a ray of hope into his vision of the future. It was suggested that even though the house of David had been removed, the throne of Judah and Israel would always be *open* to the Davidic line. This, of course, is an idea that has echoed throughout Jewish history – and formed the link between the Jewish and Christian traditons: in the latter Jesus was a descendant of the house of David.

The key fact, however, of the new, revised, Deuteronomic history was, it has been suggested, that the Jewish presence in the land was not unconditional. It depended upon observing the covenant Moses made with Yahweh. Keep Yahweh's commandments: only then will your place in the land be secure. The reviser emphasised – and re-emphasised – the exclusive worship of Yahweh as the principal commandment to be obeyed. He suggested that it was King Manasseh's reversal of Hezekiah's religious policies that finally persuaded Yahweh both to break the Davidic covenant and to punish the people of Judah with exile. This was perceived as a moral issue as well as one of religious ritual and tradition.

Rabbi Jonathan Magonet sets out this equation in simple terms – not, of course, that there is anything simple about it. 'It is a lesson from the past,' he explains, 'indicating the importance of behaving properly vis-à-vis God if you wish to remain in the land. So it goes into a much deeper thing about how you relate to God and the Covenant, and all the responsibilities that go with it. If you disobey, the land – as it says – will "vomit you out".'

As biblical commentators have pointed out, running throughout all the books of the Deuteronomic history is the understanding that the Israelite nation has a moral character. It is a morality that must be expressed at every level from the ruling political regime down to the actions of the individual. The nation – like its individual human constituents – is viewed as having not only social rights but also social responsibilities. It is, in the words of one scholar, 'a moral being whose religious beliefs cannot be separated from its daily life'. The guardians and guarantors of this pervading morality, at least within the biblical narrative, were the Prophets – uncompromising men like Elijah and Jeremiah, ever willing to point out shortfalls and to demand improvements.

This notion of a god demanding a moral obligation of his followers was, many commentators believe, something new if not unique. It is a notion that has endured and spread. The idea of God-demanded righteousness, however, was firmly connected with the idea of a God-given right to the land. And this idea has proved equally enduring. It is the nexus that generations of modern politicians have struggled either to sever or untie.

Just when, how, and how often the Deuteronomic history was revised remain much debated questions of biblical scholarship. It has been suggested that the main work of revision might have been carried out in the immediate aftermath of the fall of Jerusalem by the exiles who had fled to Egypt. Perhaps Jeremiah himself, or Baruch, was involved in the process. Others think that Babylon was a more likely place for any process of reassessment to have taken place. Certainly the exiles in Babylon had plenty of time to come to terms with their fate. 'By the rivers of Babylon, there we sat down, yea, we wept when we remembered Zion.'

No doubt for many of them the events of the recent past did seem to be proclaiming a lesson: when the Israelites worshipped only one god, Yahweh, their place in the land was safe – as it had been under Hezekiah and under Josiah. When they relapsed from this strict rule, the land was forfeit. In the face of such reckoning it would not have been surprising if the exiles began to think that they should, perhaps, have maintained Josiah's reforms. It was an idea that had some sixty years to take hold.

In 539BCE the unexpected happened. The once-mighty Babylonian empire fell – almost without a fight – to the Persians. The Persian general, Gobryas, marched unopposed into Babylon at the head of his army. The Persian emperor, Cyrus the Great, decreed that all the exiled peoples residing in the city were free to return to their homelands. They were, moreover, entitled to rebuild their temples and continue their religious practices. The following year many, though not all, of the Jews began to return to Jerusalem and the surrounding villages. They rebuilt the temple. And over the following century they also gathered together and edited the books that would make up the Hebrew Bible, or Old Testament. It is to this post-exilic period that most scholars ascribe the composition of the Pentateuch (the weaving together of the four distinct and existing strands – J, E, P and D – into a single work) as well as the final editing and ordering of the books that make up the Deuteronomic history.

According to one scholarly tradition that dates back to the fourth century BCE much of this work was carried out by the priest and scribe, Ezra. He arrived in Jerusalem from Babylon in 398BCE armed with a letter from the Persian emperor authorising him both to teach and enforce 'the torah of Moses'. In his work he was supported by the Persian-appointed governor, Nehemiah. The biblical account preserved in the book of Nehemiah describes how Ezra gathered the people of Judah in the streets of the city, near to the water gate, and, standing in a specially built pulpit, proceeded to read to them the entire book – or scroll – of the torah of Moses. It was a process that took seven days. Or seven half days, as he read only from the morning until midday. The reading was followed by a ceremony, in which the people renewed the covenant with God, agreeing to abide by the rules he had set down in the torah. The rigorous centralisation of worship in the temple at Jerusalem, the stern injunctions against foreign gods, were re-established.

Many biblical scholars from the time of Saint Jerome onwards have suggested that the scroll from which Ezra read was probably a first version of the Pentateuch, compiled and edited by Ezra himself. Certainly there are enough references in the Bible to Ezra's literary, antiquarian and theological interests to make him a likely candidate as editor. By including Deuteronomy as the last book of the Pentateuch he forged a link with the following six books of the Deuteronomic history. The resulting narrative provided the story of the Jews from the creation of the world to the beginning of the Babylonian exile. It often looks like history, but it is not.

Professor Magonet explains the need for caution: 'There are many parts of the Bible that relate to real historical moments, incidents and facts, but they are incidental to the attempt to convey a message.' That message is the special relationship between the Jewish people and the only God they recognise. It is a relationship that they projected right back through their history whether it was understood by their ancestors in that way or not. The message commanded not just that they should worship Yahweh but that they should do good and then God entitled them to the land.

The comparison put forward by some scholars between the sort of history contained in the Old Testament and the sort of history contained in Shakespeare's *Julius Caesar* may seem extreme. And certainly there are more historically verifiable incidents in the former than the latter. But there is some sense in the analogy: both texts relate to people who existed; they touch on events that happened, but they were written long after the times they describe; they include much that did not happen; and they have concerns very different from fixing the historical truth. They have their own truths – the religious and the dramatic.

The discoveries of archaeology may confirm that certain biblical characters existed and certain biblical events occurred, but they can never really touch on the central concerns of the biblical story. No matter how many stray artefacts are recovered that seem to relate –

even specifically – to the stories of the Bible, there will always be a gap between the 'facts' on – and in – the ground, and the 'facts' on the page. In the end the search for the historical truth of the Bible must be something of a wild goose chase.

The agenda of the Bible is specific and spiritual. The Bible has been a central factor in other historical phenomena – the three great monotheistic religions of the world. Religions create their own political realities and imperatives. And certainly the Hebrew Bible still plays a huge part in the politics of the Near East. But it is the spiritual message of the Bible, rather than the book's historical accuracy (or otherwise), that has exerted – and continues to exert – the greatest influence upon the unfolding drama of the region.

There is an irony in the fact that the demand to be moral is bound up with possession of the land. For many modern Israelis, religious or not, the state cannot trade land for peace without betraying its moral authority. Under such conditions questions about archaeology, about the past, about politics, about peace, all tend to end up as part of the same question. And it is difficult to see how this knot can be loosened. Can Israel become a state like any other? Would we be better off without the Holy Land? The Bible's spin on the history of this land tells the story so powerfully that it has shaped Christian and Muslim tradition as well as Jewish. It is the Holy Land for all of us. And so we argue over it – using the Bible as a weapon, a shield, and a justification.

So what is the final definitive answer on the Bible? That is still a very big question . . .

BIBLIOGRAPHY

General works

Ben-Tor, Amnon. *The Archaeology of Ancient Israel* (Tel Aviv, 1992)

Coogan, Michael D. (ed.). *The Oxford History of the Biblical World* (New York and Oxford, 1998)

Laughlin, John C.H. *Archaeology and the Bible* (London, 2000)

May, Herbert G. (ed.). *Oxford Bible Atlas* (Oxford, 1984)

Mazar, Amihai. *Archaeology of the Land of the Bible* (New York, 1990)

Metzger, Bruce M. and Coogan, Michael D. *The Oxford Companion to the Bible* (New York and Oxford, 1993)

Mills, Mary E. *Historical Israel: Biblical Israel – studying Joshua to 2 Kings* (London, 1999)

Negev, Avraham (ed.). *The Archeological Encyclopedia of the Holy Land* (New York, 1990)

Shanks, Hershel (ed.). *Biblical Archaeology Review* [*BAR*]

Chapter 1: The Book and the Spade

Athas, George. 'Minimalism': The Copenhagen School of Thought in Biblical Studies'. Edited transcript of lecture, 2nd edition, University of Sydney, 1999

Shanks, Hershel. 'Face to Face – Biblical Minimalists Meet Their Challengers', *BAR* July/August 1997

Shanks, Hershel. 'Is the Bible Right after all? *BAR* Interviews William Dever', *BAR* September/October 1996

Chapter 2: Jericho

Bienkowski, Piotr and Wood, Bryant G. 'Battle over Jericho heats up', *BAR* September/October 1990

Garstang, John and Garstang, J.E.B. *The Story of Jericho* (London, 1948)

Herzog, Ze'ev. 'Deconstructing the Walls of Jericho', *Ha'aretz*, 29 October 1999

Kenyon, Kathleen M. *Digging up Jericho* (New York, 1957)

Miller, Kevin D. 'Did the Exodus Never Happen?' *Christianity Today*, 7 September 1998

Rohl, David. *A Test of Time* (London, 1995)

Ussishkin, David. 'Notes on the Fortifications of the Middle Bronze II Period at Jericho and Shechem', *Bulletin of the American Schools of Oriental Research* 276, 1989

Wood, Bryant G. 'Did the Israelites Conquer Jericho?' *BAR* March/April 1990

Chapter 3: Judges

Dever, William G. 'Archaeology and the Emergence of Early Israel', *Archaeology & Biblical Interpretation* (John R. Bartlett ed., New York, 1997)

Finkelstein, Israel. *The Archaeology of the Israelite Settlement* (Jerusalem, 1988)

Mazar, Amihai. 'On Cult Places and Early Israelites: A Response to Michael Coogan', *BAR* July/August 1988

Shanks, Hershel. 'Two Early Israelite Cult Sites Now Questioned', *BAR* January/February 1988

Zertal, Adam. 'Has Joshua's Altar Been Found on Mt Ebal?' *BAR* January/February 1985

Zertal, Adam. 'Israel Enters Canaan – Following the Pottery Trail', *BAR* September/October 1991

Chapter 4: King David

[Biran, Avraham]. ' "David" Found at Dan', *BAR* March/April 1994

Davies, Philip R. ' "House of David" Built on Sand – the Sins of the Biblical Maximizers', *BAR* July/August 1994

Lemaire, André. ' "House of David" Restored in Moabite Inscription', BAR May/June 1994

Marcus, Amy Dockser. *Rewriting the Bible* (London, 2000)

Na'aman, Nadav. 'Cow Town or Royal Capital? Evidence for Iron Age Jerusalem', *BAR* July/August 1997

Rainey, Anson. 'The "House of David" and the House of the Deconstructionists', *BAR* November/December 1994

Shanks, Hershel. 'Everything You Ever Knew about Jerusalem Is Wrong (Well, Almost)', *BAR* November/December 1999

Chapter 5: Solomon

Davies, Graham I. 'Are Solomon's Stables Still at Megiddo?' *BAR* January/February 1994

Fargo, Valerie M. 'Is the Solomonic City Gate at Megiddo Really Solomonic?' *BAR* September/October 1983

Finkelstein, Israel. 'Hazor and the North in the Iron Age: A Low Chronology Perspective', 1998

Finkelstein, Israel. 'The Archaeology of the United Monarchy: An Alternative View', *Levant* 28, 1996

Finkelstein, Israel and Ussishkin, David. 'Megiddo', *BAR* January/ February 1994

Rothenberg, Benno. *Timna: Valley of the Biblical Copper Mines* (London, 1972)

Ussishkin, David. 'Solomon's Jerusalem: the Text and the Facts on the Ground'. Lecture delivered at the Society of Biblical Literature.

Chapter 6: Asherah

Edelman, Diana V. 'Tracking Observance of the Aniconic Tradition through Numismatics', *The Triumph of Elohim: From Yahwisms to Judaisms* (Contributions to Biblical Exegesis and Theology 13, 1995)

Handy, Lowell K. 'The Appearance of Pantheon in Judah'

Shanks, Hershel. 'Is the Bible Right after all? *BAR* Interviews William Dever', *BAR* September/October 1996

[Shanks, Hershel]. 'The Pomegranate Sceptre Head – from the Temple of the Lord or from the Temple of Asherah?' *BAR* May/June 1992

Smith, Mark S. *The Early History of God – Yahweh and the Other Deities of Ancient Israel* (San Francisco, 1988)

Chapter 7: Ezra

[Shanks, Hershel]. 'Arad – an Ancient Israelite Fortress with a Temple to Yahweh', *BAR* March/April 1987

Friedman, Richard E. *Who Wrote the Bible?* (London, 1988)

INDEX

Note: Page numbers in **bold** refer to major text sections, those in Roman numerals indicate a Timeline entry.